Managing Organizations to Sustain Passion for Public Service

Almost three decades ago, James Perry created the first survey instrument to measure public service motivation. Since then, social and behavioral scientists have intensively studied the motivating power of public service. This research relating to public service motivation, altruism and prosocial motivation and behavior has overturned widespread assumptions grounded in market-orientated perspectives and produced a critical mass of new knowledge for transforming the motivation of public employees, civil service policies and management practices. This is the first study to look systematically across the different streams of research. Furthermore, it is the first study to synthesize the research across the applied questions that public organizations and their leaders confront, including: how to recruit ethical and committed staff; how to design meaningful public work; how to create work environments that support prosocial behavior; how to compensate employees to sustain their public service; how to socialize employees for public service missions; and how to lead employees to engage in causes greater than themselves.

JAMES PERRY is Distinguished Professor Emeritus at the Paul H. O'Neill School of Public and Environmental Affairs, Indiana University. He pioneered research on public service motivation, now studied in more than fifty countries, and is recipient of the Dwight Waldo Award (ASPA), the H. George Frederickson Award (PMRA), the John Gaus Award (APSA), and the Routledge Prize (IRSPM).

Managing Organizations to Sustain Passion for Public Service

JAMES L. PERRY
Indiana University–Bloomington

CAMBRIDGE
UNIVERSITY PRESS

CAMBRIDGE
UNIVERSITY PRESS

University Printing House, Cambridge CB2 8BS, United Kingdom

One Liberty Plaza, 20th Floor, New York, NY 10006, USA

477 Williamstown Road, Port Melbourne, VIC 3207, Australia

314–321, 3rd Floor, Plot 3, Splendor Forum, Jasola District Centre, New Delhi – 110025, India

79 Anson Road, #06-04/06, Singapore 079906

Cambridge University Press is part of the University of Cambridge.

It furthers the University's mission by disseminating knowledge in the pursuit of education, learning, and research at the highest international levels of excellence.

www.cambridge.org
Information on this title: www.cambridge.org/9781108843256
DOI: 10.1017/9781108915236

First published 2021

A catalogue record for this publication is available from the British Library.

Library of Congress Cataloging-in-Publication Data

NAMES: Perry, James L., author.
TITLE: Managing organizations to sustain passion for public service / James L. Perry.
DESCRIPTION: Cambridge, United Kingdom ; New York, NY : Cambridge University Press, 2021. | Includes bibliographical references and index.
IDENTIFIERS: LCCN 2020024245 (print) | LCCN 2020024246 (ebook) | ISBN 9781108843256 (hardback) | ISBN 9781108824132 (paperback) | ISBN 9781108915236 (ebook)
SUBJECTS: LCSH: Civil service--Personnel management. | Civil service--Psychological aspects. | Public officers--Psychology. | Employee motivation. | Motivation (Psychology) | Organizational behavior.
CLASSIFICATION: LCC JF1601 .P34 2021 (print) | LCC JF1601 (ebook) | DDC 352.6/6--dc23
LC record available at https://lccn.loc.gov/2020024245
LC ebook record available at https://lccn.loc.gov/2020024246

ISBN 978-1-108-84325-6 Hardback
ISBN 978-1-108-82413-2 Paperback

This book is dedicated to my most cherished public servants, my daughters, Jennifer and Jacqueline. They have made an enormous difference to many – the people they serve, their wonderful husbands and children, and their mother and dad.

Contents

Figures

Tables

Boxes

Acknowledgments

The journey that brought me to this book began in the late 1980s. At the time I joined with my School of Public and Environmental Affairs (now the Paul H. O'Neill School) colleague Lois Wise to contribute an article to the fiftieth anniversary volume of *Public Administration Review* (*PAR*). The article, "The Motivational Bases of Public Service," launched my attention to public service motivation, an enterprise to which I have devoted a good share of time during the last three decades.

I have had the good fortune of several sabbatical leaves that were influential in shaping the path that led to this book. In fall of 1992 I worked for the late Tom McFee, Assistant Secretary for Personnel at the U.S. Department of Health and Human Services, getting firsthand exposure to federal human capital management and simultaneously thinking about measuring public service motivation. Tom was a great mentor, teacher, and person. I moved on from Washington in the winter of 1993 to the Robert M. LaFollette School of Public Affairs where I first developed a scale to measure public service motivation. I spent 1999–2000 at the Corporation for National and Community Service (CNCS) as an outgrowth of my early empirical research on public service motivation, which involved the AmeriCorps national service program. In 2006–2007, I was invited by colleagues at Katholieke Universiteit Leuven (KU Leuven) to continue my research on public service motivation as senior postdoctoral fellow. My stay in Leuven also permitted me to develop a network of colleagues across Europe (and a love for Belgian beer!).

When the volume of research about public service motivation grew during the 1990s and 2000s, I embarked with colleagues on a chapter for a book I coedited in 2008. The book chapter, "From Theory to Practice: Strategies for Applying Public Service Motivation," which I coauthored with Laurie Paarlberg and Annie Hondeghem, is a distant precursor of this book, but it was written in the spirit of coupling practice more closely to theory and empirical research.

Writing this book gained serious momentum when I coauthored a *Public Administration Review* article, "Public Service Motivation Research: Lessons for Practice," with Laurie Paarlberg and Robert Christensen. The article again focused on the question of applying research about public service motivation to management practices in public organizations. It was not long after the article appeared that I decided to write this book.

The collaborations I refer to above represent both distant and proximate stimuli for this book. Lois Wise partnered with me to get the stream of research off the ground, long before public service motivation became a common part of public administration conversations. Annie Hondeghem, Director of the Public Governance Institute at KU Leuven, collaborated on both the 2008 edited book and the chapter that appeared in it. She was my gracious host during my senior postdoctoral fellowship at KU Leuven in 2006–2007.

I owe a debt to many PhD students with whom I have collaborated over the years. Laurie Paarlberg, now the Charles Stewart Mott Chair on Community Foundations in the Lilly Family School of Philanthropy at Indiana University–Purdue University Indianapolis, collaborated with me on both of the precursors to this book. Rob Christensen, professor and George W. Romney Research Fellow at the Romney Institute of Public Management in the Marriott School of Management at Brigham Young University, collaborated on the 2017 *PAR* paper and so many other projects that I have lost track. My thanks to Laurie and Rob for their intellectual support, stimulation, and friendship over the years.

Another former doctoral student with whom I have worked frequently is Wouter Vandenabeele. Wouter and his PhD advisor Annie Hondeghem approached me to work with them in about 2004, when they visited the United States to pursue their interests in studying public service motivation. I subsequently served on Wouter's doctoral committee in 2006–2008 when I was at KU Leuven. Since receiving his PhD, Wouter has become an important contributor and leader in research on public service motivation.

My thanks, too, to scholars and practitioners who have aided me by sharing their research and other resources or reading drafts of my manuscript. They include Sergio Fernandez (O'Neill School), Jordan Gans-Morse (Northwestern University), David Garcia (Partnership for Public Service), Chet Jankowski, Steve Kelman (Kennedy School),

John Palguta (Partnership for Public Service), Adrian Ritz (University of Bern), Pablo Sanabria (Universidad de los Andes, Colombia), Rob Seidner (U.S. Office of Management and Budget), Jeannette Taylor (University of Western Australia), and Ranald Taylor (Murdoch University).

I am grateful to Valerie Appleby, Senior Commissioning Editor for Business and Management at Cambridge University Press, for her support at every step of the way during this project. I first reached out to Valerie in late summer 2019 when I began to search for a publisher. Her quick response and receptivity eased my path forward. She secured three anonymous reviews that were very helpful for improving my final manuscript.

Elise Boruvka, with whom I have worked for the last decade, assisted me with quality control on the final manuscript I submitted. She assisted with issues of editorial style, including citations and references. Devin New, my current administrative assistant at the O'Neill School, has facilitated my work on this book in many ways.

Finally, my thanks to my family for their support. My thanks, too, to my wife, Wendy. She tolerates all the time I spend in my "cave."

Foreword

For much of my career, I have called public institutions "home." Public service is enormously consequential, a critical pillar of a functioning democracy. Volcker Alliance Nonresident Senior Fellow Paul Light's research makes this point vividly. As the new millennium approached, Light surveyed the U.S. federal government's greatest achievements. Among them were rebuilding Europe after World War II, promoting scientific and technological research, and increasing older Americans' access to health care. His list of the fifty greatest achievements is impressive (www.brookings.edu/research/governments-greatest-achievements-of-the-past-half-century/).

More recently, Light turned his attention to government failures, identifying forty-eight significant failures between 2000 and 2015 (wagner.nyu.edu/files/faculty/publications/Light_Cascade_of_Failures_Why_Govt_Fails.pdf). Since 2010 alone, he points to the Deepwater Horizon Gulf oil spill, Texas fertilizer plant explosions, and the failed launch of the Affordable Care Act's Healthcare.gov. The pattern, in Light's view, is that the pace of failures is steadily increasing.

Nothing magical or mysterious determines government's successes or failures. Results do not just appear from a top hat or a black box. Successes and failures flow instead from good or bad ideas, preparation or lack thereof, and having or not having the right human capacity for the situation at hand. What I have learned from our work at the Volcker Alliance is that the human capital in government – the public service – on which we have long relied is increasingly threatened. A 2018 joint report released in collaboration with the Partnership for Public Service, *Renewing America's Civil Service* (www.volckeralliance.org/recommendations-renewing-americas-civil-service), argued that despite the enormous technological advances of the last half century, the U.S. government relies on a civil service system designed largely for a clerical workforce. Similar stories about the technological and process limitations of civil services emanate from capitals globally.

For much of his distinguished public service career, Paul A. Volcker confronted the dual realities to which I refer above. He was well aware of the noble purposes of public work and simultaneously mindful of the practical challenges to realizing them. His commitment to advancing effective management of government to deliver results that matter to citizens is what drove him to found the Volcker Alliance. His practical grounding, however, often led him to caution colleagues with a quote he attributed to Thomas Edison, "Vision without execution is hallucination."

This book, *Managing Organizations to Sustain Passion for Public Service*, by the accomplished public administration scholar, James Perry, is an encouraging bridge between the promise of reliable execution of public services and policies that advance the common good and the public sector workforce Paul Volcker envisioned – a workforce with the preparation, experience, and commitment to ensure government is accountable and delivers excellence.

Professor Perry begins by drawing from three decades of research about public service motivation, as well as research about prosocial motivation and altruism. This behavioral and social science research, Perry argues, transforms the intellectual framework for designing civil service systems.

Although Perry's journey originates from a different place, he arrives at recommendations that are comprehensive and converge with many ideas articulated in *Renewing America's Civil Service*. Among these are: using probationary periods to validate selection decisions, designing and managing job security to balance performance and property rights, making performance an important criterion for reductions-in-force, creating more pronounced wage dispersion for high-skill occupations and executives, and designing onboarding to align organizational and employee public service values.

Professor Perry observes in the concluding chapter that some of his proposals are traditional, others are novel, and still others are solidly grounded in theory but have largely been untried in the public sector. A unifying foundation for all his proposals is the merit principle: recognition that civil service systems are most effective when they are designed as autonomous units staffed by competent and experienced members. It is reassuring that merit principles remain the foundation for rediscovering the public service ethos even as new behavioral and social science evidence materializes. In fact, I am struck by the irony of

Dr. Perry's argument that the design of merit systems, which are often criticized as unresponsive and unaccountable, creates an environment for members to fulfill their basic psychological needs. This realization helps explain why well-designed civil service systems have endured and delivered effective results despite the often-heard criticisms.

A fascinating revelation of the book is the growing body of experimental evidence Dr. Perry cites how motives associated with public service can make a difference for a range of behaviors important to public employees, their leaders, and managers. Dr. Perry draws upon four dozen experimental studies of individuals, jobs, work settings, and leader behaviors. Although the experimental evidence is not definitive, it gives readers a clearer sense of consequences associated with particular policies and behaviors. His concluding chapter includes, too, a call for expanding experimentation – and more partnerships between practitioners and scholars – as a means for expanding the base of knowledge about what works.

As I note above, *Managing Organizations to Sustain Passion for Public Service* is an important bridge between public purpose and policy execution. It is also a bridge built on James Perry's thirty years of research about public service motivation. This book comes at an important time when more Americans are realizing the critical role government plays in their lives and when the focus on a well-prepared, talented, and innovative government workforce has been reawakened. The book begins to fill voids in the intellectual capital needed to redesign our civil service systems and reinvigorate human resource policies and public management. The book is a welcome addition to our tool kit for improving government performance. I look forward to observing how James Perry's spotlight on making a difference through public service inspires passion for government, public organizations, and public employees in the future.

Thomas W. Ross
President
The Volcker Alliance

Thomas W. Ross is President of the Volcker Alliance. He served as President of the University of North Carolina from 2011 to 2016, and as President of Davidson College from 2007 to 2010. Mr. Ross is also Sanford Distinguished Fellow in Public Policy at the Duke University Sanford School of Public Policy.

1 | New Foundations for Civil Service Systems

There is a debt of service due from every man to his country, proportioned to the bounties which nature and fortune have measured to him.

President Thomas Jefferson 1796

Ask not what your country can do for you – ask what you can do for your country.

President John F. Kennedy 1961

In its broadest sense, "public service" is a concept, an attitude, a sense of duty – yes, even a sense of public morality. These attributes are basic to democratic society – attributes lacking or of low priority in an authoritarian society.

Comptroller General Elmer Staats 1988

The "New Public Passion" emphasizes that officials need to be empowered, and to feel empowered, to do what they joined the public service for in the first place, namely to serve citizens.

Helen Clark, Administrator,
United Nations Development Program (UNDP) 2015

The idea of public service – the motivation of people to contribute to the good of the community and society – dates back to Aristotle. As the epigrams above imply, the idea is resilient, surviving the test of time and geography. President Kennedy's call for service may be the most often repeated epigram, certainly in the United States, especially because many living Americans remember the Kennedy years. Similar sentiments are likely to be familiar to much of the world's population. The ideas are both resilient and widespread because they capture important sentiments and values of humankind – service, giving back, and duty.

Only recently has public service come to be formally studied by social and behavioral scientists as a force in individual and group behavior. During the past two decades in particular, the motivating power of public service has been studied with respect to different concepts – among them public service motivation (Perry and Wise 1990), altruism (Piliavin and Charng 1990; LeGrand 2003), and prosocial motivation (Brief and Motowidlo 1986; Penner et al. 2005; Grant 2008b). The volume and quality of research has reached a critical mass that is hard to ignore as an important source of intellectual capital for shaping the way the public sector operates. The purpose of this book is to delimit specific applications from the knowledge base of research on these concepts.

Almost forty years ago, soon after passage of the landmark U.S. Civil Service Reform Act of 1978 (CSRA), Lyman Porter and I observed (Perry and Porter 1982) that the literature on motivation concentrated too heavily on employees within industrial and business organizations. The limitations of knowledge about the context for motivation in public organizations were borne out by failures associated with merit pay and other provisions of CSRA (Perry 1986), both in the United States and in countries globally following diffusion of the reforms (Lah and Perry 2008). Some of the research questions we identified as needing attention in 1982 – for example, the individual-organization match, the effect of goal clarity on motivation and performance, and the motivational influences of job security – have been addressed by research and are now part of the knowledge base for better understanding the motivation of public servants. Scholars have advanced our understanding of how individuals choose organizations and how organizations attract individuals and how the attitudes, beliefs, and interests that an individual brings to organizational settings affect motivation.

The creation of new intellectual capital that potentially supplants motivational practices and assumptions grounded in market enterprises is important for reasons articulated by Fabrizio Ferraro, Jeffrey Pfeffer, and Robert Sutton (2005). They argue that social science theories can become self-fulfilling and self-perpetuating. Theory shapes institutional designs, management practices, and expectations about behavior. If the theory becomes taken for granted and normatively valued, it can take on a life independent of its empirical validity. No better example exists than pay-for-performance in the U.S. federal sector. First introduced in 1978, performance pay schemes have failed and been resurrected on at least three different occasions (Perry, Engbers, and Jun 2009). They are a classic reflection of the process of normatively valued management practices that have endured, despite repeated failures to demonstrate their empirical validity.

The research on public service motivation – embedded in different assumptions about human behavior and institutional context – has gradually begun to erode the premises of the old order as evidence of empirical incidence and effects have grown. Several articles have sought to articulate new sets of assumptions, institutional rules, and management practices. One of the first was by Laurie Paarlberg, James Perry, and Annie Hondeghem (2008) and identified fourteen tactics leaders and managers could employ to strengthen public service motivation to improve behavioral outcomes in public organizations. The tactics ranged across five units of analysis: individual, job, workplace, organization, and external environment, covering motivational contexts suggested in Perry and Porter (1982).

Although research on public service motivation was already well developed when Paarlberg, Perry, and Hondeghem (2008) presented their tactics, both the quantity and quality of research evidence has improved significantly in the decade following the first applications of the research. In light of the expansion of knowledge after 2008 (Ritz, Brewer, and Neumann 2016), Robert Christensen, Laurie Paarlberg, and James Perry (2017) synthesized research published between 2008 and 2016. New to their synthesis was consideration of a threshold question: To what extent is public service motivation a changeable individual attribute? They concluded that public service motivation, based on longitudinal and experimental research since 2008, can be an influential lever in motivational strategies. They extracted five overarching general lessons and implementing tactics associated with each lesson. The practices identified in Christensen, Paarlberg, and Perry (2017) did not duplicate all the tactics in Paarlberg, Perry, and Hondeghem (2008), but they were highly consistent.

Efforts by scholars and practitioners to extract practical applications from research on prosocial behavior and altruism have also emerged over time. Hans Bierhoff (2002) discussed four areas of research application related to prosocial behavior: increasing the readiness to give first aid, solidarity in society, prosocial behavior in the workplace, and volunteerism. Some of these applications, such as readiness to give first aid, are distant from the concerns of managers and leaders in public organizations, but applications related to prosocial behavior in the workplace and volunteerism are very relevant to public leaders and managers.

The biggest impetus for basic and applied research about prosocial behavior in the workplace is the research about organizational citizenship behavior – when employees help others on the job without the overt promise of rewards (Organ and Ryan 1995; Podsakoff et al. 2000). Some dimensions of organizational citizenship behavior, specifically altruism and civic virtue, map closely to dimensions of public service motivation, specifically self-sacrifice, civic duty/ commitment to the public interest, and commitment to public values (Perry 1996; Kim et al. 2013). More recently, research by Adam Grant and his collaborators (see, e.g., Grant 2007, 2008b; Grant and Gino 2010) has injected new life and attention into research about prosocial motivation and behavior.[1]

The UNDP, under the auspices of its Global Centre for Public Service Excellence (United Nations Development Program 2015b), initiated a program dubbed the "New Public Passion," which began in 2015. The rationale for the new public passion program was concerns surrounding the implementation of the UN's 2030 sustainable development goals. Helen Clark and other UNDP leaders and stakeholders viewed effective public services as crucial for the success of the sustainable development goals, but saw public service, specifically morale and motivation, in crisis across many countries in the developed and developing worlds. As a consequence of the perceived deterioration of public services globally, the leadership of UNDP (United Nations Development Program 2015a) feared performance could spiral negatively out of control:

> Public servants seem to have little trust in their own leadership. Job commitment, professional satisfaction and ethical climate in the public service is decreasing, putting at risk fairness and impartiality. In the long term, this could threaten citizens' trust and state legitimacy, but in the short term may be resulting in increasing disengagement and lack of commitment, even misconduct. (p. 1)

The GCPSE turned to the research on intrinsic and public service motivation as a guide for the new public passion. In "The SDGs and New Public Passion: What Really Motivates the Civil Service?" (2015b), they map motivating factors for work in the public sector, emphasizing intrinsic rewards and public service motivation. Although extrinsic rewards are included in the map of motivational factors, the report acknowledges that in developing countries "the scarcity of financial resources in the public sector to support extrinsic rewards provides additional impetus for the adequate provision of less tangible rewards..." (p. 9). Among the alternative levers for improving motivation, the report suggests developing pride and recognition in public service, establishing a merit-based, professional civil service, exercising care in using performance-related pay, promoting a values-based public service, and employee engagement. Many of the levers proposed for the new public passion are direct outgrowths of applying the intellectual capital from the public service motivation and related research referred to earlier. The Global Centre for Public Service Excellence concludes that, given the many demotivating influences affecting the public sector in the developing world, many countries need strategies for strengthening public officials' passion and sense of mission.

To summarize, the idea of public service motivation is enduring, resilient, and meaningful in regimes and populations globally. The intellectual capital from social and behavioral science research has grown exponentially during the last two decades to the point where it can now sustain significant applications to improve civil service design and management practices. The supply of ideas is converging with demands for civil service reform, which have reached significant levels in both developed and developing countries.[2]

1.1 Continuing Pressure on Traditional Civil Service Systems

The sense of crisis afflicting both developed and developing countries is real. Governments around the world are under pressure. One prominent illustration of the pressure comes from *No Time to Wait*, issued by the National Academy of Public Administration (NAPA) in summer 2017. The report's executive summary begins with a dire statement about the current state of affairs:

> We launch this White Paper with a profound sense of urgency. In case after case, ranging from ensuring cyber safety to protecting the nation's borders, the federal government faces profound problems in making government work for the American people. And in case after case, these problems share a common root cause: the federal government's human capital system is fundamentally broken. (p. 1)

Despite the dire warning about the brokenness of the federal system, the federal human capital system has been on the Government Accountability Office's (GAO) High-Risk List since 2001. Although GAO credits both the U.S. Office of Personnel Management and various federal agencies with some progress in its 2017 report, many years have elapsed since GAO first cited strategic human capital management as high risk. In a 2016 report for the IBM Center for the Business of Government, Donald Kettl (2016) explored what lessons could be learned for improving government management from GAO's high-risk list. His conclusions about the centrality of human capital are startling:

> Put sharply, most of the riskiest issues on the high-risk list are rooted in human capital. The challenges are increasing, especially because of the growing policy issues and difficulty of finding the right workers to solve them. Of all the issues on the high-risk list, this is the one most likely to lead future policy areas onto the list – and make it most difficult for policy areas already on the list to escape. (p. 14)

Confronted by GAO's long-term warnings about strategic human capital management and the urgency of not one but two reports titled *No Time to Wait* (National Academy of Public Administration 2017, 2018), an obvious question arises: Why has action been delayed? In fairness to the originators of the warnings about risks associated with federal human capital systems, the current hyper-partisanship reigning in Washington, D.C. is sufficient to put a stop to the legislative action envisioned to reform federal civil service. And the capacity of the federal government to faithfully execute the laws is becoming increasingly problematic (Light 2008, 2020). The persistence of the problem, however, transcends circumstances of political consensus and rests with the stock of intellectual capital and challenges to executing large-scale change in well-established institutional arrangements.

1.1.1 *The Propensity for Civil Service Systems to Persist*

The degree to which "broken" civil service systems persist, not only in the United States but other countries worldwide, suggests that more than dysfunctions of the US political system explain the challenges facing reformers. More than two decades ago, Hans Bekke, Theo Toonen, and I (Bekke, Perry, and Toonen 1996) led a multi-investigator comparative study of civil service systems. A conclusion of the study was that civil service systems are overdetermined – caused and reinforced by a variety of external influences – which persist because they are perpetuated by the systems in which they are nested. With respect to nation-state development, for instance, we wrote: "The fact that civil service systems are outgrowths of external determinants suggests that they are not simple artifacts of their designers that can be remolded at will. Civil service systems are instead natural outgrowths of their context, in some respects organic parts of their surroundings" (p. 322).

Since Bekke, Toonen, and I first characterized civil service systems as overdetermined, scholars have routinely come to describe similar phenomena in terms of path dependence (Pierson 2000) and historical institutionalism (Thelen 1999). Kathleen Thelen (1999) offers an example of the persistence of a practice with which anyone familiar with civil service systems will be immediately familiar. She uses job classification systems as an example of a system originally imposed by employers on labor unions that subsequently became a system of union control because of rules attached to job classifications by labor unions. The ability of unions to adapt the institution to their purposes helps to explain its persistence. Thelen (1999) writes:

> This system was originally imposed on unions by employers as a way of controlling labor. Unable to change the system, emergent unions adapted their strategies to it but sought to attach rules to these job classifications, and in doing so, they eventually turned it into a system of union control. In this case, "adapting" to the institution had the effect of transforming it altogether, so much so that now it is employers who attack the system, unions who defend it. (p. 286)

Two general features of civil service systems, both elements of the system's operating rules, are consequential for their persistence. Operating rules serve to sensitize actors, particularly members of the civil service, to what they value. In doing so, the operating rules may become valued and protected. They can acquire a taken-for-granted quality, which reinforces persistence and constrains initiatives for change (Meyer and Rowan 1977; Tolbert and Zucker 1983; Scott 1987). In the U.S. federal civil service, these types of operating rules were memorialized as "merit system principles" in the 1978 Civil Service Reform Act. Any efforts to reform the system as it now stands must retain the valued operational rules or risk immediate dismissal as a viable reform option.

The second way in which operating rules affect persistence is that they usually have rational origins as appropriate technical solutions to perceived problems. Even when they fall short of performance expectations, however, they are likely to persist in the absence of a plausible technical alternative. The search for plausible alternatives is complicated by the interconnectedness of operating rules – changing one may cascade to affect many others, which increases the complexity of finding a plausible technical alternative. Position classification in the U.S. federal civil service exemplifies an operating system that persists, at least in part, because alternative technical solutions are unavailable (National Academy of Public Administration 1991).

1.1.2 *The Evolution of Motivation in the Face of Persistence*

Despite what seems at times as an imperviousness to reform, civil service systems and the organizations embedded in or linked to them do change. The reality, however, is that they are often less responsive to planned change – reform – and more likely to change as a result of processes driven by developments in their environments (March 1981). A look at the New Public Management (NPM), the name given to the movement to change the public sector beginning in the late 1970s, reveals a good deal about both change in the public sector and the evolution of public motivation.

New Public Management was the antidote for everything perceived as wrong about public bureaucracies that developed during the long period of bureaucracy's hegemony as an organizational form (Mintzberg 1979) – inefficiency, lack of responsiveness, and ineffectiveness. Although NPM is often invoked as a unitary construct, its meaning varies across the literature that invokes the construct. New Public Management has been used to refer to private sector practices imported to the public sector, approaches to organizing public services that rely on quasi-markets, and specific management practices designed to increase the efficiency and effectiveness of public services (Boruvka and Perry 2020). The diversity of meanings attached to NPM makes critiquing it a moving target, but several signature practices, among them high-powered incentives, contracting-out, and agentification, are closely identified with it (Boruvka and Perry 2020).

These signature practices were greeted with high expectations they would fix the bureaupathologies they were adopted to remedy. New Zealand and the United Kingdom, countries that were first movers on agentification and contracting-out reforms, failed to realize expectations on high-profile reform initiatives (Boruvka and Perry 2019). New Zealand's pursuit of agentification resulted in the creation of over one hundred units across government, intense attention to agency-focused goals and incentives, and, in turn, an inability to establish cooperation among units to address complex inter-unit issues. In the United Kingdom, reforms of the National Health Service in 1990 led to greater autonomy for health-care providers and less central monitoring of services delivered. Death rates increased during the course of the 1990s, leading the Blair government in 1997 to correct competitive processes introduced at the beginning of the decade.

As a lever for reform, high-powered incentives have fared even more poorly than contracting-out and agentification. Evaluations of pay-for-performance from the early 1980s to 2000s have consistently concluded that high-powered incentives usually fail to deliver expected results (Perry, Engbers, and Jun 2009).[3] More importantly, the theoretical underpinnings for high-powered incentives have increasingly been called into question (Perry 1986; Frey 1997; Frey and Osterloh 2005; Miller and Whitford 2007). Scholars have not rejected incentives, but made a compelling case for low-powered rather than high-powered incentives (see Chapter 6 for further discussion of this research).

A long-term view of the evolution of public motivation from the late nineteenth century to the present provides perspective about transitions over time. Elise Boruvka and I analyzed the evolution of public motivation from the bureaucratic model to the NPM model to the model emerging today, which we call the new public service model. Our decision to call the post-NPM era the "new public service" motivation model stemmed from its re-emphasis of democratic and constitutional values (Denhardt and Denhardt 2015). The new public service motivation model elevates the prominence of "mission," which serves to articulate public value in contrast to performance narrowly construed. Among the hallmarks of the emerging motivation model "is the centrality of socially acquired values in the motivational dynamic (Perry 2000), the stronger force of intrinsic in contrast to extrinsic motives, and the importance of personal development" (Boruvka and Perry 2020 p. 573).

Several facets of the evolution of motivation in public institutions stand out. One is the longevity of the bureaucratic model, which persisted in many developed countries for a century or more. The model's persistence masks patterns of change over time, best illustrated by Stephen Barley and Gideon Kunda's (1992) conclusion that waves of change since the 1870s have alternated between rational and normative ideologies. Despite several waves of change arriving near the end of the twentieth century, the bureaucratic motivation model remained intact, relying on the member's commitment to institutional values, job security, significant deferred compensation, and flat or pay-for-knowledge salary structures (Boruvka and Perry 2020) as the core of the motivational system. New Public Management may represent the most radical wave of change, arriving near century end and substituting rational ideology for normative (Moynihan 2008). Many of the motivational practices it brought, specifically agentification, contracting-out, and high-powered incentives, were grounded in principal-agent theory. In the aftermath of NPM, many of the motivational practices that accompanied it have been jettisoned. What remains is continuing attention to performance and symbolic action to sustain legitimacy (Boruvka and Perry 2020).

1.2 Public Service Motivation Research as a Foundation for Reform

The goal of this book is to advance change in civil service institutions and organizations throughout the public sector. Research about public service and prosocial motivation during the last two decades, however, gives me confidence that we now have the intellectual capital to lead the way to significant changes in civil service systems. Three facets of the research deserve mention as foundations for my optimism: its evidence-base, comprehensiveness, and coherence.

1.2.1 Evidence-based

A recent report from the Commission on Evidence-Based Policymaking (2017) called attention to two truisms: good government and good public policy rely on evidence; and we have too little evidence to meet our needs. The exponential growth in research on public service motivation and related concepts has crossed a critical threshold. The evidence today now provides a foundation for redesigning civil service systems and public organizations for the challenges of the twenty-first century. This observation does not mean that the research evidence is so abundant we no longer need to pursue basic and applied research to improve motivational outcomes from institutional arrangements of civil service systems. It does mean we now have evidence-based guidance to redesign institutional arrangements with good prospects for successful interventions.

Another reason for confidence about the evidence is not only the volume of evidence but its growing rigor. In their systematic review, Adrian Ritz, Gene Brewer, and Oliver Neumann (2016) identified 323 articles on public service motivation that appeared in 12 public administration journals in the period 1990–2014. Among those articles, only 12, 4.7 percent of the total, used controlled experimental methods. A simple accounting of the research that appears in this book reflects more than forty experimental studies, more than half of them appearing since 2014, the last year included in Ritz, Brewer, and Neumann's (2016) systematic review.[4]

That much of the recent research on public service and prosocial motivation is experimental is not a great surprise given developments in the modern search for solutions to public problems. The United Kingdom's Behavioural Insights Team and President Obama's Social and Behavioral Sciences Team are two examples of relatively intensive efforts to experiment to find novel and sustainable alternatives to current civil service practices. Current evidence, coupled with the openness of many public organizations to rigorous experimentation, is a formula for making significant progress toward civil service reform.

Although we have no fixed standards for whether the volume and quality of research has reached a threshold for reforms of management practice, my reflection about the meaning of evidence-based management (Rousseau 2012; Rousseau and Olivas-Luján 2015) leads me to conclude we have arrived at the threshold. Denise Rousseau and Miguel Olivas-Luján (2015) write that "the central idea of evidence-based management is that scientific knowledge is systematically applied in management practice and, as a result, managers will make better decisions, decrease the inefficiencies with which they operate, and improve the consistency and level of organizational outcomes" (p. 1). The ideas presented in this book adhere closely to the first of four characteristics Rousseau and Olivas-Luján (2015) associate with evidence-based management – use of scientific knowledge. Rather than turning to traditional foundations like managers' experience, much of the evidence in this book is drawn from scientific knowledge "based on controlled observations, large samples sizes (N), validated measures, statistical controls, and systematically tested and accumulated understandings of how the world works (i.e., theory)" (p. 1).

Scientific knowledge is only one element of evidence-based management, it is with regard to the other attributes of the construct that the knowledge accumulated from recent developments in social and behavioral science research passes the threshold to drive reform. Rousseau and Olivas-Luján (2015) argue that using facts, i.e., organizational evidence, is an integral part of evidence-based management. All too often, however, stakeholders in public settings dismiss the reliability and validity of evidence proffered by "bureaucrats" or other knowledgeable stakeholders, owing to either stereotypes or the presumed superiority of practices in the private economy. The research streams (e.g., public service motivation, prosocial motivation, positive organizational behavior) contributing to the foundation of this book have a healthy respect for organizational evidence generated by actors and agents within public institutions. We also know that the other two attributes Rousseau and Olivas-Luján (2015) associate with evidence-based management – reflective judgment and decision aids, and making ethical decisions with consideration of stakeholders – are valued in public organizations.

1.2.2 Comprehensiveness

At the beginning of this chapter, I commented about the surging volume of research on public service motivation (Ritz, Brewer, and Neumann 2016) and prosocial motivation (Grant and Berg 2011). As the research has evolved (Perry 2014), it has expanded to address a range of issues that are pivotal to redesigning civil service systems specifically and public organizations more broadly. The breadth of the accumulating evidence provides an impressive foundation to drive the redesign of civil service systems. A sampling of the issues addressed in the research (Perry 2019) is listed as follows:

- Job choice decisions (Wright and Christensen 2010; Christensen and Wright 2011; Kjeldsen and Jacobsen 2013; Holt 2018; Sanabria-Pulido 2018);

- Absenteeism (Jensen, Andersen, and Holten 2019; Gross, Thaler, and Winter 2019);
- Incentives (Frey and Jegen 2001; Burgess and Ratto 2003; Miller and Whitford 2007);
- Job design and performance (Grant et al. 2007; Grant 2008b; Bellé 2013);
- Performance (Brewer and Brewer 2011; Warren and Chen 2013; Andersen, Heinesen, and Pedersen 2014; Callen et al. 2015; Mostafa and Leon-Cazares 2016; Van Loon et al. 2016; Miao et al. 2019);
- Ethical behavior (Brewer and Selden 1998; Choi 2004; Stazyk and Davis 2015; Meyer-Sahling, Mikkelsen, and Schuster 2019);
- Collaboration (Esteve, van Witteloostuijn, and Boyne 2015);
- Innovative behavior (Wright, Christensen, and Isett 2013; Miao et al. 2018).

1.2.3 Coherence

By coherence, I mean the extent to which the key ideas associated with public service motivation are logical, consistent, and form a unified whole. Three forms of coherence are important. The first is how well the models of individual motivation fit with values embodied in public institutions. As I noted in the opening paragraph, the epigraphs heading this chapter capture values important in public institutions – service, giving back, and duty. The alignment of these values with motivational theories for public service represents *institutional coherence*. As argued earlier, the values of public service were misaligned with the theories used to motivate public employees. If theory shapes institutional designs, management practices, and expectations about behavior (Ferraro, Pfeffer, and Sutton 2005), then theory grounded in values such as the public interest and common good is far better suited to the public sector than theory grounded in self-interest and opportunism.

A second type of coherence that applies to public service motivation is *theoretical coherence*. During the past forty years, scholars from sociology (Knoke and Wright-Isak 1982), social psychology (Deci and Ryan 2000), economics (Frey 1997; Francois 2000), organizational behavior (Schneider, Goldstein, and Smith 1995; Grant 2008a), and public administration (Perry and Wise 1990; Perry 2000; Perry and Vandenabeele 2008; Wright and Pandey 2008; Christensen and Wright

2011) have advanced theories and empirical research that is logical, consistent, and sums to a unified whole. These theories are discussed in greater depth in Chapter 2. The point is that theories advanced across several disciplines and the empirical research they spawned have created a coherent body of compelling evidence.

The third type of coherence is *synergy*, which represents consistency across practices that contributes to self-reinforcing effects when they are implemented.[5] The self-reinforcing effects across the policies and practices mean the systemic outcomes are likely to be greater than the sum of effects from individual practices, emulating outcomes identified for high-performance work practices (Combs et al. 2006). Two questions are at the core of identifying synergy across practices. Does the practice enhance public service or prosocial motivation among employees and across the workforce? Does the practice undercut or detract from public service or prosocial motivation? A high degree of synergy means the practices collectively will contribute constructively and minimize detracting from public service and prosocial motivation.

1.2.4 *Organization of the Book*

Chapter 2, Theoretical and Empirical Foundations for Public Service Motivation, examines the primary theories animating public service motivation research. The discussion is organized around three clusters of theory: (1) predisposition-opportunity theory and related theories about attraction–selection–attrition and person-fit, (2) self-determination theory and related theories associated with motivation-crowding, and (3) goal-setting theory. The chapter calls attention to both the theories that are most prominent in public service motivation research and relevant findings from the empirical research related to each research stream.

Following the broad review of theory and empirical research foundations for public service motivation, Chapters 3–8 are devoted to articulating practical principles and findings that flesh out new directions for civil service design and public management strategy and practice. The six chapters are organized around a classification of analytic units used previously (Perry and Porter 1982; Paarlberg, Perry, and Hondeghem 2008; Christensen, Paarlberg, and Perry 2017) to identify characteristics that affect motivation: (1) individual,

(2) job, (3) work environment, and (4) organization. Chapters 3–8 are organized around units of analysis rather than the theories presented in Chapter 2 to capture the full expanse of ways in which interventions can alter employee motivation. The practical principles call attention to management practices that tap into the motivational potential of public service to energize, direct, and sustain employee behaviors. These chapters engage direct ways to motivate by selecting people predisposed to public service motivation and designing their work to activate prosocial behavior. They also examine ways to support value systems that motivate individuals to engage in public service behaviors. The model of value management extends to managing such values in all aspects of the organization, from work environment to organizational mission. The proposals reach beyond formal human resource management systems to look at leadership, culture, and interpersonal relationships that shape employees and their attitudes and behaviors.

Chapter 3, Selecting for High Public Service Motivation Is a Priority, focuses on attracting individuals whose predispositions will create a foundation for high-quality service to citizens. Arguing for public organizations to attract individuals with high public service motivations means that merit, which has traditionally been associated with competence alone, would be defined more broadly, to include service predispositions. This chapter identifies methods for attracting and selecting staff with high public service motivation.

Chapter 4, Leveraging the Meaningfulness of Public Work, looks at another avenue for energizing public service motives, that is, the work itself. The potential of public work to motivate employees begins with an understanding that governments are different: They are entrusted, especially in democracies, by society to make and enforce the rules of a society. Public institutions create and provide access to public goods, oversee the stewardship of common-pool resources, and promote fairness and access for citizens. Assuring the public interest and sustaining the common good are among the most cherished prosocial goals in a society. That government is the institution entrusted with the public's work is a significant structural advantage for energizing, directing, and sustaining the behaviors of employees situated in this context. The chapter identifies systematic ways for leveraging the meaningfulness inherent in public work to exploit its motivational advantages.

Chapter 5, Creating a Supportive Work Environment, looks at attributes of the work environment that encourage employees to develop strong ties between their values and the organization's. Creating a supportive work environment provides a context in which employees can pursue and realize their innate needs for competence, autonomy, and relatedness. An environment within which employees can pursue their basic psychological needs creates a foundation for psychological health and well-being that, in turn, permits employees to connect their values and goals with those of the organization without diversions. The chapter examines steps to intentionally nurture public service motivation and, on the other side of the ledger, to purge practices that are harmful to creating a supportive environment and assure a freer rein for employees to connect their values and the organization's.

Supportive managers, coworkers, and policies represent the "soft" side of the work environment. The "hard" side is represented by compensation systems, which are the subject of Chapter 6, Aligning Compensation Systems and Public Service Motivation. Compensation and public service motivation have intersected frequently in research, particularly research on pay-for-performance. Although intersections between performance-based pay and public service motivation are most prominent, many areas of compensation policy are highly relevant to public service motivation. This chapter highlights principles for aligning compensation policy and public service motivation, assesses inferences that professionals can draw from research for compensation policy and practice, and identifies compensation strategies that align compensation policy with public service motivation.

Although public organizations should strive to recruit staff with high public service motivation, leaders need to assume that some employees will arrive who are not predisposed to public service or that, over time, employees will benefit from continuing socialization to public service values because both organizations and staff change. Chapter 7, Providing Opportunities for Newcomers to Learn Public Service Values, recognizes the need for socializing both new and established staff. Several mechanisms available for strong culture creation are considered in this chapter, among them new-employee orientation, onboarding, and mentoring. The processes discussed in Chapter 7 represent ways to fill gaps in selection systems and broaden and strengthen public service values across the workforce.

Chapter 8, Leading with Mission, Inspiration, and Communication, explores the roles of leaders in stimulating the salience and responsiveness of staff to public service values. Many employees sustain their motivation through self-regulating processes. Others benefit from stimulation of their aspirations. This chapter discusses two general paths worth pursuing as ways to enhance public service motivation through leadership. The first of these paths involves leaders articulating mission and vision as a means to stimulate, reinforce, and direct staff toward salient public service values. The second path is for leaders to pursue value-based leadership.

The book concludes with Chapter 9, Designing Civil Service to Unleash Public Passion. A central issue taken up in the conclusion is whether the perspective conveyed in the first eight chapters may be either too optimistic or overlook a dark side to the enthusiasm for public service motivation as the intellectual capital for rethinking how we motivate public employees and design our civil service systems. Although my answer may be easy to anticipate, I believe there is value in visiting whether the case built here either has been too optimistic or has ignored a dark side of public service motivation. The book concludes with a summary of key ideas about how to advance the redesign and realignment of public services.

1.3 Conclusion

This book navigates well-traveled territory with a goal of advancing civil service reform. What distinguishes this enterprise is that it begins from a new foundation, one built on recent social and behavioral science research about public service. Because of the research, we now possess a critical mass of intellectual capital to rethink civil service designs, policies, and management practices to change civil service systems around the globe. I explain in Chapter 2 the theories that are prominent in public service motivation research and relevant findings that serve as a new foundation for civil service systems.

Notes

1 The research by Grant and colleagues is referred to throughout the book, particularly in Chapters 4 and 8.
2 Although I believe many of the concepts, theories, and organizational practices presented in this book are broadly applicable, managers and other users of the ideas will need to assess their appropriateness for specific contexts. This caution is consistent with advice provided by

experts on evidence-based management (Rousseau 2012; Rousseau and Olivas-Luján 2015). As I emphasize in this introductory chapter, I believe the book's contents are germane to problems across a diverse population of organizations globally. I am cautious, however, not to overstate the applicability of the ideas, in part because the boundary conditions for many of them are uncertain or may not be fully established.

I am mindful of the difficulties of specifying the boundaries to which ideas in this book apply. The challenge of specifying boundaries is shaped both by the heterogeneity of governments and the public sector globally and the fact that the public sector is increasingly about governance rather than government alone (Rhodes 1996). A world in which governance is the operative descriptor of who is engaged in the delivery of public goods and services is an environment in which it is difficult to arrive at a completely satisfactory nomenclature for focal units of analysis. Although government organizations are at the core of the population of organizations targeted by this book, the boundaries of the public sector are shifting and also vary significantly cross-nationally. The contents of the book, therefore, are also likely to have value for quasi-governmental and nonprofit enterprises that are engaged in implementing public policies, often as integral parts of public governance systems.

In some places in the book, I use terms such as "government" or "civil service systems" to refer to the primary institutional context for which my generalizations are relevant. I am especially inclined to use these terms when discussing rules or practices that are closely identified with governments or civil service systems. One example is traditional job security systems (see, especially, Chapter 7) that are closely identified with civil service systems globally.

In other parts of the book, I use terms such as "public sector" and "public organizations" to convey a scope of application broader than organizations controlled by government or civil service laws, rules and regulations (see, e.g., Perry and Rainey 1988). Although much of the content of Chapter 4, for example, which focuses on work design, originates from research in both public and private organizations, I refer to public sector and public organizations to convey that I believe the ideas are broadly applicable throughout large segments of the public sector.

3 The most recent synthesis of research on public performance pay is more positive than prior syntheses, but still calls for caution and additional research. See Zahid Hasnain, Nick Manning, and Jan Henryk Pierskalla (2014). I return to the issue of incentives in Chapter 6.

4 The experimental studies cut across a range of disciplines and fields, including economics, organizational behavior and public administration (Grant et al. 2007; Grant 2008a, 2008b, 2012; Grant and Gino 2010; Tonin and Vlassopoulos 2010; Brewer and Brewer 2011; Grant and Hofmann 2011; Kosfeld and Neckermann 2011; Muralidharan and Sundararaman 2011; Bellé 2013, 2014; Christensen et al. 2013; Dal Bó, Finan, and Rossi 2013; Moynihan 2013; Arieli, Grant, and Sagiv 2014; Ashraf, Bandiera, and Jack 2014; Ashraf, Bandiera, and Lee 2014; Banerjee et al. 2014; Fehrler and Kosfeld 2014; Banuri and Keefer 2015, 2016; Barfort et al. 2019; Bellé and Cantarelli 2015; Callen et al. 2015; Esteve, Van Witteloostuijn, and Boyne 2015; Pedersen 2015; Burbano 2016; Esteve et al. 2016; Neumann 2016; Smith 2016; Tepe 2016; Hanna and Wang 2017; Linos 2018; Asseburg, Homberg, and Vogel 2018; Jensen 2018; Resh, Marvel, and Wen 2018; Bromberg and Charbonneau 2020; Deserranno 2019; Jensen, Andersen, and Jacobsen 2019; Marvel and Resh 2019; Meyer-Sahling, Mikkelsen, and Schuster 2019; Olsen et al. 2019; Weske et al. 2019; Asseburg et al. 2020; Vogel and Willems 2020).

5 Implicit in my use of the idea of synergy is that some motivational strategies and tactics (i.e., work motivators) will better fit with others in a cluster of strategies and tactics. My world view – and I believe world view is an appropriate description for what I have in mind because a body of evidence does not exist to test my conjecture – is that this form of coherence has consequences. This is somewhat different than the inference I draw from Marc Esteve and Christian Schuster's (2019) typology of work motivators. They identify six work motivators (prosocial motivation, group-organization identification, incentives, warm glow, relatedness, and enjoyment) by cross-classifying two continua, other- to self-regarding and outcome- to activity-motivated. The implication is that organizations and their leaders and managers can avail themselves of practices associated with all types of work motivators. I can envision circumstances, however, when practices across the six types may cancel or detract from one another. Organizational leaders and managers should therefore be attentive to the dynamics across practices, implied by my use of the term synergy.

2 | Theoretical and Empirical Foundations for Public Service Motivation

Motivation usually stands for that which "energizes, directs and sustains behavior" (Perry and Porter 1982). It is the degree and type of effort an individual exhibits in a behavioral situation. As the definition implies, motivation is not simply the sheer amount of effort, it also involves the direction and quality of that effort. By whatever mechanisms, individuals must be stimulated to expend effort, channel it in constructive directions, and sustain it over an appropriate time.

The concept of public service motivation originates from belief in a public service ethic, that what motivates public servants goes beyond the factors that motivate others in the private sector. When Lois Wise and I first wrote about public service motivation, we expressed some caution about its motivational power. We wrote: "Calls for a recommitment to values associated with government service, among them personal sacrifice and duty to the public interest, raise practical questions about the power of these values to stimulate and direct human behavior. At their core, calls for a renewal of public service motivation assume the importance of such motivations for an effective and efficient public service" (Perry and Wise 1990, 367). One reason for our caution was that public service had been depicted throughout most of history as an ideal. Sylvia Horton (2008) concludes, based on a review of history: "... the concept of public service is well established in the history of political and moral philosophy mainly as a prescriptive or idealistic idea – a higher calling, an unselfish activity, a duty and responsibility of the good citizen that individuals are motivated to perform" (p. 22).

Public service motivation has been defined formally "as an individual's predisposition to respond to motives grounded primarily or uniquely in public institutions and organizations" (Perry and Wise 1990, 368). In the original formulation, motives referred to psychological deficiencies – needs – that an individual feels some compulsion to eliminate. Individuals are exposed, in varying degrees, to experiences, social groups and networks, and institutions that inculcate logics and values that shape their rational, normative, and affective identities (Perry 2000). The consequence is that people will bring different levels of public service motivation with them to their organizations. Those whose identities are consistently and strongly public in character will bring with them an inherent interest in and valuing of public service (Perry and Vandenabeele 2008).

The formal definition of public service motivation mentioned earlier has given way to a variety of measures of the construct (Perry 1996; Wright 2008; Kim et al. 2013; Wright, Christensen, and Pandey 2013), which both define it more concretely and link it back to some of the historic ideals identified by Horton (2008). The first multidimensional scale to measure public service motivation consisted of four dimensions (Perry 1996): attraction to public policy making, civic duty/commitment to the public interest, compassion, and self-sacrifice (see Table 2.1). The four dimensions have remained relatively consistent across subsequent alternative measures. Sangmook Kim and a group of international collaborators (Kim et al. 2013) introduced a measure created from a twelve-country sample. The new measure also consisted of four dimensions: attraction to public participation, commitment to public values, compassion, and self-sacrifice (Table 2.1). The number and content of dimensions closely track the original scale, with two identical dimensions, compassion and self-sacrifice, and two dimensions, attraction to public participation and commitment to public values, closely aligned with the institutional logic of the original.

In addition to the multidimensional measures of public service motivation, a variety of unidimensional measures have also been developed (Wright, Christensen, and Pandey 2013). The unidimensional five-item scale presented in Table 2.1 was derived from a list of forty items appearing in James Perry (1996) and was first fielded by the U.S. Merit Systems Principles Survey (Naff and Crum 1999). The short scale has appeared frequently in subsequent merit-principles surveys, conducted about every three years by the U.S. Merit Systems Protection Board.

For purposes of comparison, Table 2.1 presents survey items for two other scales associated with prosocial motivation and altruism. The four-item prosocial motivation scale was introduced by Richard Ryan and James Connell (1989) and used subsequently by Adam

Table 2.1 *Survey items for public service motivation, prosocial motivation, and altruism scales and subscales*

Public service motivation, original (Perry 1996)	Public service motivation, international (Kim et al. 2013)	Public service motivation, short form (Perry 1996; Naff and Crum 1999)	Prosocial motivation (Ryan and Connell 1989; Grant 2008a)	Altruism (Ruston, Chrisjohn, and Fekken 1981; response options: never, once, more than once, often, and very often)
Attraction to public policy making	*Attraction to public service*	1. Meaningful public service is very important to me.	*Why are you motivated to do your work?*	1. I have helped push a stranger's car out of the snow.
1. I don't care much for politicians. (Reversed)	1. I admire people who initiate or are involved in activities to aid my community	2. I am often reminded by daily events about how dependent we are on one another.	1. Because I care about benefiting others through my work.	2. I have given directions to a stranger.
2. The give and take of public policy making doesn't appeal to me. (Reversed)	2. It is important to contribute to activities that tackle social problems	3. Making a difference in society means more to me than personal achievements.	2. Because I want to help others through my work.	3. I have made change for a stranger.
3. Politics is a dirty word. (Reversed)	3. Meaningful public service is very important to me	4. I am prepared to make enormous sacrifices for the good of society.	3. Because I want to have positive impact on others.	4. I have given money to a charity.

Commitment to the public interest/civic duty

1. Meaningful public service is very important to me.
2. I unselfishly contribute to my community.
3. I would prefer seeing public officials do what is best for the whole community even if it harmed my interests.
4. It is important for me to contribute to the common good.
5. I am not afraid to go to bat for the rights of others even if it means I will be ridiculed.

Commitment to public values

1. I think equal opportunities for citizens are very important.
2. It is important that citizens can rely on the continuous provision of public services.
3. It is fundamental that the interests of future generations are taken into account when developing public policies.
4. Because it is important to me to do good for others through my work.
5. I have given money to a stranger who needed it (or asked me for it).
6. I have donated goods or clothes to a charity.
7. I have done volunteer work for a charity.
8. I have donated blood.
9. I have helped carry a stranger's belongings (books, parcels, etc.).

Table 2.1 *(cont.)*

Public service motivation, original (Perry 1996)	Public service motivation, international (Kim et al. 2013)	Public service motivation, short form (Perry 1996; Naff and Crum 1999)	Prosocial motivation (Ryan and Connell 1989; Grant 2008a)	Altruism (Ruston, Chrisjohn, and Fekken 1981; response options: never, once, more than once, often, and very often)
4. It is hard for me to get intensely interested in what is going on in my community. (Reversed)	4. To act ethically is essential for public servants.			10. I have delayed an elevator and held the door open for a stranger.
5. I consider public service my civic duty.				11. I have allowed someone to go ahead of me in a lineup (at Xerox machine, in the supermarket).

1. It is difficult for me to contain my feelings when I see people in distress.

2. Most social programs are too vital to do without.

3. I am often reminded by daily events of how dependent we are on one another.

1. I feel sympathetic to the plight of the underprivileged

2. I empathize with other people who face difficulties

3. I get very upset when I see other people being treated unfairly.

12. I have given a stranger a lift in my car.

13. I have pointed out a clerk's error (in a bank, at the supermarket) in undercharging me for an item.

14. I have let a neighbor whom I didn't know too well borrow an item of some value to me (e.g., a dish, tools).

15. I have bought "charity" Christmas cards deliberately because I knew it was a good cause.

Table 2.1 (*cont.*)

Public service motivation, original (Perry 1996)	Public service motivation, international (Kim et al. 2013)	Public service motivation, short form (Perry 1996; Naff and Crum 1999)	Prosocial motivation (Ryan and Connell 1989; Grant 2008a)	Altruism (Ruston, Chrisjohn, and Fekken 1981; response options: never, once, more than once, often, and very often)
4. To me, patriotism includes seeing to the welfare of others.	4. Considering the welfare of others is very important.			16. I have helped a classmate who I did not know that well with a homework assignment when my knowledge was greater than his or hers.
5. I have little compassion for people in need who are unwilling to take the first step to help themselves. (Reversed)				17. I have before being asked, voluntarily looked after a neighbor's pets or children without being paid for it.

6. There are few public programs that I wholeheartedly support. (Reversed)

7. I seldom think about the welfare of people I don't know personally. (Reversed)

8. I am rarely moved by the plight of the underprivileged. (Reversed)

Self-sacrifice

1. I am prepared to make enormous sacrifices for the good of society.

2. I think people should give back to society more than they get from it.

Self-sacrifice

1. I am prepared to make sacrifices for the good of society

2. I believe in putting civic duty before self.

18. I have offered to help a handicapped or elderly stranger across a street.

19. I have offered my seat on a bus or train to a stranger who was standing.

20. I have helped an acquaintance to move households.

Table 2.1 (*cont.*)

Public service motivation, original (Perry 1996)	Public service motivation, international (Kim et al. 2013)	Public service motivation, short form (Perry 1996; Naff and Crum 1999)	Prosocial motivation (Ryan and Connell 1989; Grant 2008a)	Altruism (Ruston, Chrisjohn, and Fekken 1981; response options: never, once, more than once, often, and very often)
3. I am one of those rare people who would risk personal loss to help someone else.	3. I am willing to risk personal loss to help society.			
4. Making a difference in society means more to me than personal achievements.	4. I would agree to a good plan to make a better life for the poor, even if it costs me money.			
5. Serving other citizens would give me a good feeling even if no one paid me for it.				

6. Doing well financially
   is definitely more
   important to me than
   doing good deeds.
   (Reversed)
7. Much I do is for a
   cause bigger than
   myself.
8. I believe in putting
   duty before self.

Grant (2008a). The twenty-item altruism scale was developed by J. Philippe Rushton, Roland Chrisjohn, and G. Cynthia Fekken (1981). The developers refer to it as a "self-report" scale because respondents indicate the frequency with which they engage in twenty specific behaviors. The scale predicts peer ratings of altruism and measures of prosocial orientation (Rushton, Chrisjohn, and Fekken 1981).

As my presentation throughout this book will illustrate, I view the research and evidence flowing from the study of the constructs represented in Table 2.1 as complementary, especially for illuminating a path to a positive and renewed public service globally. Despite my interest in emphasizing and highlighting useable knowledge flowing from the research, scholars and others have legitimate disagreements about the multiple and complementary concepts. Barry Bozeman and Xuhong Su (2015), for example, raise a number of questions related to the differentiation of public service motivation and altruism. Their questions arise from both the proliferation of definitions of public service motivation and ambiguities surrounding the definition of altruism. A similar controversy arises with respect to self-interest and other orientation. Bruce Meglino and Audrey Korsgaard (2004) proposed other orientation as an alternative to self-interest as a motivational foundation for theories of attitudes and behavior. Carsten De Dreu (2006) agrees, in part, with Meglino and Korsgaard's critique, but suggests that self-interest and other orientation are not bipolar opposites. De Dreu suggests instead that because individuals in organizations confront a combination of competitive and cooperative incentives that self-interest drives self-concern, and self-concern and other orientation are orthogonal and unipolar. Previous disagreements involved the origins and diversity of prosocial motives and behavior (Batson and Shaw 1991; Batson 1994).

I do not try to sort out or, even more ambitiously, resolve fundamental disagreements in this book. My goals are instead pragmatic and applied: identify institutional arrangements, organizational policies, and management practices that can reform civil service systems to enhance public service significantly. Any fundamental disagreements will resolve themselves over time as different communities of scholars and practitioners pursue their distinct lines of inquiry, coming together occasionally to inform one another and creating opportunities for new understandings. At the same time, I believe the application of existing intellectual capital and knowledge can advance movement toward resolving key theoretical questions (see Chapter 9 for an elaboration of this point). The choice is not either–or. Waiting for all the conceptual and theoretical questions to be answered should not deter us from exploiting opportunities for learning and improvements that come from applying knowledge we now possess, even if imperfect.

Assuming that public institutions serve distinctive individual needs, another question is central to the motivational equation: What are the behaviors that leaders, managers, and governments are seeking to motivate? Following Daniel Katz's (1964) seminal article about behaviors that effective organizations must elicit, three classes of behaviors are relevant for answering the question. First, effective organizations must motivate individuals to join and sustain their membership with the organization. Second, effective organizations must motivate reliable role behaviors, the cluster of behaviors associated with the mission of the organization that are performed to fulfill expectations of coworkers, supervisors, external stakeholders, and others that the routines associated with work in the organization are being performed. Finally, effective organizations must motivate innovative and spontaneous activity to achieve organizational objectives beyond role specifications. With regard to motivation, these three concepts, that is, membership, reliable role behaviors, and innovative and spontaneous activity, encompass the behaviors required by effective organizations.

When Wise and I published the "Motivational Bases of Public Service" (Perry and Wise 1990), we relied primarily on a single, sociology-based theory, predisposition-opportunity theory (Knoke and Wright-Isak 1982) to sustain our core arguments about distinctive motivations in public service and their behavioral outcomes. In the years since our article appeared, theoretical support for public service motivation has broadened to other disciplines and become more compelling. The remainder of this chapter discusses these theoretical foundations and some of the empirical research associated with them. The discussion is organized around three clusters of middle-range theory (Abner, Kim, and Perry 2017): (1) predisposition-opportunity theory and related theories about attraction–selection–attrition (ASA) and person-fit, (2) self-determination theory and related theories associated with motivation-crowding, and (3) goal theory.

2.1 Predisposition-Opportunity Theory

David Knoke and Christine Wright-Isak (1982) proposed what they called a predisposition-opportunity theory in search of an answer to the question: "Why do people contribute varying amounts of personally-controlled resources to organizations?" (p. 211). On the predisposition side of the equation, they conceive of individuals as acting upon appropriate external cues tied to three types of social motives: rational choice, normative conformity, and affective bonding. Rational motives involve actions grounded in individual utility maximization. Norm-based motives refer to actions generated by efforts to conform to norms. Affective motives refer to stimuli of behavior that are grounded in emotional responses to social contexts.

The opportunity side of the model is the incentives that organizations offer in return for the personally controlled resources that individuals commit to the organization. Knoke and Wright-Isak (1982) developed a typology of organizational incentives, reproduced in Table 2.2, based upon all combinations of the presence or absence of each of the three types of social motives, resulting in eight types, from a nonincentive system (i.e., none of the three incentives present) to a full-incentive system (i.e., all three of the incentives present). It is only when organizational incentive systems match individual motivation that commitment to the organization is achieved and results in organizational behavior and contribution. Knoke and Wright-Isak summarize the logic of the

Table 2.2 *A typology of organizational incentive systems*

| System | Types of incentives | | |
	Utilitarian	Normative	Affectual
1. Nonincentive	Not offered	Not offered	Not offered
2. Pure utilitarian	Offered	Not offered	Not offered
3. Pure normative	Not offered	Offered	Not offered
4. Pure affectual	Not offered	Not offered	Offered
5. Partisan	Offered	Offered	Not offered
6. Solidarity	Offered	Not offered	Offered
7. Service	Not offered	Offered	Offered
8. Full incentive	Offered	Offered	Offered

Source: Knoke and Wright-Isak (1982).

predisposition-opportunity model: "Whether a member decides to commit himself or herself to the group depends upon the relationship between the individual's motivational predisposition and the type of organizational incentive system. That is, individual predispositions must match the organizational opportunity structure before action is initiated" (p. 210).

The "matching" feature of predisposition-opportunity theory, which links individual to organizational characteristics, has led to its association with two theories of organizational behavior, ASA, and person–organization fit. These theories are discussed in turn to understand their similarities and differences from predisposition-opportunity theory.

2.1.1 Attraction–Selection–Attrition Theory

Attraction–selection–attrition theory is most closely identified with psychologist Benjamin Schneider, who introduced the theory in a series of articles in the 1980s. Benjamin Schneider, Harold Goldstein, and Brenth Smith (1995) summarize key features of this theory:

- Three interrelated dynamic processes – attraction, selection, and attrition – determine the kinds of people in an organization.
- The personality, attitudes, and values of an organization's founder and colleagues – and the goals, structures, processes, and culture that emerge surrounding them – determine the kinds of people who are attracted to the organization.
- Attraction to the organization is a function of prospective members' judgments about the congruence between their personalities and the organization's goals, structures, processes, and culture.
- During the selection cycle, organizations use formal and informal procedures in recruitment and hiring to select people with attributes the organization desires.
- People leave the organization – the attrition part of the cycle – if they do not fit.
- The consequence of ASA dynamics is increasing homogeneity of personalities within an organization.

The ASA model associates both positive and negative consequences with the homogeneity of personalities within organizations. Among the positive consequences associated with the homogeneity are fewer interpersonal conflicts and better communication and cooperation. The negative consequences include an absence of diversity that may reduce adaptability and lack of critical judgment in decision-making processes.

2.1.1.1 Comparisons to Predisposition-Opportunity Theory

The ASA model has important similarities and differences with predisposition-opportunity theory. The dynamic processes are likely to be common across the two models. Attraction, selection, and attrition cycles are at work in predisposition-opportunity theory. The core of the theory contends that individuals with particular predispositions are attracted to organizations offering appropriate incentives. Organizations select in accordance with convergence between individuals who approach them and the incentives they offer. Although the attrition cycle is less prominently part of predisposition-opportunity theory, it is reasonable that individuals who join an organization will hold it accountable to deliver on the incentives they expect and organizations will similarly hold individuals to conform to their expectations. The failure of either individuals or organizations to conform is likely to trigger attrition.

The two models also diverge in important ways. Attraction–selection–attrition theory emphasizes that the personalities, attitudes, and values of an organization are at the heart of individual judgments surrounding their attraction. The heart of individual attraction to organizations in predisposition-opportunity theory are the types of incentives – utilitarian, normative, affectual – offered by the organization. The salient attributes may converge in some areas, for instance when values or norms are relevant to the choice situation, but the attributes associated with attraction are generally different.

Another distinction between the models involves the ASA model's focus on an organization's founder and the personalities with whom the founder surrounds herself or himself. Predisposition-opportunity theory is largely silent about an organization's origins and the cadre of people who compose it. In fact, Knoke and Wright-Isak's (1982) original presentation of predisposition-opportunity theory was framed in terms of voluntary associations rather than corporate or government organizations because of their judgment that voluntary associations were understudied relative to the other organizational types and offered a broader range of primary incentives. It is not that founders are irrelevant to voluntary associations (see, for instance, research on "founder's syndrome" in the nonprofit sector, Block and Rosenberg 2002) or governments, but rather that they may be much less consequential for long-term attributes of the organization.

The divergence of the two models around the centrality of founders may mask an implicit difference with respect to the institutional nexus in which organizations are situated and the ways in which institutions affect motivational processes. Knoke and Wright-Isak's (1982) decision to emphasize voluntary associations because of their broader range of primary incentives calls attention to organizational differences associated with underlying ownership and funding that today distinguish not only voluntary associations but governments, too, from their market-based counterparts (Perry and Rainey 1988). Previous research (Perry and Porter 1982; Shamir 1991; Perry 2000; Vandenabeele 2007; Perry and Vandenabeele 2008) has critically assessed the institutional blindness of most motivation research. Boas Shamir (1991) observes that values and moral obligations, which are central to the meaning of institutions, are excluded from conceptions of intrinsic motivation. Theories of work motivation give little recognition to either moral obligation or to values as conceptions of the desirable. Theory and research about public service motivation, which originates from predisposition-opportunity and its precursors in sociology (Etzioni 1988), has begun to remedy the exclusion of institutions.

2.1.1.2 Empirical Research about ASA and Public Service Motivation

Although few empirical studies using the ASA model looked at public service motivation as recently as 2008 (Leisink and Steijn 2008), scholars have addressed ASA-related research questions more frequently during the last decade. Peter Leisink and Bram Steijn (2008) concluded, based on limited research from the Netherlands: "Public service motives are the most important motive for a substantial share of public sector employees..." (p. 130).

Several studies published following Leisink and Steijn's conclusion support the influence of public service motivation on individual ASA in public service organizations. In cross-sectional research, Wouter Vandenabeele (2008), using a sample of advanced masters students from Belgian colleges and universities, concluded that individuals with high public service motivation were more likely to seek public employment. Jacqueline Carpenter, Dennis Doverspike, and Rosanna Miguel (2012) support these findings about attraction in subsequent research. They conducted three studies with student samples that found public sector motivation was positively related to attraction to both public and nonprofit organizations. They also concluded that public sector motivation predicted attraction when controlling for the general personality factor of agreeableness, which was closely aligned with facets of public service motivation such as compassion and self-sacrifice.

Longitudinal research related to the ASA model provides a more nuanced perspective about the influence of public service motivation. Bradley Wright and Robert Christensen (2010) assessed the ASA model using panel data on attorneys. They found that an individual's interest in social service and helping others did not predict the employment sector of a lawyer's first legal job. Proxy measures of an individual's public service motivation were related to a greater likelihood of subsequently taking a job in the public sector. Wright and Christensen (2010) concluded that while public service motivation was influential in an individual's sector choices, the attenuated relationships were evidence that other factors, such as personal financial situation and family circumstances, moderated the influence of public service motivation. In a study of Danish university students in economics, political science, and law, Mogens Jin Pedersen (2013) concluded that the academic field of study also moderated the public sector motivation decision.

Paul Gregg et al. (2011) studied unpaid overtime, as an indicator of donated labor, in caring industries in the United Kingdom. They found that people with high public service motivation were more likely to move to firms in the public or nonprofit sector. They concluded that increasing the wage raises the probability of attracting workers with lower prosocial motivations. A study by Georgellis, Iossa, and Tabvuma (2011) used data from the first fourteen waves of the British Household Panel Survey covering the period 1991–2004. Their analysis focused on 747 transitions from the private to the public sector within the data. They concluded that a significant share of individuals move to the public sector because of the higher likelihood of fulfilling their public service motivation.

The nuances first suggested by Wright and Christensen (2010) from their research on attraction are developed further by Anne Mette

Kjeldsen and Christian Bøtcher Jacobsen (2013) and Anne Mette Kjeldsen (2014) in two panel studies of professionals in Denmark, which looked at attraction–selection and socialization. The two studies, one on physiotherapists and the other on social workers, arrived at similar conclusions related to dynamics associated with public service motivation, sector, and work values. They found that the work itself is more influential than whether the work is in the public or private sector. Both the work and organization environments affected postentry changes in public service motivation. They concluded from the studies that the dynamics of attraction–selection effects differed from socialization effects. In a subsequent study of teachers in the United States using the National Longitudinal Study – 1972, Yujin Choi and Il Hwan Chung (2017) arrived at conclusions similar to Kjeldsen and Jacobsen (2013).

A recent study sought to extend understanding of ASA dynamics to the Russian Federation. Jordan Gans-Morse et al. (2019) pose the question: Do findings from Western countries about the attraction of public employment to individuals with high public service motivation explain behavior in developing countries, particularly post-communist states. Questioning the generalizability of the findings from Western countries about a public service ethos is entirely appropriate given the lack of established norms and traditions, uncertainties surrounding public values like the "public interest," and the tendency of public officials to pursue self- or corrupt interests. Gans-Morse and colleagues engaged 1,180 students from two universities to assess the generalizability of the previous findings. Their data collection included both surveys and experimental games. Their results about the generalizability of past research are encouraging. They found that both traditional measures of public service motivation and a measure of altruism derived from the experimental game were positively and strongly associated with student preferences for public employment. Follow-up research using panel data showed that public service motivation predicted career paths two years after graduation. These results make a strong case for the generalizability of previous findings.

2.1.2 Person–Environment Fit Theory

Predisposition-opportunity theory is manifest in another cluster of frameworks that have also played a prominent role in research about public service motivation. Person–environment theory covers a bundle of frameworks for assessing the effects of congruence between an individual and the environments in which they are situated. Among the environments that have been studied for how their fit with individuals affects individual-level criteria (e.g., attitudes, performance, withdrawal behaviors) are jobs, supervisors, groups, organizations, and vocations (Kristof-Brown, Zimmerman, and Johnson 2005). The central tenet of person-fit theory is as follows: The causes of behavior are best understood by looking at the relationships between individuals and their environments.

It is worth noting that what scholars commonly call person-fit or person–environment theory has a long tradition, dating to personnel selection research from the early 1900s. Benjamin Schneider (2001) classifies his ASA research as one among the many types of person–environment theories, providing further support for grouping together the predisposition-opportunity, ASA, and person–environment models.

Scholars have frequently studied public service motivation in the context of person–environment fit models. I call attention to some of that research later. Before reviewing findings from that research, however, it will be helpful to place the findings in the context of challenges of person–environment models to date. Two challenges identified by Kristof-Brown et al. (2005) merit mention. The first limitation is the lack of valid measurements for person–environment fit. Kristof-Brown et al. (2005) lament the absence of multidimensional measures for a concept as complex as person–environment fit. The absence of valid multidimensional measures is not surprising given the complexity of environments relevant to the fit construct, but the lack of measures stand in the way of progress for assessing how organizations and managers can use the fit concept. The second challenge is what "fit" means. Kristof-Brown et al. conclude that "... a better understanding of what it means to people to 'fit' and the mechanisms that stimulate fit are long overdue" (p. 321).

I highlight the two challenges mentioned earlier as a cautionary note about relying heavily on person-fit research to advance understanding of public service motivation. Although the research stream has spawned many studies, many measurement and conceptual issues need resolution for it to be highly productive for future public service motivation research.

2.1.2.1 Empirical Evidence about Person–Environment Fit and Public Service Motivation

The body of research about person–environment fit is far more extensive than the research on ASA. Given the distinct "environments" from which investigators have to choose, however, discovering central tendencies and consistencies in the results is a bigger challenge than drawing inferences from ASA research. Most of the research also fails to address the general challenge of valid multidimensional measures, which confounds any search for consistencies.

One of the first studies of person–environment fit related to public service motivation predates most other studies by almost five years. Katherine Karl and Barbara Peat (2004) took up the issue to address what educators in public affairs could do to prepare students to develop congruence between what a student brings to the employment in terms of values, motives, and skills and the requirements and rewards of a job. Although their study invoked the research on public service motivation, its primary emphasis was that students pursuing public service as a profession were in touch with their values and motives as they entered public service work. Karl and Peat's research anticipates a proposal introduced in Chapter 3, suggesting the benefits of realistic job previews for increasing congruence between organizations and the values, motives, and reward preferences of their employees.

Karl and Peat's study was followed by four studies in 2007 and 2008, including a study by Bram Steijn (2008) in the Netherlands that looked at vocational outcomes. Leonard Bright (2007, 2008) contributed two of the four studies. His research focused on person–organization fit and its relationship to job satisfaction, turnover intentions, and job performance, with a sample of 250 public employees randomly selected from a public health-care agency, and city and county governments in Indiana, Kentucky, and Oregon. The two cross-sectional studies used direct measures of person–organization fit, using survey items to measure the extent to which employees perceived fit with the organizations' values, goals, and culture. Bright concluded that public service motivation contributed significantly to person–organization fit and that fit was the key determinant of job satisfaction, turnover intentions, and job performance. Confidence in these findings is tempered by the cross-sectional nature of the studies and the common methods limitations of the measures.

Bradley Wright and Sanjay Pandey (2008) also framed fit in terms of the person–organization relationship. Their goal was to clarify the dynamics by which public service motivation affects performance through antecedent employee attitudes. Their study sample included state and local government employees from seven organizations in two northeastern US states. Wright and Pandey found that the public service motivation–job satisfaction relationship was mediated by the perceived congruence between an employee's values and those of the organization. They inferred from their findings that fostering employee–organization value congruence was an effective strategy for optimizing benefits from employee public service motivation.

Robert Christensen and Bradley Wright (2011) broadened the analysis of person–environment fit by investigating independent effects of two types of fit, person–organization, which to this juncture had dominated the research, and person–job. The sample for the policy-capturing study was first-year law students. Christensen and Wright concluded that public service motivation more strongly influenced person–job than person–organization fit. "Consistent across three sectors of employment, individuals with stronger PSM [public service motivation] were more likely to accept jobs that emphasize service to others – whether that be pro bono work (private sector), client interaction (public sector), or client representation (nonprofit sector)" (p. 723). In fact, once the influence of person–job fit was controlled, they found that public service motivation had no significant effect on person–organization fit. Like the research by Wright and Pandey (2008) that illuminated the causal dynamics of relationships among predisposition, job attitudes, and performance, this study illuminates dimensions of fit that are consequential for individual choice.

Many subsequent studies, originating from diverse countries (e.g., China, Egypt, Iran, Korea, Pakistan), have used the person–environment fit framework.[1] Several of the studies technically represent constructive replications of previous person–environment fit empirical research (Kim 2012; Liu, Tang, and Yang 2013; Quratulain and Khan 2015; Jin, McDonald, and Park 2016; Salajegheh, Mouseli, and Jaghdari 2016; Jin et al. 2019) and others (Ryu 2017) efforts to refine conceptual models. Others broke new ground by introducing new variables, dimensions of fit, and theory perspectives. Rusi Sun, Shuyang Peng, and Sanjay Pandey (2014) introduce goal ambiguity into a dynamic model explaining relationships between person–environment fit and a variety of individual control variables, including public service motivation. Stephen Teo et al. (2016) placed public sector change at the center of their study of public service motivation, change-induced stressors, and person–organization fit. Gould-Williams, Mostafa, and Bottomley (2015) introduced a new outcome variable, organizational citizenship behavior, into their model of the mediating effects of person–organization fit. Neumann (2016) used prospect theory to inform his conceptualization of person–job fit and integrated public service motivation with the model's motivational dimensions.

2.1.3 Summary

Several complementary theoretical frameworks explain what attracts individuals to organizations and why individual attitudes and performance vary. At the core of each of the theories is a matching principle. Predisposition–opportunity theory emphasizes a match between individual predispositions and organizational incentives to explain individual–organization attraction. Attraction–selection–attrition theory posits that matching mechanisms are influential with respect to attraction, selection, and attrition. A range of variables, including personalities, attitudes, and values, within an organization are consequential to the matching processes at different stages of an individual's relationship to an organization. Person-fit theory also posits the importance of fit, involving a variety of analytic pairings, including job, supervisor, work environment, and organization. Empirical research supports the importance of public service dimensions within each of these frameworks, helping to explain an individual's choice of incentives associated with public institutions, variations in work attitudes such as organizational commitment and job satisfaction, and behavioral differences like job performance.

2.2 Self-Determination Theory

Self-determination theory originated from Edward Deci's (1971) research about the effects of extrinsic rewards on intrinsic motivation. The theory has evolved over time as a collaboration between Deci and his colleague Richard Ryan (Deci and Ryan 1985, 2000). It has two fundamental components, one involving basic psychological needs that motivate individual growth and change and another that focuses on how different types of motives affect an individual's motivation to act.

The basic psychological needs aspect of self-determination theory posits that individuals possess three needs that are innate and universal,[2] reminiscent of needs models associated with Abraham Maslow (1943) and, later, Clayton Alderfer (1972). The first of the three needs is competence, which involves the mastery of skills for the situations an individual encounters. Deci and Ryan equate competence with self-efficacy, an individual's belief in their innate ability to achieve goals.

The second basic need is autonomy, individuals' perceptions that they have choices about how to act. The opposite of autonomy is control, where external forces dictate an individual's options. Autonomy is essential for, and to some extent equated with, self-determination, which gives the theory its name.

The third of the psychological needs Deci and Ryan consider foundational for self-determination theory is relatedness, the need for connection to others and belonging. This need reflects the innate social nature of humans.

The second component of self-determination theory, which garners greater attention in most scholarly discussions of the theory, is how different types of motives affect the individual's motivation to act.[3] The dynamics of this component are explained by how different motives affect an individual's ability to realize their basic needs. Deci and Ryan identify a continuum of motives, ranging from controlled to autonomous.

- Amotivation: A state in which the individual lacks any intention to act, that is, the absence of motivation.
- External regulation: The least autonomous type of extrinsic motivation. It is a response to external demands, which may include externally imposed rewards.
- Introjected regulation: Acting because of pressure as a way to avoid guilt or to maintain self-esteem.
- Identification: An individual acts out of identification with the importance of a behavior, thereby accepting it as his or her own.
- Integration: The individual acts because the action is congruent with his or her own values and needs, that is, internalized and integrated.
- Intrinsic: Doing an activity for its inherent enjoyment or satisfaction rather than a separable consequence.

Deci and Ryan (2000) characterize some types of extrinsic motivation along this continuum as "impoverished" and others as "active, agentic states" (p. 55).

Convergence between self-determination theory and public service motivation. Scholars studying public service motivation have borrowed from self-determination theory, but infrequently. Chung-An Chen and Barry Bozeman (2013), Chengwei Xu and Chung-An Chen (2017), and Breaugh, Ritz, and Alfes (2018) have proposed using the "lens" of self-determination theory for understanding motivation in public service. Crossovers between public service motivation and self-determination theory could prove enlightening for scholars identifying with each of these research fields. Three potential benefits deserve highlighting (1) self-determination theory's language for framing mixed-motives research about public service; (2) public service motivation theory's capacity to inform motivational states at the autonomous end of the motivation continuum; and (3) strengthening the institutional foundations of self-determination theory, with respect to both its basic psychological needs and its individual-motive components.

Chen and Bozeman (2013) focus on the utility of using self-determination theory's motives continuum for framing mixed-motives research about public service. Their argument is straightforward: nonintrinsic motivation has been neglected in public and nonprofit management and self-determination theory helps fill a gap in research on such motivations (p. 599). James Perry (2014) echoed Chen and Bozeman's call for more mixed-motives research in summarizing foundations for what he called a third wave of public service motivation research: "An essential next step for research about public service motivation is to conduct more studies that investigate natural, multi-incentive settings" (p. 40).

Beginning early in its development, public service motivation theory (Perry 2000) emphasized the social origins of the motivational process. The disproportionate attention public service motivation theory gives to identified and integrated motives in the self-determination theory motivation continuum creates an opportunity to learn more about these relatively unexplored motives. Thus, public service motivation research has the capacity to inform understanding about motivational states at the autonomous end of the self-determination theory motivation continuum.

A by-product of the process theory of public service motivation (Perry 2000) is recognition that motivational situations or contexts (Perry and Porter 1982) are often dictated by institutions – laws, rules, and external expectations. Like the de-emphasis of nonintrinsic motives in recent public and nonprofit management research, institutions have been neglected in most motivation research (Perry and Porter 1982; Perry 2000; Perry and Vandenabeele 2008). A convergence between traditional psychology-based motivation theories and social- and institution-grounded theories offers opportunities to explore fundamental questions that could inform motivation theories generally. Among the fundamental questions is the extent to which basic psychological need theory can be empirically confirmed and the extent to which institutional environments support or thwart optimal or maladapted functioning. One piece of this larger investigation, involving autonomy, may be particularly engaging for traditional debates about accountability in public administration, which are often framed in terms of accountability and control (Friedrich 1935; Finer 1941).

2.2.1 Motivation-Crowding Theory

The findings of Deci, Ryan, and associates about the decline of intrinsic motivation in the face of extrinsic, especially monetary, rewards triggered subsequent research by economists (Frey 1997; Frey and Jegen 2001). The reasons for the subsequent research are evident: The results of the research by social psychologists fly in the face of a fundamental economic principle – raising monetary incentives reduces, rather than increases, supply. Economists and scholars from other fields such as political science (Gailmard and Patty 2007) have studied both the crowding-out effect, identified in Deci's early research and repeatedly confirmed thereafter by others, and the crowding-in effect. This body of empirical research is given more attention in Chapter 6 when compensation and financial incentives are discussed.

Motivation-crowding theory posits two distinct effects (Frey and Jegen 2001; Weibel, Rost, and Osterloh 2010) that determine the overall influence of financial incentives on intrinsic motivation. The first is a price effect, created by the cognitive shift associated with calling attention to the influence of financial rewards for behavior. The cognitive shift simultaneously diminishes the meaning of work content for behavior, which is the crowding-out effect. The sum of the price effect and crowding effect determines the overall effect of pay for performance on employee motivation.

2.2.1.1 Empirical Research about Motivation Crowding and Public Service Motivation

Although motivation crowding has been used frequently to account for findings in public pay-for-performance research (Perry, Engbers, and Jun 2009; Weibel, Rost, and Osterloh 2010), the theory has been used less frequently a priori to empirical research about public service motivation. Anthony Bertelli's (2006) study of the U.S. Internal Revenue Service (IRS) is the first public sector study to assess the motivation-crowding phenomenon. Bertelli estimated latent intrinsic motivation for employee samples in IRS and the Office of the Comptroller of the Currency (OCC). The two agencies were differentiated by the fact that the IRS had introduced high-powered incentives in the form of a pay-banding system for supervisory personnel that was not used in the OCC. Acknowledging limitations in his underlying data source (i.e., the 2002 Federal Human Capital Survey), Bertelli found crowding-in of intrinsic motivation at the lowest levels but crowding-out at the highest levels in the IRS. Although the motivational consequences differed along the pay-band, Bertelli came to no conclusion about the overall effects of the pay-banding system.

Yannis Georgellis, Elisabetta Iossa, and Vurain Tabvuma (2011) indirectly tested motivation-crowding theory in a study of the sorting of employees between the public and private sectors, which was discussed earlier in this chapter in relation to ASA research. Their conclusion about motivation crowding was based on a finding that more intrinsically motivated individuals in the British Household Panel Survey were less likely to accept public sector employment when offered higher extrinsic rewards. The finding applied only to the higher education sector and the National Health Service. They interpreted this finding as an indication of crowding out of intrinsic motivation.

The most recent public sector study touching on motivation crowding used a US local government sample to test predictions about performance-related pay, public service motivation, and job satisfaction (Stazyk 2013). Results for the sample of city managers, assistant city managers, and department heads arrived at some conclusions different from preceding studies. Edmund Stazyk used both logistic regression and Monte Carlo simulations in arriving at his findings. He did not find evidence of motivation crowding. He reports: "Instead, results indicate employees with the highest job satisfaction and strongest reported service motives are most likely to work in cities with performance-related pay" (p. 265). He acknowledged, however, that the cross-sectional sample he used was not a robust test of the relationships.

2.3 Goal Theory

Goal theory is based upon the idea that motivation is purposeful (Locke and Latham 1990). The core concept of the theory is goals. These are conceived as "applications of values to specific situations" (Locke 1991, 292). Although goal-setting theory does provide some indications about how goals are acquired, this is not the central focus of the theory. More attention is devoted to how goals influence individual behavior and performance.

Goal-setting theory contends that people differ in motivation and consequently in performance because they tend to have different goals (Latham and Locke 1991). The basic components of goal-setting theory are goal content and goal commitment. Goals that are specific and difficult are theorized to increase motivation and performance. The theory focuses on the content of the goal or task one wants to achieve. This part of the theory is general and makes no reference to the value component of the goal. Goal commitment involves commitment to a goal and its effects on motivation and performance. Values play an important role here. Commitment is, on one hand, influenced by the individual's self-efficacy, that is, the belief people have that they can achieve the goal. On the other hand, commitment is influenced by the belief that achieving the goals depends on the importance of the goal. This last element can be associated directly with institutions and identities, especially given the way Latham and Locke have defined the relationship between goals and values. Therefore, goal commitment will be enhanced by the presence of public identities.

Bradley Wright's research has been instrumental in tying research on goal setting to public service motivation. An early contribution from Wright (2004) sought to put goal setting squarely at the center of middle-range theory about public sector context and public service. Drawing from both goal and social cognitive theories, Wright developed a model incorporating salient aspects of the public sector work context, including goal conflict, goal ambiguity, and procedural constraints, consistent with goal theory. With respect to the logic of goal theory, Wright posited that the specified challenges of public sector context could diminish work motivation by affecting antecedents identified in goal theory, including job goal specificity and job difficulty. Although Wright did not specifically incorporate public service motivation into his model, he argued that public service could be investigated within the goal theory framework. A key link is the relationship between public service and the importance employees attach to the goals they and their organizations pursue. Wright (2004) argues: "... if public sector employees perceive their own work as important to accomplishing agency goals that benefit society, then they may strive harder to achieve their job level goals" (p. 73).

2.3.1 Mission Valence as a Proxy for Goal Characteristics

One construct that has become prominent because of Wright's (2001, 2004) line of research is mission valence. In a follow-on study to test the utility of goal theory for explaining the dynamics of work motivation in the public sector context, Bradley Wright (2007) introduced mission valence as an antecedent variable in a model incorporating key goal theory variables. Mission valence represents the importance of organizational goals. Its role within goal theory is that individuals who are energized by their organization's mission will perceive their job goals as important and therefore put forth greater work effort. Wright's analysis of surveys from 807 employees in a New York State agency supported the mission valence→job importance→work motivation relationships. The relationships were significant even when controlling for performance-related extrinsic rewards. The research confirmed the view that mission valence influences work motivation by enhancing job meaningfulness. In subsequent research, Bradley Wright and Sanjay Pandey (2011) identified that mission valence varied with organizational goal clarity, public service motivation, and work impact, but affirmed its importance as a determinant of organizational outcomes.

The line of research about the effects of mission has gained momentum recently. Sebastian Fehrler and Michael Kosfeld (2014) conducted two laboratory experiments with interesting results. In the first experiment, they found that when subjects selected the mission for their job, they did not provide higher effort than the control group. The unexpected finding in the first experiment led to a second in which subjects were given a choice whether to work on a job with their preferred mission. A subgroup of those who chose the preferred mission were willing to do so even when receiving lower wages and they simultaneously exerted substantially higher effort. As a result of the two laboratory experiments, Fehrler and Kosfeld concluded "that some workers can be motivated by missions and that selection into mission-oriented organizations is an important factor to explain empirical findings of lower wages and high motivation in these organizations" (p. 99).

Three subsequent studies strengthen the conceptual and empirical foundations about research on missions and public service motivation. James Gerard Caillier (2015) surveyed a representative sample of 3,500 for which he received 913 usable surveys, a response rate of 26.1 percent. He concluded that respondent public service motivation had a direct effect on mission valence and extra-role behaviors. Jason Smith (2016) and William Resh, John Marvel, and Bo Wen (2018) conducted real-effort experiments that tested mediated models of mission matching. Smith was interested in better identifying psychological mechanisms that explained the positive motivational effects of matching missions and workers. He identified meaningfulness as the intervening mechanism between mission matching and effort. The mission→meaningfulness→effort relationship was mediated by the extent to which subjects were well matched (matched vs. mismatched) and their level of prosociality. Resh, Marvel, and Wen (2018) built on Smith's mission-matching research. The new variable they introduced to the research was the extent to which mission match explains *persistent* prosocial work effort. They found that a subject's narrow identification with the mission was an important determinant of persistence, supporting Smith's findings.

The research on public service motivation, mission match, and their effects on work effort has also been the subject of studies on leadership. This research is addressed in more detail in Chapter 8.

2.4 Conclusion

The theory behind the surge in research about public service motivation is robust. Predisposition-opportunity, self-determination, and goal theories, and several additional complementary frameworks, offer collective support for many of the predictions embedded in public service motivation research. More important than the robustness of the theories is that their practical implications offer new ways for designing and managing public human resources. I begin to illuminate these practical implications in Chapter 3.

Notes

1 Among the studies are: Sangmook Kim (2012), Bangcheng Liu et al. (2015), Geunpil Ryu (2017), Rusi Sun, Shuyang Peng, and Sanjay Pandey (2014), Stephen Teo et al. (2016), Quratulain Samina and Abdul Karim Khan (2015), Julian Gould-Williams, Ahmed Mohammed Sayed Mostafa, and Paul Bottomley (2015), Oliver Neumann (2016), Sanjar Salajegheh, Morteza Mouseli, and Ali Moradpour Jaghdari (2016), Myung Jin, Bruce McDonald, and Jaehee Park (2016), and Myung Jin et al. (2019).
2 Edward Deci and Richard Ryan (2000) refer to this part of self-determination theory as a "subtheory," which emanates from cognitive evaluation theory.
3 This component of self-determination theory is another subtheory, which Deci and Ryan (2000) refer to as organismic integration theory.

3 | Selecting for High Public Service Motivation Is a Priority

In a blog post, Steve Kelman (2015) aptly summarized what I infer from the substantial body of research related to public service motivation: "Again, there is a managerial takeaway from this: If you want to harness the ability of public service motivation to improve the performance of your employees, you need to be looking for people with that motivation to join your organization in the first place."

Kelman's observation carries a more subtle, implied message as well. Managers and human resource professionals in public organizations often ignore public service motivation as a determinant of outcomes such as attraction, retention, ethical behavior, and performance because of their fixation on knowledge, skills, and abilities as the explicit objects of recruitment processes and their adherence to policy and regulatory guidance. An experimental study by Daniel Bromberg and Etienne Charbonneau (2020) starkly makes the point about the misplaced attention of human resource professionals. Bromberg and Charbonneau begin by observing that many who have studied public service motivation, like Kelman (2015), recognize the value of using public service motivation in the selection process for public service jobs. They recruited 238 human resource professionals from the International Public Management Association for Human Resources (IPMA-HR) for their experiment. The professionals were asked to rate three cover letters that varied on expressed public service motivation and five personality traits. The result was that public service motivation had no effect on the ratings, indicating that variations in the attribute had no influence on the human resource professionals. Accumulating evidence indicates that ignoring public service motivation in recruitment processes is a serious omission.

Selecting for high public service motivation is likely to have several favorable consequences for public organizations:

- The predispositions of employees are likely to be better aligned with the types of incentives offered by the organization;
- The person selected is more likely to fit the job and team.
- The person selected is likely to be a good fit for the organization;
- Employee motives are more likely to reflect identification or integration with the organization's values; and
- Employees are likely to have greater commitment to goals embedded in their job and organization.

The direct result of these favorable consequences is greater likelihood of retaining staff, more reliable role behaviors, and higher employee performance.

Kelman's assertion about the importance of selecting for high public service motivation is borne out by research. Adrian Ritz, Gene Brewer, and Oliver Neumann (2016) found that selecting for public service motivation was the most frequently mentioned practical implication in a global synthesis of 323 peer-reviewed publications about public service motivation that appeared from 1990 to 2014. More than 18 percent of all publications, 59 in total, proposed considering an individual's public service motivation in selection decisions.

The studies Ritz, Brewer, and Neumann (2016) link to selecting for public service motivation identify several reasons why the recruitment and selection of employees who possess high public service motivation makes a difference to how public organizations function, echoing perspectives articulated when the construct first appeared (Perry and Wise 1990). Simon Anderfuhren-Biget, Frédéric Varone, and David Giauque (2014) are adept in condensing the primary reasons for selecting for public service motivation to three: value congruence, the reduction of principal-agent problems, and civil servant identification.

The three mediating variables identified by Anderfuhren-Biget, Varone, and Giauque are integral to the theories discussed in Chapter 2. The value congruence argument, for instance, captures rationales from predisposition-opportunity, attraction–selection–attrition, and person-fit theories and research, the first streams of research addressed in Chapter 2. When employee values are congruent with organization values, then employees are more likely to be stimulated by identification and integration, two of the higher order extrinsic motivations identified in self-determination theory (Ryan and Deci 2000; Paarlberg and Perry 2007). Recruiting a workforce where principal-agent problems are minimized reduces the need for monitoring employees, which, in turn, increases the likelihood that employees operate with greater autonomy, particularly from internal stakeholders, creating another condition for self-determination (Ryan and Deci 2000). Finally, civil servant identification increases employee ownership, enhancing the quality of effort applied. Employee ownership of goals is a dynamic central to goal theory (Locke and Latham 1990). Ownership translates directly to greater goal commitment and quality of effort, which are keys for realizing high levels of employee motivation.

3.1 Attracting High Public Service Motivation Staff

Public organizations have a variety of options for policies and systems that can be introduced to realize the goal of attracting a staff with high public service motivation. Four general steps for attracting high public service motivation staff can be gleaned from the research: project attractive missions and organizational images to prospects; tailor position descriptions and advertising to emphasize mission and public values; screen in candidates with high public service motivation; and screen out candidates with motivations that crowd out intrinsic or prosocial orientations (Christensen, Paarlberg, and Perry 2017). It is conceivable that one of these general steps alone may succeed in attracting a staff with high public service motivation (see, e.g., the effects of the organizational image of the U.S. Bureau of Prisons [BOP] discussed later), but public organizations are likely to realize greater success by pursuing multiple options.

3.1.1 Project Organizational Images to Attract High Public Service Motivation Prospects

Two streams of research point to close ties between an organization's image and the types of people who are attracted to the organization. The first stream focuses on the concept of mission mystique, which emanates from public and development administration represented best in contributions from Merilee Grindle (1997) and Charles Goodsell (2011). The second stream of research, captured by the rubric organizational identification, flows from organization behavior, and is best encapsulated in research by Jane Dutton, Janet Dukerich, and Celia Harquail (1994). These streams echo themes from theories introduced in Chapter 2, specifically predisposition-opportunity theory and attraction–selection–attrition theory.

Grindle's contribution is less developed than the other two, but is intriguing because of its origins, both temporally (i.e., the mid-1990s) and geographically. Grindle arrived at her inferences when trying to understand why organizations in the developing world were able to perform at high levels in very difficult circumstances where the public sector performed poorly as a whole. She arrived at her conclusions after she and her team studied twenty-nine organizations in six countries, sorting organizations based on whether their performance exceeded expectations or fell short of the standard.[1] Her primary conclusion was that what she referred to broadly as organizational culture – but also as organizational mystique and mission mystique – was a significant contributor to unexpectedly positive performance under difficult conditions. Grindle describes the mystique in the following way: "In each case, a sense of mission or a mystique about the activities of the organization was an important factor in accounting for the commitment of workers to the goals of the organization and in eliciting hard and consistent effort from them, even in the midst of often severe resource shortages and sometimes poor working conditions" (p. 489). Grindle identifies several components of mission mystique. Among these components were that employees behaved according to professional norms and standards and identified with them, they possessed a strong sense of service to the missions, and the mission was not only organizational but personal. Grindle concluded that many of the features her team found in effective organizations in developing countries were similar to features John DiIulio (1994) documents in the BOP, which is discussed later.

Charles Goodsell (2011) embraced and developed the concept of mission mystique more than a decade after Grindle (1997) first referred to the idea from her research in developing countries.[2] The proximate source of Goodsell's inferences about mission mystique were six case studies of US public organizations,[3] but he also drew upon a large body of interdisciplinary research accumulated during his more than fifty-year scholarly career. Consistent with Grindle's discussion, Goodsell defines mission mystique as follows:

> ... a quality of public agencies that can serve as a reference point for promotion of animated and reflective administration. It lays the basis for conscious development of strong institutional *belief systems* for agencies that center on a compelling *public mission*. In the mission mystique organization, employees labor not merely to implement laws faithfully or to run programs efficiently, as critical as these requirements are. The act of carrying out the mission itself kindles passion. Men and women work hard and creatively because they want to make the most emphatic mark as possible on the community and world with respect to their mission. (p. 2)

Goodsell uses his definition of mission mystique to develop a template for a mission mystique belief system. By template, he means general guidance, to distinguish it from a model or explicit instructions. His template, reproduced in Table 3.1, has nine components, created by cross-classifying tri-partite rows and columns. The three rows represent the substantive core of the template: endowed with a sense of purpose (a purposive aura), presence of passion and commitment (internal commitment), and sustain the institution over time (sustaining

Table 3.1 *The mission mystique belief system: a template[a]*

System requirements	Prime qualities	Essential elaborations	Temporal aspects
A Purposive Aura	1 A central mission purpose permeates the agency	2 The societal need met by the mission is seen as urgent	3 Has a distinctive reputation based on achievement
Internal Commitment	4 Agency personnel are intrinsically motivated	5 Agency culture institutionalizes the belief system	6 Agency history is known and celebrated
Sustaining Features	7 Beliefs are open to contestation and opposition	8 Qualified policy autonomy to permit appropriate change	9 Agency renewal and learning are ongoing

[a] From Goodsell (2011), 14.

features). A review of many of the cell entries reveals notable features that Goodsell's mission mystique shares with public service motivation, among them that agency personnel are intrinsically motivated.

Dutton, Dukerich, and Harquail (1994) developed a model about ties between organizational images and member identification that provides a foundation for thinking about how public organizations can more effectively attract high public service motivation prospects. Dutton et al. posit that two distinct organizational images influence a member's organizational identification. The first of these two organizational images is *perceived organizational identity*, which is based on a member's beliefs involving what is distinctive and central about the organization. The other image is *construed external identity*, which is defined by Dutton and colleagues as a member's beliefs about how outsiders perceive the organization. The thesis is the joint attractiveness of the two images, that is the attractiveness of perceived organizational identity and attractiveness of construed external identity go a long way toward explaining the strength of member organizational identification.

Although my summary of the Dutton et al. (1994) model is simplified, the model gives public managers some rules for what they can do to attract staff with high public service motivation. The first rule is that "organizations should project clear images about their missions, how the missions advance outcomes valued by society, and the distinctiveness of what the organization contributes" (Christensen, Paarlberg, and Perry 2017, 533). This first rule is largely focused on mission valence, which represents the importance of organizational goals, a concept introduced in Chapter 2. Many factors influence the attractiveness of perceived organizational identity, but the first rule leaves no doubt that organizational members need to be attentive to attractiveness and how member conduct, public communications (e.g., websites, print media, and job advertisements), and administrative systems affect it (Carpenter 2010). Public organization leaders bear a special responsibility for maintaining and enhancing the attractiveness of perceived organizational identity, an issue addressed in Chapter 8.

Public organizations, their leaders, and members have far less control over the attractiveness of construed external identity, but they can act to frame the narrative about construed external images. Although public and media criticisms are routine for public programs and organizations, leaders can seek to place criticisms in a larger context. The U.S. Internal Revenue Service (IRS) illustrates what an organization might do. The IRS can cultivate perceived organizational identities in professional circles that are attractive to prospective employees. At the same time, the IRS will face challenges in managing construed external images because of the coercive nature of its mission, which makes it an object for critical public and political assessments (Christensen, Paarlberg, and Perry 2017). One tactic the IRS could pursue to mitigate images generated by public attacks is messaging to prospects, staff, and other stakeholders explaining the rationales and sources of its policies (see, e.g., the discussion later in this chapter about the IRS's realistic job previews).

Many public organizations effectively project images that cultivate their attractiveness to prospects who develop strong organizational identification. One agency that succeeded at this strategy for more than sixty years is the U.S. Federal Bureau of Prisons, which is discussed in Section 3.1.2.

3.1.2 Affirmative Use of Organizational Image: The U.S. Federal Bureau of Prisons

John DiIulio's analysis of "principled agents" in the BOP makes a case for how an organizational image can transform an organization's transactions with employees, prospective and current, from a rational to a moral enterprise (DiIulio 1994). DiIulio argues that in the Bureau of Prisons he chronicled sixty-three years after its founding, principled agents were the rule, not the exception, for the behavior of staff. The principled agents to which DiIulio refers mirror the characteristics I associate with public service motivation in this volume. DiIulio (1994) writes about:

> … "principled agents" – workers who do not shirk, subvert, or steal on the job even when the pecuniary and other tangible incentives to refrain from these behaviors are weak or nonexistent, and who often perform "thankless tasks" and make virtual "gifts" of their labor even when the pecuniary and other tangible rewards for behaving that way are highly uncertain at best. (p. 282)

DiIulio characterizes the Bureau of Prisons as a "strong culture" organization, one that rests on beliefs and values, which he associates with descriptors that have become increasingly common in public organizations – "sense of mission," "distinctive competence," and "reputation." Rather than relying on exchanges or pecuniary incentives, such organizations represent a normative order that drives individuals to act on behalf of the institution and identify with it. Self-sacrifice for the institution is an attribute of member behavior.

The story of the BOP DiIulio recounts begins in late November 1987 when two federal detention centers, one in Oakdale, Louisiana, and a second in Atlanta, Georgia, were the venues of major disturbances that occurred just a few days apart. The disturbances resulted in millions in damage to government property and an almost equal cost to quell the riots and relocate rioters.

Although the events at Oakdale and Atlanta headlined media globally, the reactions of BOP staff and retirees revealed what the organization meant to people familiar with the organization. DiIulio (1994) describes the personal reactions of retirees: "They telephoned one another, gathered together, and remained glued to their radios and television sets for the latest news on the riots. Some retirees squeezed into their old uniforms in a symbolic show of support. A contingent of retirees even rushed to the scene" (p. 284). Even junior staff were moved by events. An Atlanta correctional officer commented: "But it's sort of like watching the flag burn or something. It's especially that way for the guys who've been with the outfit for years. You can just see it in their faces.... Hell, I saw a lot of important BOP folks crying out there the other day" (p. 285).

A reality to which DiIulio calls attention, one visible and meaningful to people inside and outside BOP, was the aftermath of the Oakdale and Atlanta disturbances. Despite prospects for strongly negative emotions about the disturbances, "not one act of extralegal vengeance was taken by a BOP correctional officer against a rioter" (p. 286). The restraint of the correctional officers was matched by their intense commitment to and effort made in reconstructing the Atlanta facility. In 1988, the person who managed Atlanta's reconstruction received BOP's first annual award for exceptional managerial performance (DiIulio 1994, 287). A warden summarized the consequences of BOP's responses to adversity: "You see, when something happens in any organization, you can always find a scapegoat. But we don't want scapegoats. We want excellence. We want the director, the Congress, the attorney general on behalf of the president, and the public at large to be proud of federal prisons. But above it all, we want to be proud of ourselves, from top to bottom – the director, these wardens, the officers out there on the line everyday. We want to get the job done" (p. 287).

3.1.2.1 Administrative Uniformities in BOP

Another distinctive feature DiIulio describes, which has roots in both the staff's beliefs about what is distinctive and central about BOP and their attention to external images, is the extraordinary operational uniformities across geographically disparate BOP units. DiIulio uses administrative uniformities of US Penitentiaries in Lewisberg, Leavenworth, and Lompoc to illustrate his point. Three administrative areas in which differences are common across facilities in other systems exhibited remarkable uniformity, what DiIulio calls "the centripetal character of operations."

The first administrative uniformity is the wardens' administrative behavior, noteworthy because of variability across so many variables, including diverse wardens, geographic distribution, and the physical characteristics of the facilities. Within BOP, the trademarks of administrative uniformity are the consistent routines of "standing on line" and "walking and talking." Standing on line and walking and talking are the BOP equivalent of "management by walking around," that is, talking to inmates and staff, seeing and being seen. The consistency of these routines across the diverse units of BOP is, according to DiIulio, because wardens "have very similar ideas about the 'right way' to run a prison, and a shared commitment to running it 'right'" (p. 293).

The second administrative uniformity is unit management, which refers to "physically and administratively distinct housing units that generally hold between 50 and 250 inmates" (DiIulio 1994, 298). Unit management is team-based, with a staff consisting of a unit manager, and one or more case managers, correctional counselors, and correctional officers who are collectively responsible for custodial and other functions. Clerical support, teachers, psychologists, and other specialized assistance, depending on the unit's mission, typically augment the core custodial team. U.S. Bureau of Prisons Director Norm Carlson instituted team-based unit management, about which DiIulio writes, "even the weakest forms of unit management are easily distinguishable from traditional, custody centered, command-and-control forms of penal administration" (p. 299). Carlson's unit management philosophy had far-reaching consequences both for how insiders and outsiders viewed the BOP. One warden summarizes these consequences, about which scores of senior administrators came to a shared understanding: "Norm believed in sanitation and in a spit-and-polish appearance for employees. He didn't have to persuade any of us that good sanitation contributes to an orderly, professional operation and to a positive image of the BOP with visitors and the press" (p. 300).

The third administrative uniformity is the administration of disciplinary actions against inmates. If any feature of life in BOP created context for variations and the exercise of seemingly unlimited discretion, inmate discipline is the candidate. But even in the realm of inmate discipline, "the disciplinary process conforms to official agency policy, is valued by employees, and is administered in a way that minimizes discretion and results in like infractions receiving like penalties" (p. 301). DiIulio expressed surprise at his findings:

> But to find that the staff at all levels seemed to prize the process as a tool of correctional management left me a bit incredulous. After all, in many if not most prison systems, the dominant correctional ethos, at least among line security staff, has favored curbstone justice, not bureaucratic procedure, as a means of handling inmates who violate the rules or seriously challenge official authority in other ways. (p. 307)

What was the cumulative effect of the surprising administrative uniformities and ability to recover from adversity recounted by DiIulio? It was an organizational image that BOP staff valued, in which they took pride, and for which they were prepared to contest unfair attacks. A veteran warden summarized the sentiments: "That pride [for BOP] is in our agency symbols, it's in our respect for people who have retired after contributing to the Bureau, and in the way we respond to media cheap shots or public lies about who we are and what we do" (p. 311).

Over time, the organizational image that stimulated employees and to which they responded attracted an extensive cadre of staff with strong commitments to public service as represented by BOP. A warden articulated the motivational sentiments shared by many BOP employees: "The history, the pride in the seal, is a big part of why most people like working for this agency, and will bust their butts to get the job done even when it's no bed of roses, and even when, around Christmas, you feel like you're not paid nearly enough.... You feel like you're doing something important, the best it can be done, and doing it with others who feel the same" (p. 314).

3.1.2.2 Post 1990s Aftermath: Changes to BOP's Image and Member Identification

Building a government organization whose history, values, and performance generates an organizational image that attracts quality, highly motivated talent is a difficult task, but, as the Federal Bureau of Prisons example illustrates, it is possible.

An organization's image is not immortal, however, and BOP illustrates that point too. Although no one has recently conducted the type of on-the-ground research John DiIulio did in the early 1990s, here is what can be pieced together from public records. First, if the Partnership for Public Service's Best Places to Work in the Federal Government is an indicator, then the Federal Bureau of Prisons has been on a steep slide since the Partnership began reporting composite employee engagement scores in 2007.[4] In 2007, BOP ranked 67 out of 222 agencies,[5] which placed it high in the second quartile. By 2012, BOP's ranking was 185 out of 292 agencies, more than a full quartile lower than in 2007. When another five years had passed in 2017, BOP ranked 298 among 339 agencies, well into the fourth quartile of all agencies. For the most recent year for which data were available, 2018, BOP is 372 of 415 agencies, close to the bottom decile of all federal units, well below where it stood in 2007.

The survey evidence is more a result than a cause. So what has contributed to the steep decline? Several factors appear to be at play.

3.1.2.3 Overcrowding

One factor is likely the expansion of inmate population. The U.S. Bureau of Prisons experienced extraordinary growth in inmate population in the years following DiIulio's (1994) analysis. The inmate population grew from 26,000 in 1980 to 201,000 by 2008 (Friel 2008). The growth in inmate population was not accompanied by commensurate growth in guards. In 1998, the employee-to-inmate ratio was 1 to 3.57. In 2008, the ratio was 1 to 4.92. A story not told by these numbers concerns the effects of growing workloads on outcomes like safety risks to staff and staff's ability to control inmate populations. The U.S. Government Accountability Office (2014) (GAO) called attention to links between prison population growth and officer safety in 2014: "... BOP is 30 percent crowded overall and more than 50 percent crowded across its highest security institutions. Additionally, BOP's inmate to staff ratio has increased since 2000 and officer safety is continuously at risk." Increases in both risks to staff and inmate outcomes (e.g., violence among inmates and lack of rehabilitation) are likely to have adversely affected the way BOP was perceived by both staff and significant stakeholders.

3.1.2.4 Activation of New Installations

Overcrowding and aging facilities have also created the need for new prison facilities. The U.S. Bureau of Prisons began in the early 2000s to add new facilities, largely to reduce the rate of overcrowding. The U.S. Government Accountability Office reported in 2014 that BOP had added six facilities, five newly built and one purchased from the State of Illinois, but the activation of the new facilities, that is getting them fully functional, was falling short of BOP's goals, resulting in underutilization of the facilities. The underutilization of new facilities was exacerbated by aging facilities. The U.S. Department of Justice (2014) reported that a third of BOP's facilities were more than 50 years old and 220 major maintenance projects were estimated to cost $430 million. Deferred maintenance was affecting institutional security, adding to "increased risk of escape, inability to lock down cells, and violence over inadequate living conditions" (p. 12).

3.1.2.5 Private Prisons' Growth

Contracts with private prisons were initiated in 1997 to address the growth in BOP's inmate population. Their use grew to 22,600 inmates, 12 percent of BOP's inmate population and cost $639 million in fiscal 2014. In 2016, the Obama Administration announced it would phase out private prisons. At the time, Deputy Attorney General Sally Yates wrote, based on a Department of Justice Inspector General report, that private prisons "... simply do not provide the same level of correctional services, programs and resources.... They do not save substantially on costs ... and they do not maintain the level of safety and security" (Yates 2016, 1). Regardless of the critical assessment in 2016, the decline of private prisons was short lived. By February 2017, new Attorney General Jeff Sessions reversed direction. By January 2018, the Trump Administration had proposed to cut BOP officers by 6,000 and increase contracts with private prisons despite the evidence-based assessment of 2016 that private prisons did not provide the same level of correctional services as BOP-run institutions (Katz 2018a).

The period since DiIulio's intensive research on BOP is a story of declining attractiveness of the agency on two fronts, perceived organizational identity and construed external identity, the result of deterioration of both internal service standards and external pressures associated with shortcomings surfaced by audit agencies and magnified by private competitors for public funding. Recent trends do not undo the long-term record that made BOP an exemplar among public agencies for creating an organizational identity that helped to attract and retain high public service motivation staff. The U.S. Bureau of Prison's long-term success in managing the attractiveness of its organizational images is a model to which other public agencies can aspire.

3.1.3 Shape Job Advertising to Emphasize Mission and Public Values

Christian Waldner (2012) and Torben Beck Jorgensen and Mark Rutgers (2014) investigated empirically the job advertisement, which they contend is an underutilized tool for shaping organizational images. Waldner begins his article by contrasting two labor market strategies that he considers polar opposites. At one pole is the New Public Management, which assumes individuals are self-interested and public employers will pursue strategies aligned with the private sector. At the other pole is a labor market strategy that stresses the publicness of public institutions, which he associates with public service motivation (Perry and Wise 1990), thereby differentiating it from private sector employers. In his study, Waldner looked at job advertisements for lawyers from both the public and private sectors. His content analysis of job advertisements identified 473 distinct job requirements and job benefits. He found that the job advertisements differed across the sectors. Public employers promoted specific public characteristics, but few of the public characteristics employers emphasized involved differences related to public service motivation, like service to citizens and the social significance of the work. In addition, despite public–private differences, public employers positioned themselves close to private counterparts, which indicated public strategies were not highly differentiated from private strategies.

The Jorgensen and Rutgers' (2014) study covered a significant expanse of time in two European countries, Denmark and the Netherlands. Over a five-decade period, covering the 1960–2000s, they found that the job advertisements in both countries followed similar patterns. They were attentive both to merit as a core value, which they defined as expertise/professionalism, and to organizational branding, which they defined as emphasis on human resource values and national identity. Jorgensen and Rutgers found a significant rise over time in job advertisement content related to the New Public Management end of the labor market poll identified by Waldner (2012). This temporal shift was accompanied by what they interpreted as a new conception of merit: "the capacity to act in a political environment and to have a public service motivation" (p. 69).

Two experimental studies build on the research by Waldner (2012) and Jorgensen and Rutgers (2014). Ulrike Weske et al. (2019) sought to assess the effects of using public service motivation to promote public jobs. Their experiment, with a sample of master's students at the University of Bern (Switzerland), used vignettes that differed according to the values they emphasized. The public-values vignette differed from the control and private-values vignette with respect to three values: impartiality, incorruptibility, and lawfulness. The private-values vignette branded the employer according to three distinct values: innovativeness, profitability, and competitiveness. Public service motivated participants showed no differences in their expressed attraction to public or private values, but individuals highly motivated by extrinsic factors were more likely to be attracted by private values branding. Although Weske et al.'s findings were unexpected, they offered several theoretical and statistical explanations for the results. Among the statistical explanations was the power of the model to detect interaction effects because of a sample size of sixty-six and high average values for the public service motivation variable (commitment to public values) that exhibited low variation across participants. Given these statistical and other theoretical limitations of the experiment, the authors offer recommendations for future research to remedy them.

The second experimental study, using a sample of 600 students in Germany, investigated a chain of relationships, beginning with the framing of recruitment messages, to prospects' perceptions of fit, to the moderating influence of public service motivation on intentions to apply. Julia Asseburg, Fabian Homberg, and Rick Vogel (2018) manipulated key variables in a survey experiment that contrasted inspirational messages with rational messages related to both job tasks and organizational missions. They found that the inspirational messages increased perceptions of fit, which mediated applicant intentions. An applicant's level of public service motivation influenced perceptions of fit. They also found that inspirational messages about job tasks, mediated by person-job fit, were more influential than messages focused on organizational mission, mediated by person-organization fit.

The studies by Waldner (2012), Jorgensen and Rutgers (2014), Asseburg, Homberg, and Vogel (2018), and Weske et al. (2019) identify several paths by which job advertisements, employer branding, and values are important for signaling and shaping organizational images in processes of recruiting high public service motivation staff. The research to date, however, is more suggestive than definitive and needs to be expanded and extended experimentally so that clearer guidance is available for public organization recruiters, managers, and executives.

A recent story in *Governing* reveals how some local government organizations perceive what projecting mission and public values does for attracting staff. "San Francisco started using its 'choose purpose' language specifically to court technologists, in 2016, after focus groups and market research suggested they were willing to give up a higher-paying job for one they found more meaningful" (Vyse 2019). The trade-off between a job's pay and its meaningfulness is one that is familiar to those who follow the research on public service motivation (see, e.g., Fehrler and Kosfeld 2014; Banuri and Keefer 2015; Hu and Hirsh 2017; Deserranno 2019). The lesson is not lost on Susan Gard, who directs policy in San Francisco's Human Resources Department: "We can't offer you stock options but we can offer you purpose" (Vyse 2019). Cities in many parts of the world have turned to branding campaigns with slogans such as, "Be a part of the city that you love," "Choose purpose," and "Serving community, Building careers" (Vyse 2019) to attract civic-minded, quality talent. As Patience Ferguson, Minneapolis's human resources director, observed, "Our aim is to attract people who have a value of public service" (Vyse 2019).

The fact that communities like San Francisco and Minneapolis have made the leap to project a competitive advantage to potential job applicants holds an important lesson for other public jurisdictions: Incorporate mission and public value into media to convey your image and, by extension, the rewards of working for the jurisdiction. Another recent story in *Governing* asked and answered the big question: "Want to Attract Talented Workers? Find a Better Way to Tell Your City's Story" (McKissen 2019).

Adrian Ritz and Christian Waldner (2011) surveyed a sample from the University of the Federal Armed Services in Munich (Germany) and came away with strong conclusions about the value of appealing to public service motives and using them in the marketing of public positions. Ritz and Waldner write: "Public administration must be more conscious of public service motives and use them purposefully in human resource marketing because they, as this study shows, have a high attraction potential. As public administration also simultaneously has a 'quasimonopoly' in this regard, public service motives can be addressed predominantly by public administration" (p. 308). In a subsequent study, Waldner (2012) elaborated the potential benefit of emphasizing the distinctiveness of public mission and values: "As part of a differentiation strategy in the labor market public employers must continue using PSM in the recruitment and selection stage, and also provide opportunities that individuals believe satisfy their public services motives."

The evidence about appealing to public service motives, however, is not universally consistent with the support for it from Ritz and Waldner (2011), Waldner (2012), and others (Asseburg et al. 2020). Elizabeth Linos (2018) conducted a field experiment using job advertisements for police officers in the Chattanooga, Tennessee, Police Department. She hypothesized that appealing to serving the community would not attract more applicants because this motive was already shared by most prospects and so would not increase applications. Linos confirmed this hypothesis. She confirmed hypotheses that making salient to applicants the challenge of the work and its career benefits would positively influence applications. The challenge and career benefits messages also increased the diversity of applicants. Thus, though Linos did not confirm that serving the community attracted applicants who otherwise would have applied, the content of advertising messages did influence the number and diversity of applicants.

A subsequent study by Asseburg, Hattke, Hensel, Homberg, and Vogel (2020) places the Linos experiment into context. Asseburg et al. observe:

> In the field experiment by Linos (2018), it was not possible to collect personal information on all recipients of recruitment messages, including their individual levels of PSM or any other type of motivation. It is thus not clear from this study if and how recruitment campaigns resonate differently in different target groups. The results of our moderation analyses establish an interaction between PSM and perceptions of

prosocial employment attributes among nonstudents. In contrast to Linos (2018), we conclude that it is still worth sending such messages because they foster the self-selection of strongly public service motivated candidates into public sector jobs.... According to our results, designing appropriate recruitment messages is one means to create this effect.

Asseburg et al. (2020) therefore offer the following advice for human resource managers:

1. If HR managers wish to facilitate sorting effects between candidates with high and low levels of public service motivation already at the early stages of the recruitment process, messages in job advertisements should highlight prosocial employment attributes.
2. Our results suggest that highlighting prosocial attributes of public sector jobs (such as societal impact, public values, higher purposes) is advisable only as a supplemental rather than an exclusive strategy because employment incentives that are perceived as extrinsic and intrinsic are considerably more appealing to potential applicants than prosocial incentives.
3. Recruiters who aim to attract public service motivated applicants should send prosocial signals preferably to candidates with work experience. The same recruitment strategy is largely ineffective among students because sorting effects between individuals with high and low levels of public service motivation do not occur in this target group (pp. 14–15).

3.1.4 Screen in Candidates with High Public Service Motivation

As the discussion to this juncture illustrates, public managers can take affirmative steps to make their organizations attractive to high public service motivation prospects by establishing an attractive organizational image and by projecting their mission and public values in the recruitment process.

In addition to these steps to enhance the selection pool, public managers can take deliberate steps to select candidates with high public service motivation. Among the steps public organizations and managers can take in the selection process are:

- Use selection procedures that are predictive of public service motivation.
- Seek out applicant pools comprised of individuals committed to public service.

- Use situational interviews to identify which applicants are most willing to engage in behaviors epitomizing public service.
- Use validated tests to identify individuals with attributes that predispose them to public service.

These practices of selecting for public service motivation reflect an underlying shift in perspective shared by another proposal in this book: hiring for the organization, not the job (Bowen, Ledford, and Nathan 1991). This shift toward hiring for the organization, not the job, has precedent in the high-performance, high-involvement movement of the 1980s and 1990s. David Bowen, Gerald Ledford, and Barry Nathan (1991) described a new approach to selection where employees are hired to fit the characteristics of an organization, not just the requirements of a particular job. The more holistic selection perspective permits organizations to build cultures of self-motivated, committed people similar to the staff infused with the mystique documented by DiIulio (1994), Grindle (1997), and Goodsell (2011). The new hiring practices may be more expensive than the traditional selection model, but the positive consequences reach from retention to organizational effectiveness. The reality is that investments that improve the quality of employees selected is likely to provide significant returns.

At least one recent study suggests that traditional, job-focused selection tests may, in fact, undermine attracting and selecting high public service motivation job candidates. Chung-An Chen et al. (2019) surveyed more than 3,000 individuals holding a polytechnic diploma or a bachelor's degree from the 2015 college-level (C-level) Public Service Exam in Taiwan. They examined two scenarios related to the highly competitive civil service exam (Chen et al. report a pass rate of about 5 percent). One scenario is that high public service motivation candidates are demonstrably better able to pass the exam, assuring that new entrants to public service are more likely to have high rather than low public service motivation. They also entertain a contrary scenario: "high-PSM individuals are less likely than low-PSM individuals to be screened into the public sector through competitive public service exams" (p. 12). Chen et al.'s (2019) statistical analysis supports the latter scenario, that is, high public service motivation exam takers are less likely to be screened into the public sector. They also found that those passing the exam spent less time volunteering than those who failed. The authors interpret their results as evidence that the form of highly competitive exams used in Taiwan and, by extension, many other Asian countries (e.g., China, India, and Bangladesh) may serve to winnow out of the public sector individuals with desirable attributes, like high public service motivation. They also argue that winnowing out high public service motivation candidates runs contrary to evidence about tendencies in many other countries, where institutionalized processes screen in high public service motivation candidates (Van de Walle, Steijn, and Jilke 2015).[6]

Although scoring job candidates using currently available public service motivation survey instruments (Perry 1996; Kim et al. 2013) is one option for identifying and sorting candidates based on their levels of public service motivation, simple selection screening is not sustainable in the long term. Simple surveys may be gamed by applicants who adjust their responses based on social desirability cues in the selection setting.

Another potential avenue for selection testing is using personality traits as a proxy for characteristics related to respondent public service dispositions or behaviors. A recent study sought to identify, for example, correspondence between public service motivation, prosocial motivation, and personality traits. Arjen van Witteloostuijn, Marc Esteve, and George Boyne (2017) investigated personality–public service motivation relationships with a sample of 320 first-year undergraduate students in business and economics from a major Netherlands university. They distinguished two types of motives underlying public service motivation: affective and nonaffective. The affective motives encompassed the compassion and self-sacrifice dimensions of public service motivation (Perry 1996; Kim et al. 2013). The attraction to policy-making and commitment to the public interest were classified as nonaffective motives, encompassing instrumental and normative facets of public service motivation (Perry and Wise 1990). They used a six-dimensional model to measure personality traits. Based upon ordinary least-squares regression models to test their hypotheses, van Witteloostuijn et al. concluded that public service motivation is strongly related to personality traits. Their results for nonaffective components of public service motivation were significantly related to four personality traits – positively to honesty-humility, emotionality, and agreeableness and negatively to conscientiousness. The nonaffective facets of public service motivation were positively related to only one personality trait, openness to experience.

Although other studies have pursued related lines of inquiry about personality traits and public service motivation (Jang 2012; Hamidullah, Van Ryzin, and Huafang 2016; Bromberg and Charbonneau 2020), they are only suggestive rather than definitive about potential public service motivation/prosocial motivation relationships. More importantly, alternatives to standard public service motivation, prosocial motivation, or altruism surveys or personality tests are available that are demonstrably more valid and reliable, which is imperative for selection tests. Among these tests are scored biographical data, behavior-based interviews, and implicit social cognition tests.

3.1.4.1 Biographical Data

The well-established principle that past behavior is a likely indicator of future behavior is a strong rationale for considering a variety of ways to identify applicants' prior behaviors. Equally important from a selection perspective is that biodata is one of the best predictors of employee performance and turnover (Breaugh 2009). Thus, incorporating biodata into a search for employees with high public service motivation makes great sense. Prior research also shows the success of selection processes using biodata to select employees to enhance employee citizenship behaviors (including altruism and prosocial behavior toward others) (Bolino, Turnkey, and Averett 2003), which is moderately correlated with public service motivation.

The understanding that biodata are valid indicators of future performance is important foundational evidence for building biodata into selection. Additional evidence is found in what public service motivation research tells us about behavioral differences between people pursuing public versus private careers. Gene Brewer (2003) and David Houston (2006) conducted early studies that helped to shape our understanding of behavioral differences between public and private employees. Brewer's distinctive contribution involved his analysis of civic participation. His behavioral measure of civic participation combined indicators of involvement and financial contributions to nonpolitical organizations and membership and participation in twenty-two types of civic associations. Using data from the 1996 American National Election Study, Brewer (2003) found public servants scored significantly higher than other citizens on all five indicators of civic participation, indicating public servants are more engaged.

Houston (2006) used data from the nationally representative 2002 General Social Survey. He compared government, nonprofit, and for-profit employees on three self-reported behavioral measures, gifts of time, blood, and money to charitable organizations. Government employees were more likely than for-profit employees to volunteer and donate blood, but Houston found no differences in philanthropy. Houston concluded that public service motivation was more prominent in public than private organizations.

Sebastian Barfort et al. (2019) suggest another potential reason for using biodata in the selection process – reducing corruption. Barfort and colleagues conducted a survey experiment to study self-selection into public service. They looked at the world's least corrupt country, Denmark, and found more honest people self-selected into public service. What can public organizations do with this and other research evidence about corruption? One implication is to build awareness about what factors are associated with attraction and self-selection related to honesty and integrity. A second implication is more proactive. Just as selection mechanisms can be designed to identify attributes positively related to public service motivation, indicators related to honesty and integrity or its obverse, dishonesty and corruption could be built into the selection process.

Scoring biographical data from résumés or other sources is a valid way to connect public service motivation with the prior behaviors of applicants. Critical incidents offer another avenue for assessing behaviors associated with public service motivation. The difference between biographical data and critical incidents is that the latter can include observable behaviors that either have been or could be exhibited on the job. Thus, critical incidents associated with a particular job may be used in both the selection process and subsequent appraisal of job incumbents, which may give them more versatility than biographical data alone. Robert Christensen, Laurie Paarlberg, and James Perry (2017) suggest another benefit of using résumés and critical incidents in tandem: "Both the scoring of résumés and critical incidents can also be geared to particular jobs and contexts, which may further enhance validity" (p. 533).

These types of behavioral measures have limits. One is the cost for their development, which may constrain their value to high-volume positions. Another limitation is if their use has a demonstrable, adverse impact on a protected class of applicants. Aside from potential concerns related to these limitations, scoring résumés or critical incidents can be proactive and effective ways for public organizations to screen candidates for desirable public service behaviors (Brewer 2003; Houston 2006; Christensen, Paarlberg, and Perry 2017).

3.1.4.2 Behavior-based Interviews

An approach that can be used either independently or in conjunction with biographical data is the behavior-based interview. Behavior-based interviews are a structured approach to link past performance to future behavior. They offer a systematic, objective method to build public service motivation into the selection decision. Although behavior-based interviews may be used to verify specific job behaviors, they are also useful for garnering other information relevant to performance in public service, specifically determining fit for the agency or work unit and how the applicant will contribute to the team and the agency's mission.

The following types of behavioral items may reveal a great deal about a candidate's public service motives and orientation toward others:

- Tell me about a time when you really identified with an organization's values and goals.
- Talk about a time when you made a personal sacrifice for an organization for which you worked previously.
- Tell me about how you helped a citizen or someone outside your organization in a prior job.
- Talk about a time when you gave back more than you got in return.
- Talk about how your participation in an organization made it better.
- Tell me about the last time you volunteered to do something extra.

If individuals without prior experience are being interviewed, then the items could be adjusted to inquire about situations in which the applicant might behave in a particular way.

3.1.4.3 Implicit Social Cognition Tests

In the last twenty-five years, scholars have intensively engaged a line of research involving implicit social cognition. The research establishes that social judgments and behavior are guided by attitudes and other cognitions for which actors may lack awareness (Greenwald and Lai 2020). Although most of the research emanates from psychology,[7] research about implicit social cognition also appears in scholarly journals of applied disciplines such as education, business, and public administration.

John Marvel and William Resh (2019) recently developed an implicit association test (IAT), a specific form of implicit social cognition, for prosocial motivation. They view their measure, which they call Pro-IAT, "as a complement to existing, survey-based measures of prosocial and public service motivation" (p. 65). Although the delivery of their implicit association test is moderately complex, Marvel and Resh describe Pro-IAT in the following terms:[8]

> Implicit Association Tests that are designed to measure self-concepts typically pair the categories ME and THEY or ME and NOT ME with two other categories that represent whatever construct is of theoretical interest.... Our version of the Implicit Association Test pairs ME and THEY with SERVICE and PROFIT. Stimulus items representing the ME category are the words I, me, myself, and mine. Items representing the THEY category are the words they, them, their, and theirs. For the SERVICE category, we used the words compassion, sacrifice, duty, give, and helping. For the PROFIT category, we used the words gain, win, money, take, and capitalize.

The Pro-IAT, consistent with the prosocial and public service motivation constructs it seeks to test, aims to contrast other-regarding orientation (e.g., duty, sacrifice, compassion) with self-regarding, profit-driven orientation (e.g., money, winning, gain). Pro-IAT scores are derived from respondents classifying items into categories as quickly as possible. The test is usually administered online and consists of seven rounds in which respondents classify items. One of the advantages of the Pro-IAT is that it is an indirect way to identify an individual's public service and prosocial motivations, thereby avoiding the manipulation or social desirability triggered by more direct survey measures.

Marvel and Resh (2019) report encouraging results about the validity of Pro-IAT on several fronts. Their validity tests include:

- *Known groups validity.* Pro-IAT discriminates for implicit prosocial motivation on groups with known differences on prosocial and public service motivation; MPA students, MBA students, M-Turk adults, and California local government employees. Using fourteen samples across these four categories, MPAs and local government employees score the highest, followed by M-Turk adults, and MBAs score the lowest. They also found no significant differences among samples in each of the four categories.

- *Relationship between implicit and explicit measures.* Correlations between Pro-IAT and explicit measures of prosocial and public service motivation are weak, suggesting that Pro-IAT and the explicit scales may be measuring different facets of other orientation.
- *Predictive validity.* Pro-IAT explains only a small portion of variation in subjects' charitable donations, which was used as a proxy for altruism.
- *Resistance to social desirability bias.* When subjects were randomly exposed to prosocial priming from a video presentation on the Peace Corps, no differences were found in Pro-IAT between subjects exposed to the treatment and subjects who did not view the Peace Corps appeal. No differences were found for an explicit five-item summary measure of public service motivation (see Table 2.1 in Chapter 2), suggesting that social desirability bias affected neither the implicit nor the explicit measures.

Although the evidence at this juncture of research concerning implicit cognitive tests about other orientation is limited, the results are sufficiently promising to consider them among a battery of selection instruments for employee selection.

3.1.5 Screen Out Candidates with Motivations Likely to Crowd Out Intrinsic or Prosocial Motivations

Screening candidates is not only a matter of finding applicants with positive attributes for public service and including them in the applicant pool but it is also about finding applicants with negative attributes and selecting out candidates who exhibit these characteristics (Christensen, Paarlberg, and Perry 2017). Some methods for screening out candidates, like realistic job previews, rely on self-selection dynamics, with individuals opting to exit the candidate pool, perhaps because of the normative or affective obligations attached to public service (Clerkin and Coggburn 2012).

Christensen, Paarlberg, and Perry (2017) propose a proactive variant of realistic job previews. They write:

… screen out candidates with significant self-interest motivations that stand in contrast to motivations associated with public service motivation, such as self-sacrifice and civic duty. Candidates with high needs for security or money might be screened out if these are their primary needs in the absence of strong public service motivation. An experiment reported by Fehrler and Kosfeld (2014) offered a lower wage to assess the willingness of participants to opt for mission-oriented jobs. About a third of the subjects took the lower-wage option, proving it to be an effective screening device. (p. 533)

Several concrete methods are offered below to facilitate screening candidates: screening for corruption (and honesty), implementing realistic job previews, using probationary periods to validate hiring decisions, and using internships to create positive recruitment and selection opportunities.

3.1.5.1 Screening for Corruption (and Honesty)

Several studies indicate that institutional arrangements may attract candidates who perceive personal advantages from their public employment, thereby undermining a public service ethos and, instead, putting corrupt agents in place to serve their personal interests (Banerjee, Baul, and Rosenblat 2015; Finan, Olken, and Pande 2017). A study of students in India is revealing. Using laboratory experiments, Rema Hanna and Shing-Yi Wang (2017) found that students who cheated on a simple laboratory task were more likely to prefer public employment and those who expressed prosocial preferences were less likely. Hanna and Wang found no difference in sector preferences between high-ability and low-ability students, implying that "screening on ability would neither exacerbate nor mitigate the selection problem among government workers in this context" (p. 264). The results for students were replicated with a sample of nurses working for the government, validating the simple laboratory task (a dice game, which is discussed later) as a potential selection device. Based upon the overall results, Hanna and Wang conclude: "These findings provide novel evidence highlighting that the variation in the levels of observed corruption may be driven, in part, by who selects into government service. They also imply that recruitment processes may be improved by increasing the emphasis on screening along characteristics other than cognitive ability, as long as the measures are not too explicit to be gamed" (p. 265).

Selection research suggests at least two methods for screening for honesty and corruption that are already available to public organizations. Robert Klitgaard (1988) called attention to selecting agents using integrity tests when the idea was first gaining momentum in the 1980s. Saul Fine (2010) offers evidence about the cross-cultural validity of integrity testing. He compares mean average integrity scores from 60,952 job applicants from 27 countries. The mean integrity scores for countries vary consistently with a comparative index of country-level corruption, supporting the validity of integrity tests.

Asmus Olsen et al. (2019) suggest another method that uses the dice game employed in laboratory experiments, like Hanna and Wang's (2017) research about selection in India discussed earlier. Olsen et al. (2019) explain the logic behind the dice game. They begin by pointing out the stark reality about doing research on corruption in the real world: "Measuring dishonesty is difficult.... Data on rule-breaking, arrests, or convictions will be systematically biased by the very same latent concept that the measures aim to capture. Asking about dishonesty and self-reported unethical behavior in surveys will also be severely biased due to social desirability, self-serving bias, and strategic behavior" (p. 574). Among key details Olsen and colleagues provide about the dice game paradigm[9] are:

- *Basic structure of dice games.* The dice game typically structures tasks in one of two ways that permit subjects to increase their rewards dishonestly without the experimenter knowing they did so. In the "game-in-private" version, the subject first observes the outcome of a private die roll and reports the results to receive a reward based on the report. The "game-in-mind" variant proceeds in three steps. The subject first makes a private prediction regarding the die roll but is not required to record the prediction. Then the roll occurs and is observed by the experimenter and the subject. On the third step, subjects report their predictions and are rewarded based on closeness to the actual outcome.
- *Binary versus varied reward structure.* In dice games with a binary reward structure, subjects receive a fixed reward or none at all. A varied reward structure permits subjects to receive a reward that varies depending on what they report. The binary-reward structure is better suited for calculating a cheat rate, whereas the varied-reward structure permits assessment of different degrees of dishonest behavior;
- *Likelihood of winning honestly.* How likely subjects are to win if they report honestly affects the statistical precision with which dishonest behavior can be measured.

- *Implementation settings.* Users of the dice game paradigm can choose among lab, online, and field implementation, permitting a variety of contexts for applying the dice game.
- *One-shot versus repeated implementations.* A one-shot game can provide useful information about the overall level of dishonesty or differences in dishonesty across groups if the number of subjects is large. When subjects repeat the dice games multiple times, however, users can increase statistical precision and power without increasing the number of subjects.
- *External validity.* The dice game paradigm has been validated against real-world dishonest behavior, including Hanna and Wang's (2017) research reported earlier.

Olsen et al. (2019) report two studies using the dice game: one about prospective public employees in Denmark and another on prospective public employees in ten countries with different levels of corruption. The study of prospective public employees in Denmark ($n = 441$) shows strong correlations between (dis)honesty on the dice game and public service motivation. Overall, public service motivation is strongly and negatively correlated with dishonesty. Olsen et al. also found significant and substantive correlations with behavioral honesty across all public service motivation subscales, particularly commitment to the public interest and self-sacrifice. Olsen et al. emphasize that these findings apply to a subgroup of prospective Danish public employees who are relatively honest, illustrating "the ability of the dice game paradigm to capture quite subtle differences in (dis)honesty within relatively homogeneous groups" (p. 579). Olsen et al.'s general findings about the strong relationship between public service motivation and honesty in a low-corruption country like Denmark are supported by a subsequent study using incentivized experimental games with a sample of 1,870 university students in Russia and Ukraine, two countries well known for high levels of corruption. Jordan Gans-Morse et al. (2019, 2020) provide evidence for a robust positive association between public service motivation and altruistic behavior and a negative association between public service motivation and willingness to engage in corrupt behavior.

The second study seeks to assess results from the dice game with regard to corruption in ten countries with varying levels of corruption. The ten countries are Denmark, Singapore, Sweden, the United Kingdom, Germany, Morocco, Egypt, Algeria, Indonesia, and Thailand. Five of the countries (Denmark, Singapore, Sweden, the United Kingdom, and Germany) are among the least corrupt countries based on Transparency International's corruption perceptions index from 1998 to 2017. The other countries represent the opposite end of the corruption spectrum, exhibiting high levels of corruption from 1998 to 2017. How well does the cheat rate among subjects with a preference for a job in the public sector correlate with the macro-level rates of corruption in each country? Olsen et al. (2019) conclude: "Corruption perception index and control of corruption both show strong and robust correlations with the estimated cheat rate.... In sum, country-level measures of corruption are strongly correlated with the average cheat rate of prospective public employees in a country" (p. 584). Based on their two studies, particularly the links they identify between micro-level honesty and macro-level corruption, Olsen and colleagues conclude that the dice game paradigm is a relevant selection tool.

3.1.5.2 Use Realistic Job Previews

A central idea of this chapter is that the values embraced by both organizations and prospective employees should be the basis for evaluating whether an organization and an applicant are well matched (Bowen, Ledford, and Nathan 1991; Cable and Judge 1996). Chatman (1991) observes, "... individuals and organizations ought to get as much information as possible about each other during the selection process" (p. 481).

A realistic job preview is just what the name implies. A realistic job preview offers a look into what a job and the organization in which it is situated entails, showing the positives and the negatives so a candidate gets a window into the skills and qualifications needed for the job, what a typical day on the job entails, and a look at the context and challenges for job incumbents. Realistic job previews are typically a tool for candidate self-evaluation, not a traditional selection device (U.S. Office of Personnel Management 2019a). They let candidates know the organization's expectations, which makes them better able to assess if this fits what they are looking for. The realistic job preview makes the process less one of "tell and sell" by the organization than a "two-way street" between the organization and the candidate.

Realistic job previews have been shown to make a difference across several important behavioral and attitudinal outcomes. They affect self-selection, an immediate behavioral outcome, which is consistent with the expectation that realistic job previews are tools for candidate self-evaluation (Premack and Wanous 1985; Phillips 1998; Earnest, Allen, and Landis 2011). Realistic job previews also affect other attitudinal and behavioral outcomes, including the level and accuracy of initial job expectations and increasing organizational commitment, job satisfaction, performance, and job survival.

Although research shows that realistic job previews can produce desirable outcomes, including self-selection that might screen out candidates with low public service motivation, they are not part of the recruitment and selection tool kit for most public sector employers. There are exceptions:

- The Internal Revenue Service uses realistic job previews for a variety of jobs, among them special agents (www.youtube.com/watch?v=YZZfKfT8TwM),[10] which are available on the IRS YouTube account;
- The Transportation Security Administration uses a realistic job preview video for transportation security officers (www.youtube.com/watch?v=NQoPmWIYytQ)[11]
- The State of Texas Department of Family and Protective Services uses realistic job previews for case workers (www.dfps.state.tx.us/Jobs/CPS/working_at_cps.asp)
- The Cherry Hill New Jersey Fire Department uses a brochure for firefighter jobs (www.cherryhill-nj.com/261/Fire-Employment-Opportunities)

Public organizations seeking to implement realistic job previews to enhance the motivational fit of their staff must consider a number of factors, among them:

- How the realistic job preview will be created;
- How the realistic job preview will be distributed;
- How to present both positive and negative aspects of the job; and
- When in the recruitment process to introduce the realistic job preview (U.S. Office of Personnel Management 2019a).

Decisions about these factors will give organizations many options for delivery format. They include:

- videos
- booklets or brochures;

- meetings with current employees or stakeholders;
- multimedia presentations; and
- structured observations.

In addition to the delivery format, implementing realistic job previews involves a host of other decisions important for developing effective programs (Wanous 1989; U.S. Office of Personnel Management 2019a). Several other decisions are likely to be particularly consequential when realistic job previews are used for the purpose of enhancing staff public service motivation. Assessing the situation is critically important to identify the outcomes sought for realistic job previews. Realistic job previews can be used proactively to secure staff who are prosocial and committed to public service or the social goals of the organization. Designers may also need to be attentive to identified problems such as high turnover among new hires, a second outcome that may make design of the realistic preview more complex.

Designers of realistic previews also need to identify issues addressed by a job preview (U.S. Office of Personnel Management 2019a). These issues may involve specific job duties, relationships with customers, coworkers and external constituencies, and situations employees may face that will challenge their coping skills. The jobs of Transportation Security Administration airport screeners, for example, require frequent repetition of low skill tasks, with a need for high accuracy, in a paramilitary context with intensive monitoring by supervisors and low autonomy. This type of information helps inform what should be covered in the realistic job preview.

Properly assessing the situation and accurately identifying issues that need to be addressed are critical concerns for those implementing realistic job previews. Matching realistic job preview methods with the organizational outcomes of interest is essential for achieving effectiveness.

3.1.5.3 Using Probationary Periods and Alternative Selection Processes to Validate Hiring Decisions

We seldom think of an employee's probationary period as a time to validate hiring decisions, but that is precisely how it can be viewed (Elliott and Peaton 1994; U.S. Merit Systems Protection Board 2005; PDRI 2010). What often makes public employment unique are the property rights that attach to the appointment in civil service, including full job protection appeal rights after a year or less of employment. In a 2005 report, the U.S. Merit Systems Protection Board (2005) referred frequently to agencies and supervisors serving the public interest by being sure probationers are carefully assessed during the probationary period before confirming their final appointments to civil service.

The probationary period provides an excellent opportunity for public organizations to assess the adequacy of their judgments about hiring decisions. The initial period of employment offers the organization an opportunity to observe an employee's job performance, the likelihood of the employee becoming a long-term asset for the organization, and the conduct of the employee relative to superiors, subordinates, coworkers, and the public. Given the stakes associated with final civil service appointments, using the probationary period to validate hiring decisions makes good sense.

Terminating employees before the end of their probationary period reduces the bar for the public employer's burden of proof regarding employee performance or conduct. The public employer, however, is not without substantive and ethical obligations to employees. Among the steps public employers must take to integrate the probationary period effectively and ethically into their selection process are (U.S. Merit Systems Protection Board 2005):

- Be clear in statute, ordinance, and/or regulation that the probationary period is a time to assess candidates before appointments are final.
- Tailor probationary periods to the unique characteristics of positions and training programs.
- Public employers should establish procedures where affirmative action must be taken to certify probationers so they do not automatically become an employee in the absence of meeting affirmative requirements.
- Supervisors should be accountable for the effective use of the probationary period.
- Supervisors should be trained to fulfill their responsibilities.
- Probationers should be notified, before accepting a job offer, what their status means and that a finalized appointment is not guaranteed.
- Probationers whose level of performance and conduct fail to meet organizational and supervisory standards are terminated.

3.1.5.4 Use Internships to Create Positive Recruitment and Selection Opportunities

Organizations with concerns about validating hiring decisions by exercising their discretion during the probationary period have alternatives. One is to integrate temporary arrangements (Forde 2001), such as internships, directly into the recruitment and selection process. The most common of these alternatives is internships. In a report commissioned by the Partnership for Public Service, PDRI (2010), an international human resource consulting company, emphatically endorsed internships: "Agencies must take greater advantage of intern programs by seizing the opportunity to assess the potential of young candidates while they are on the job – one of the best indicators of employees' future performance – and hire those who have demonstrated they have the right qualifications and abilities for vacant positions" (p. 16). The *Wall Street Journal* (Feintzeig 2014) reported that 89 percent of Pathway interns at NASA's Johnson Space Center accepted jobs after completing their internships.

A nonprofit in Brazil, Vetor Brazil, is using internships as one of its primary ways to attract talent to government, which suffers from stereotypes that it is rule bound and corrupt. Some of Vetor Brazil's initiatives are described in Box 3.1. What Vetor Brazil hopes to accomplish with a small number of internships is to change governments by changing the people who serve within them. The Vetor Brazil program, which its director describes as Brazil's equivalent to the United States-based Teach for America program that seeks to transform public schools by attracting high-quality, high-commitment teachers to inner city school districts, has attracted only a dozen recruits to state governments in its early stages. The director's goal, however, is to attract 800 transformative staff to governments across Brazil to change performance and stereotypes on a grand scale.

Box 3.1 How to make government work more attractive

Vetor Brasil Matches Leaders with
Opportunities in the Public Sector

With one of the world's largest economies and a population of more than 200 million people, Brazil is Latin America's giant. The country's government is large and provides essential services to its people, but Brazil struggles to strengthen and consolidate its public institutions.

The Problem

"If we really want to have impact on people's lives, we can't do it working only with the private sector," says Joice Toyota. "If we want to have scale, we have to change the government."

However, changing the government is a herculean task and it's difficult to attract skilled government employees who are up to the job. People often steer clear of government work because of pervasive stereotypes that Brazil and its unbridled bureaucracy are corrupt. "That's something that people don't want to deal with," says Toyota, who earned her MBA from Stanford GSB in 2015.

The Solution

Toyota's nonprofit Vetor Brasil aims to develop leaders who can change Brazil's public sector and how services are provided to the public. Think of it as Teach for America for government work. "We believe that there are thousands of high-potential university graduates who want to have social impact and give back to their country," Toyota says.

What's keeping them from rolling up their sleeves? These young workers don't know of the opportunities available in public management, Toyota says. Vetor Brasil selects workers and places them in temporary government jobs. "The idea is to change the system by changing the people," she says.

Toyota put out her first call for applicants last summer. She received 1,700 applicants and placed 12 trainees in state and local governments in four different states in Brazil.

Vetor Brasil will provide resources and counseling after their service to help them acquire jobs in the public sector or other types of public service organizations. Toyota's goal is to staff a total of 800 people in the public sector within the next five years.

Original report by Lily B. Clausen
Insights by Stanford Business
September 2, 2015
http://stanford.io/1PLO90s

3.2 Conclusion

A direct way to find public servants who are motivated to make a difference for the missions of their organizations and those who care about the public good is to recruit and select them in the first place. This chapter described strategies and methods for achieving that end. An organic means for attracting such staff is to build an organization whose image appeals to individuals high in public service motivation. For many decades, the BOP was an exemplar, an organization that attracted "principled agents" who were committed to the organization in good times and bad, chose consistently to do the right thing, and sacrificed tangible rewards because they valued the social goods of their work. Building a positive organizational image is a direct way by which many public organizations extract member identification that elicits high public service motivation.

In addition to relying on organizational images to attract high public service motivation prospects, public organizations have a variety of other tools to increase the prospects for recruiting and selecting the right people. In recruiting, they can shape job advertising to attract high public service motivation staff by including messages that emphasize mission and public values.

The process of screening applicants provides additional opportunities for inclusion and exclusion of candidates based on public service motivation behaviors. Candidates with high public service motivation may be screened in by selecting based on biographical data and behavioral interviews that indicate future behaviors. Implicit social cognition tests are another method for identifying individuals with prosocial and public service motivation.

Proven methods, including testing for integrity and dishonesty, are among methods that may be used to screen out candidates. Realistic job previews rely on candidates opting out of the selection process because they decide they do not fit the job or the organization. Public organizations can take a more active role in the screening process by using internships to give both the organization and individual opportunities to assess fit prior to decisions about career status. For individuals who have accepted positions, the probationary period can similarly be used by the organization to determine that it has made the correct selection decision.

Although more research and experimentation is needed to further develop our understanding of recruiting and selecting the right people for public service, the evidence reviewed in this chapter clarifies two facets of this challenge. First, the evidence reinforces the view that what individuals bring to public service makes an important difference to their performance and needs to be managed thoughtfully and rigorously to achieve the best results. The overall body of evidence reinforces this conclusion from a review of experimental evidence in developing countries: "... these studies establish that the characteristics of individuals are an important determinant of performance and they suggest how governments could change the applicant pool" (Finan, Olken, and Pande 2017, 491). Second, the evidence considered here also suggests the challenge of selecting and recruiting the right people for public service may be more demanding and costly than previously assumed. This inference is consistent with Bowen, Ledford, and Nathan's (1991) conclusion in the early 1990s that hiring for the organization was a more demanding and costly challenge than hiring for the job alone. We still have more to learn about how governments should screen to improve who occupies positions in public service. The directions proposed in this chapter represent a strong start toward necessary reforms.

Notes

1 The six countries Grindle studied were Bolivia, Central African Republic, Ghana, Morocco, Tanzania, and Sri Lanka. Among the organizations Grindle categorized as good performers were central banks in Bolivia and Sri Lanka, an agricultural extension institute in Ghana, budget offices in Ghana, Morocco, and Sri Lanka, and health service delivery nongovernmental organizations in Bolivia.
2 Although both Goodsell and Grindle use the concept of mission mystique, their contributions appear independent. Goodsell does not cite Grindle in the book. The one place their contributions intersect is with reference to DiIulio's research on the BOP.
3 The six organizations Goodsell studied are the U.S. National Park Service, the U.S. National Weather Service, U.S. Centers for Disease Control and Prevention, the Department of Social Services, Mecklenburg County, North Carolina, the Virginia State Police, and the U.S. Peace Corps.
4 My thanks to David Garcia, Senior Research Program Manager at the Partnership for Public Service, for providing the composite rankings for BOP from 2007 to 2018.

5 The Partnership uses the term "subcomponents," which aligns with what once were called "bureaus." I use the generic term "agencies," which is more appealing intuitively.

6 The countries in the twenty-six-country study are Australia, Belgium (Flanders only), Bulgaria, Canada, Cyprus, Czech Republic, Denmark, Finland, France, Germany, Hungary, Ireland, Israel, Japan, Korea, Latvia, Mexico, New Zealand, Norway, Portugal, Slovenia, Spain, Sweden, Switzerland, the United States, and the United Kingdom (Great Britain only).

7 Anthony Greenwald and Calvin Lai (2020) report that a search of the PsycNET database at the end of 2018 produced 1,483 peer-reviewed articles about implicit social cognition published since 2003.

8 Marvel and Resh refer to a general source for information about IAT. See https://implicit.harvard.edu/implicit/iatdetails.html.

9 Olsen et al. (2019) repeatedly refer to the "dice game paradigm," but do not define explicitly what they mean by paradigm. I interpret their use of the word as encompassing a class of games with the following structure. "A standardized measure of individual- and group-level dishonesty. The dice game paradigm involves experimental tasks in which subjects can increase their winnings by lying about the outcome of a die roll but face no risk of the researcher detecting their lie. Because the expected distribution of die rolls is known, however, the distribution of reports across repetitions of the game can benchmark what should have been observed if subjects were honest" (572).

10 The special agent job previews convey a variety of messages with a bearing on points made throughout this book. They include using internships to attract public service motivated staff and connecting staff with the outcomes they produce (e.g., arrest of law violators).

11 The transportation security officer video emphasizes several important public service messages, including the Transportation Security Administration's mission and the importance of the job for the country's protection from antiterrorism.

4 | *Leveraging the Meaningfulness of Public Work*

Janice Lachance (2017), President Bill Clinton's Director of the U.S. Office of Personnel Management, recounts a tale about President John F. Kennedy's chance encounter with a janitor at Cape Canaveral in 1962, soon after Kennedy committed the National Aeronautics and Space Administration (NASA) to putting a man on the moon before the end of the decade. Kennedy encountered the janitor sweeping the floor and asked, "What is your job?" The janitor replied, "Oh, Mr. President, I'm putting a man on the moon."

This story has been retold frequently since the 1960s. It has been recounted in many media outlets, but its authenticity is uncertain. Some have called it an urban legend.[1] The name of the janitor is not known. Did President Kennedy actually have such an encounter or did the President use the story to inspire employees across the federal bureaucracy?

The story about the janitor has become legendary, but it is not alone among the oral and written narratives about the meaning of public service. My youngest daughter, Jackie, is a proud Master of Social Work, who has been practicing her profession for more than fifteen years. In 2008, she shared with me a letter from another social worker (Arrington, 2008) that reflected their sentiments about "worth" and social "value":

> A group of friends and I were sitting around one evening discussing life. One guy there (whom I had just recently gotten to know) decided to explain the problem with social services and how they help those who won't help themselves.... He argued, "How's a person going to benefit from someone who has decided their best option in life is to become a social worker?" He reminded everyone what they say about social workers – "bleeding heart liberals." To stress his point, he said to me, "You're a social worker, Karen. Be honest. What do you make?"

I, having a reputation for honesty and frankness, replied, "You want to know what I make?" I paused for a moment and began, "Well, I have made safe places for abused children. In the process, I did my best to make them feel that they didn't deserve the treatment they got, so they could go out and do better in their lives."

"I now make arrangements for the terminally ill to stay at home in their last days with exceptional end of life care. I see that caregivers don't burn out making the patient and caregivers last days comfortable and worry-free."

"When a young widow or single mother doesn't know where to turn, social workers make sure they know (whether people like it or not) what benefits they are eligible for. And we try to make sure she doesn't get lost in the bureaucracy. We make plans with clients so they can get jobs and homes."

This is only a start. "You want to know what social workers make?" I asked again. "We make visits in neighborhoods that most people won't go to on a bet, because we know people there are in need, and we make friends there who invite us back to their weddings, cookouts, and openings of community centers we have campaigned for."

"We make time to listen to the elderly, the mentally ill, the lonely. And we have the knowledge and skills to help them make improvements in their lives." "We make appointments with officials and testify before legislature to get everyone in the community a fair shake."

"Some of us teach, to make the next generation's social workers."

"And sometimes, we make plans with our families and friends – only to break them because there is an accident, a fire, a disaster or death and a social worker is needed."

I then paused one last time and then continued. "So, when people want to judge me by what I make, I hold my head up high and say, "I make a difference…..What do you make?"

Both the often-shared story of the janitor at Cape Canaveral and the letter from the Alabama social worker ring true to many who have worked in public service. The fact these stories are so frequently shared testifies to the belief systems of those who tell them. The stories also speak to a broader phenomenon, personal significance reinforcement, introduced to public administration by Bruce Buchanan in the mid-1970s (Buchanan 1974, 1975). Personal significance reinforcement involves the extent to which individuals perceive they make contributions to organizational success. Buchanan argued that it is especially difficult for public agencies to inculcate employees with a sense of personal significance. A primary reason is the difficulty in establishing a line of sight between the work of public employees and the success of their organizations. The difficulty of establishing a line of sight is a product of many factors, including the size of many governments and the pluralism of policy implementation. The challenge of reinforcing personal significance is even more daunting when attitudes of personal significance must be developed within large-scale organizations where general standards of performance may be contested. Institutional rules, such as separation of executive and legislative authorities of government, which can produce intense executive-legislative conflicts, are an added challenge to establishing and reinforcing personal significance.

Despite seemingly insurmountable odds against reinforcing personal significance in the public sector, public employees, like the janitor and social worker, are often able to establish a clear line of sight. This chapter identifies methods for facilitating personal significance by establishing strong connections between work and the differences it makes for other people and society. Leveraging the meaningfulness of public work creates several positive results for public organizations, in particular:

- Employee motives are more likely to be aligned with autonomous rather than controlled incentives.
- Increased meaningfulness is likely to increase goal difficulty, enhancing the motivational potential of the work.
- Work meaningfulness, mediated by value and mission salience, increases goal commitment and thereby employee motivation.

4.1 Meaningfulness of Public Work: The Public Sector's Competitive Advantage

The stories of the NASA janitor and Alabama social worker call attention to the meaningfulness of work as an extraordinarily powerful motivator. A more subtle implication is the potential links between meaningfulness and institutional identity. Is the nature of public institutions an advantage for creating meaningful work? Several research streams suggest there may indeed be an institutional advantage. These streams involve research on public work and socially useful and useless jobs.

4.1.1 Public Work

In *Building America: The Democratic Promise of Public Work*, Harry Boyte and Nancy Kari (1996) leave no doubt about the social value of public work. Boyte and Kari write, "Public work, work that makes things of value and importance in cooperation with others, is the taproot of American democracy. Linking everyday work to democracy gives work larger meaning and makes citizenship serious" (p. 2). Whether the work employees perform throughout the public sector globally is thought of as fundamental to regime development is uncertain, but the very nature of most work in the public sector ties value creation to cooperation with others. Thus, many public sector workers might be inclined to embrace the meaning of their work and its relationship to citizenship.

Boyte and Kari's search for a practical theory about democratic renewal through work begins with their simple observation about work. Boyte and Kari observe:

> Today, people are supposedly "overworked." In fact, work has become simply a means to an end – one "has to work" to feed the family, to pay for the vacation, to survive economically. Few worksites discuss the larger significance of what one makes or produces. We are convinced that in fact people are "underworked." However many hours, work has lost its tie to larger public purposes, challenges, and possibilities. (pp. 3–4)

The critique of work advanced by Boyte and Kari is not bounded by sector, but is infused across sectors and, by extrapolation, perhaps even across nations.

Boyte and Kari offer tools for democratic renewal that traverse sector boundaries, but may be more salient for renewing public work. They identify three strands of the meaning of public that resonate within public institutions. "*Public* is a diverse group acting together – a public; *public* is a quality of space that is open, visible, and accessible to view; and, finally, *public* suggests broad purposes of general importance, for example in public goods or public interests" (Boyte and Kari 1996, 11–12). These strands have long been identified with public institutions and organizations (Perry and Rainey 1988). From Boyte and Kari's view, the failing is that the fundamentals of public – and the meaning they bring to work – have been lost in current everyday life. But pursuit of the public ideal is the institutional identity that frames much of the work that is done by governments, communities, and interest groups that gives meaning to public spirit (Kelman 1988).

4.1.2 Socially Useful/Useless Jobs

A source of evidence about whether public institutions are at an advantage for creating meaningful work comes from research about socially useless jobs. The concept of socially useless jobs originates with anthropologist David Graeber (2013). A socially useless job is defined by Robert Dur and Max van Lent (2019) as one that makes no or a negative contribution to society. Graeber's (2013) critique of capitalism, looking back to John Maynard Keynes' (1930) prediction of a fifteen-hour work week by the century's end, is less polite. He labels socially useless jobs, "bullshit jobs," and writes: "It's as if someone were out there making up pointless jobs just for the sake of keeping us all working" (p. 2).

Dur and van Lent's (2019) study of socially useless jobs used a large representative dataset, the *International Social Survey Program, Work Orientations Waves*, covering more than 100,000 workers from 47 countries in 1989, 1997, 2005, and 2015. Their study employed the 2015 wave only, which included 27,000 workers from 37 countries. They operationalized socially useless jobs with a subjective assessment, using a respondent's disagreement or strong disagreement with the survey item: My job is useful to society.

Overall, Dur and van Lent found about 75 percent of workers agreeing or strongly agreeing with the survey item. A relatively large portion of the sample, 17 percent, neither agreed nor disagreed, suggesting ambivalence about the usefulness of their jobs. Public sector workers were much less likely to report having a socially useless job than workers in the private sector. The average for private sector workers was 8 percent. The average for the public sector was 6 percent lower than the private sector. For some public sector occupations – firefighters, police officers, social benefits officials, health workers, and teachers – the proportion of socially useless work is close to or equal to zero. The public sector advantage was not universal. Dur and van Lent report that government clerks and armed forces members, for instance, were closer to the sample average.

Although Dur and van Lent's research relies on subjective assessments of work, they discover that government workers are far less likely to perceive their work as useless than their private sector counterparts. The difference reflects one type of systematic sorting between sectors. The takeaway is that public managers, and probably nonprofit managers, too, have an edge when seeking to leverage the meaningfulness of work.

Lea Cassar and Stephan Meier (2018), summarizing evidence about the meaningfulness of work, point to interesting results from another study that, like Dur and van Lent's (2019) research, gives public-sector jobs and occupations an edge for meaningfulness. Andrew Bryce (2018) analyzed *eudaimonic well-being*, the extent to which certain jobs or types of work foster meaning and purpose for an individual. Bryce used two major data sets from two countries, the Time Use Survey from the United States and the United Kingdom's Annual Population Survey. Two findings are particularly relevant here. First, Bryce found that work was more meaningful than many other uses of time, specifically consumer purchases, socializing, relaxing, and leisure, suggesting that work is one of the primary ways people find meaning in their lives. Second, the most meaningful jobs were those high on personal autonomy and prosocial impact, among them health professionals, therapists, nurses, teachers, and social workers. Although Bryce presents no evidence about the sector-locus of these jobs, simple inspection indicates that most or all of them are likely public-sector dominated occupations (e.g., health professionals, nurses, teachers, and social workers).

4.1.3 Summary

Work intended to better the common good, what Boyte and Kari passionately call "public work," appears to make a difference in the lives of people who are engaged in it, judging both from the stories people tell and survey research. The "ideal" or "aspirational" significance about which Boyte and Kari write appears to extend to how incumbents of public-sector jobs perceive their work. Based on research by Dur and van Lent (2019) and Bryce (2018), the public sector has a disproportionate share of work that is meaningful. Eudaimonic well-being, the extent to which types of work foster meaning and purpose for individuals, is well represented across jobs in the public sector. It is ironic that the "reputation" of work in the public sector so often seems to fall outside both the potential and reality of public work.

The strategies discussed next have two purposes. Where employees experience the meaningfulness of public work, the strategies are useful for realizing and reinforcing that meaningfulness. In situations where the meaningfulness of the work goes unexperienced, the strategies are a means to reconnect employees with the passion of public service.

4.2 Strategies for Leveraging the Meaningfulness of Public Work

Although conceptual arguments can be mounted and empirical evidence marshaled, I recognize that not everyone will share my positive view about the competitive advantage of public work. One counterargument is primarily institutional, asserting that institutional factors alone, in total, have only modest effects, if any, on the meaningfulness of work. This counterargument merits acknowledgement and attention. Institutional sorting is variable across societies and labor markets, which likely affects its influence in different settings (Kerckhoff 1995). At the same time, institutional arrangements appear to have real consequences for the meaningfulness of work, as research by Dur and van Lent (2019) and Bryce (2018) suggests.

Another counterargument is primarily practical. It goes something like this: "Any advantages that acting on behalf of citizens and the public interest may create for work's meaningfulness can be undercut by the realities of the public sector. Low budgets, meddling politicians and interest groups, and a host of other implementation barriers mean that the meaningfulness of public work is very hard to experience." These barriers are real and often part of life in the public sector. Although reviews of motivation research that touch on the meaningfulness of public work (Perry and Porter 1982; Perry, Mesch, and Paarlberg 2006) conclude that work design is an important influence on the motivations of public employees, these reviews also acknowledge that "moderators and implementation are important influences on the efficacy of job design" (Perry, Mesch, and Paarlberg 2006, 508).

These threats to the optimism expressed about public work are legitimate. At the same time, even when work may not be inherently public or practical barriers stand in the way of employees experiencing the meaningfulness associated with public work, public managers and organizations can take action to enhance meaningfulness and leverage the motivational potential of meaningful work. At least four strategies provide avenues to leverage the meaningfulness of public work: designing work for direct contact between employees and beneficiaries; using self-persuasion to enhance meaningfulness; facilitating job crafting by employees; and providing career counseling to strengthen meaningfulness.

4.2.1 Designing Work that Allows for Direct Contact between Employees and Beneficiaries

The idea that work design has an important influence on employee motivation is well established, dating at least to Frederick Herzberg's (1968) research on job enrichment, that is, building more "satisfiers" or motivators into work and reducing the influence of "dissatisfiers" or hygiene factors. Richard Hackman and Greg Oldham (1976, 1980) advanced Herzberg's research when they developed a formal model of motivation and work design. Their model posits that five characteristics of work are influential for stimulating internally motivated psychological states. These psychological states, like the experienced meaningfulness of the work, lead to desirable personal and work outcomes, among them high internal work motivation, quality work performance, and lower absenteeism and turnover.

The job characteristics most germane to the discussion here are autonomy and task significance, sometimes referred to as social significance, which Hackman and Oldham (1976) defined as "the degree to which the job has a substantial impact on the lives or work of other people, whether in the immediate organization or in the external environment" (p. 257). When the job characteristics model first appeared (Hackman et al. 1975), Hackman and colleagues proposed establishing client relationships as a way to reinforce ties between work and critical psychological states like experienced meaningfulness and experienced responsibility for outcomes. The implementing concept of establishing client relationships was seen as a mechanism for reducing fractionalization that prevents workers from contact with or awareness of end users.

Adam Grant (2007) reenergized interest in work design by introducing a model of relational job design. Grant's relational model begins with a recognition that "... many employees describe the purpose of their work in terms of making a positive difference in others' lives" (p. 393). Grant argues that the relational architecture surrounding work – the structures that "shape employees' opportunities to connect and interact with other people" (p. 396) – has an enormously important influence on the motivation to make a prosocial difference. Unlike the job characteristics model, which gave greater attention to task structures and the characteristics of job incumbents, the relational model emphasizes the structure of relationships and how that structure contributes to making a prosocial difference.

The extent to which individuals perceive their jobs to be meaningful is influenced significantly by the extent to which employees perceive the impact their work has on its beneficiaries, which is the core principle of relational job design (Grant 2007; Grant and Parker 2009). Adam Grant (2008b) has demonstrated the importance of connecting employees with their prosocial impact in a number of studies, several involving public employees. One of his first studies was a quasi-experiment set in a public university. Subjects were telephone fundraisers seeking to secure funds for scholarships. Grant arranged for the experimental group to meet scholarship recipients who benefitted from the telefund campaign. The scholarship recipient shared a testimonial about the difference funding meant for their pursuit of higher education. After a month, the members of the experimental group achieved results superior to the control group for both pledges and donations. The results for the control group did not change. Grant concluded that connecting public service employees to the prosocial impact of their work was motivating and the effects of such connections are powerful.

Grant's findings have been replicated with public service employees outside the United States. Nicola Bellé (2013) conducted a true experiment with nurses in a public hospital in Italy. Bellé's study investigated relationships among two variables and two experimental conditions. The focal variables were public service motivation and job performance. The first experimental condition was the nurses' exposure to contact with beneficiaries of their work. The second experimental condition was exposure to self-persuasion, essentially the nurses' preparation of an advocacy presentation about the importance of their work. Both beneficiary contact and self-persuasion positively influenced several motivational outcomes, specifically persistence, output, productivity, and vigilance. Nurses who entered the experiment with higher public service motivation demonstrated stronger effects for each of the experimental conditions. Bellé identified an additional benefit from both experimental interventions. They increased public service motivation that, in turn, partially mediated the intervention's positive effects on job performance. Bellé's experimental results support the case for work redesign interventions that explore ways to enhance direct contact between employees and beneficiaries and substitutes for such direct contacts using self-persuasion mechanisms.

Aside from these direct experiments testing interventions involving relational structures, many other studies of public employees support both the logic of the model and power of enhancing beneficiary contacts. A sampling of the research includes:

- John Brehm and Scott Gates (1997), in a wide-ranging study of bureaucrats across all levels of government, found that service recipients exerted more influence over public employees with whom they had regular contact than their supervisors.
- In a qualitative study, Janet Vinzant (1998) sought to answer a general question about the difficult work of child and protective services workers: Why did they do what they did? Interviewees responded about their commitments to protecting the vulnerable, helping families, and serving communities. Vinzant writes: "One worker simply said, 'I love helping people.' Another said, 'I love working at CPS. It's challenging, different, and I'm saving children's lives. I am making a difference.' Still another said, 'I am here to help. I am here to help kids. I am committed to that purpose, and that's why I am here. This isn't just a job'" (p. 358).
- Studies of teachers show they are motivated by their ability to see and experience their contributions to improvements in their students (Kelley 1999).
- In a study of civilian employees at a Department of Defense installation, Laurie Paarlberg (2007) explored relationships between "customer orientation," motivation, and employee performance and motivation longitudinally across work roles. Customer orientation was an additive scale constructed from survey questions about "awareness of customer needs, organizational systems in place to interact with customers, and goals to encourage action in response to customer needs" (p. 210). Paarlberg found that customer service orientation had a significant positive influence on employee performance and motivation. Customer service orientation provided a connection to the organization's goals that supported employees' values of public service. She concluded, however, "... efforts to create a

more 'market'-based orientation focused on institutional customers who purchase services may have limited impact, or even a deleterious effect on, employee performance and motivation, unless also accompanied by formal linkages to service beneficiaries" (p. 201).

- Jeannette Taylor (2014) studied Australian local government workers' perceptions of two relational work structures – impact on citizens and contact with citizens – to ascertain the effects on public service motivation and job satisfaction. She found that employees who perceived that their jobs provided avenues for impact on citizens were more satisfied with their job. She found that job contact with service recipients had no mediating or moderating effects on the public service motivation–job satisfaction relationship. On its face, Taylor's finding could be interpreted as conflicting with Grant's (2007) relational job design theory. Another plausible explanation is that relational work structures can be complex, especially in the public sector (see the discussion later about street-level bureaucrats, a stream of research that makes this interpretation of Taylor's results plausible), and the complexity needs to be carefully managed to generate positive outcomes.

While public organizations and their managers may not be able to connect all employees with the beneficiaries of their service, other avenues are available to tie employees to beneficiaries. Stories shared within the organization by word-of-mouth, for instance, that reinforce the social impact of the work may favorably influence employees' behaviors. Social interactions with service beneficiaries may also positively influence employee motivation by providing a face for employees' public service values, translating abstract organizational goals into significant action (Paarlberg 2007). The World Bank developed two programs that give development professionals opportunities to observe firsthand the lives of the poor (World Bank 2003; Irvine, Chambers, and Eyben 2004). The objectives of the Grass Roots Immersion Program and the Village Immersion Program are similar. They take development professionals from the comfort of their offices to the places where the poor live. Immersions (Irvine, Chambers, and Eyben 2004) are

> ... distinct from normal brief field visits to a village, slum or project. Such visits, often highly structured and "red carpet" in style, are vulnerable to a rigid pre-planned schedule, formality, shortage of time, a constraining

political environment, and behaviour designed to please or gain benefits from the visitor as a funder. As one expatriate informant put it "the whole process is highly ritualised and fraught with political significance around what foreigners can and cannot see". (p. 5)

Professionals participating in immersion live with their hosts for several days, often directly shadowing the host "to see the reality of poverty and vulnerability through the eyes of a particular individual and to understand how that individual copes with the circumstances of their poverty and vulnerability" (World Bank 2003, 5). The immersion facilitates development professionals' knowledge of the environments they are seeking to change and current conditions in rapidly changing situations, opportunities for questioning and reflecting about complex development processes, and energy and commitment to make policy based on face-to-face encounters (Irvine, Chambers, and Eyben 2004). The descriptions of the cognitive and affective consequences of the immersion mirror how interventions associated with work designs that bring together employees and beneficiaries are frequently described.

Although much of the research related to connecting employees with beneficiaries to stimulate the motivational power of their prosocial impact involves public services, the tactic is also effective for employees attracted to government because of their interest in influencing the public policy process. In an early study of public service motivation and work characteristics, Peter Leisink (2004) investigated what happens at the intersection between the dispositions individuals bring to their work and work characteristics. Leisink points to the observations of a Dutch secretary general to illustrate how important it is for employees to see their actions influence the policy process. "What motivates individuals at work is the wish to see what their efforts have produced, for instance to find their text in a communication which the Minister sends to the parliament. They wish to see their stamp on some piece of policy making" (p. 8).

Although work design tactics such as Grant's (2007) relational job design can be influential for motivating prosocial behaviors among public employees, such efforts are likely to have a ceiling. A variety of organizational, occupational, and social factors may constrain employees' responses to job design (Perry, Mesch, and Paarlberg 2006; Grant 2007, 402). Attributes of beneficiaries could, for example, decrease employees' affective commitments toward them. Robert Christensen, Laurie Paarlberg, and James Perry (2017) point to the example of U.S. Internal Revenue Service clients who have avoided filing taxes for long periods and are presumptively treated as "tax cheats." Christensen et al. observe: "... structural characteristics of jobs affect social information about beneficiaries that moderates the effect of contact on affective commitment to beneficiaries. Social information is therefore an important variable that affects choices about whether job design can be an effective strategy for increasing public service motivation" (p. 535).

4.3 Using Self-Persuasion or Other Self-Administered Interventions to Connect Employees to Beneficiaries

Self-persuasion eschews direct attempts at convincing an individual of something using external sources. Instead, self-persuasion relies on individuals convincing themselves that something is the case. Elliot Aronson (1999), the originator of self-persuasion, contrasts direct and self-persuasion in the following way: "What characterizes a self-persuasion situation is that no direct attempt is made to convince anyone of anything. Rather, individuals find themselves in a circumstance where it becomes efficacious to convince themselves that a particular thing is the case: for example, that a particular group they have joined is attractive...." (p. 882).

The logic of self-persuasion mirrors self-determination theory in that the more powerful motivation comes from within, that is, self-regulation rather than from another, that is, extrinsic sources.[2] The underlying psychological processes that make self-persuasion effective are beyond the scope of this book, but inducing cognitive dissonance is a key feature of the dynamic. Peter Heslin, Gary Latham, and Don Van de walle (2005) assert: "A key finding in the self-persuasion literature is that inducing cognitive dissonance, by drawing attention to how people have not acted in accordance with the ideas they have espoused, serves to substantially increase the effectiveness of self-persuasion" (p. 850). Bradley Wright and Adam Grant (2010) suggest that self-persuasion interventions may take many different forms:

> Typical self-persuasion interventions involve the processes of idea reflection and advocacy. For example, researchers might ask employees to reflect on the importance of public service, and then publicly advocate, both in writing and in person, why it is critical for each person to engage

in public service. In doing so, they may convince themselves of the importance of public service, making a private and public commitment to furthering public institutions in the future. (p. 696)

A self-persuasion intervention was a second experimental condition in Bellé's (2013) study of Italian nurses in a public hospital. Bellé's self-persuasion intervention used the principle referred to earlier of putting the nurses in a position to persuade themselves about the importance of their work. Nurses in the self-persuasion treatment wrote "a few lines – to be included in a presentation that ... would [be delivered] to all hospital departments and to all of the other hospitals belonging to the same local health authority – describing how they thought the project would help health care practitioners in the target area improve the lives of their patients" (p. 146). The self-persuasion participants were also required "to promote the project within their departments and to do their best to recruit at least three volunteers willing to perform the same work in the future" (pp. 146–147). Bellé found that the self-persuasion intervention increased performance among employees reporting high public service motivation in advance of the experiment.

Another study points to the utility of self-persuasion in shaping dispositions that are highly relevant to, but conceptually distinct from, public service motivation (Arieli, Grant, and Sagiv 2014). Sharon Arieli, Adam Grant, and Lilach Sagiv conducted experiments with both US and Israeli samples. The object of Arieli et al.'s study was benevolence values, "which reflect the motivation to help and care for others" (p. 15). They developed interventions that combined self-persuasion and consistency maintenance, which required effort from subjects, with priming, an automatic stimulus for value change. The results of their three experiments produced compelling results. All three experiments produced increased benevolence values. The second experiment, conducted with business students in Israel, involved a check for whether values translated to behavior. The subjects revealed willingness to volunteer to help others, thus indicating the value change translated to behavior change, too. The third experiment (with US undergraduate subjects, like the first experiment) tested whether the value change persisted. Arieli et al. found that increased benevolence was still evident after four weeks.

In another experiment relevant to the efficacy of self-persuasion that focuses on public services, Dominik Vogel and Jurgen Willems (2020) conducted three "micro-interventions," which were intended to assist "employees in recognizing their job's prosocial and societal impact...." (p. 2). Although the meaning of microintervention is broader and distinct from self-persuasion, Vogel and Willems repeatedly described their interventions as "reflection tasks," which involve processes of self-persuasion. They assessed the effects of three microinterventions on the influence of employees' prosocial (specific others) and societal (generalized others) impacts on employees' well-being, intentions to stay, and willingness to recommend their job to others. They concluded that microinterventions to sensitize employees to their jobs' societal impact did influence the outcomes they studied.

Public managers may not turn to self-persuasion routinely, but it is a tool at their disposal for influencing motivational outcomes for public employees. Given the types of results from experiments reported earlier, self-persuasion (or microinterventions) deserves much more frequent use by managers than it receives currently. Self-persuasion may be a substitute for interventions like relational job design when such alternatives are constrained or costly. Self-persuasion might also be considered to augment or reinforce alternatives, as in Bellé's experiment with nurses in Italy. Self-persuasion may also be a tactic useful in the context of career counseling, which is discussed later in this chapter.

4.4 Job Crafting

Job crafting, employee-initiated job changes to infuse meaning into work, has not surfaced in the context of public service motivation research until recently, but the concept deserves attention. In a recent study of work–family conflict as a potential "dark side" of public service motivation, Julia Asseburg (2018) proposed using job crafting as a method to mitigate tensions for high public service motivation staff. Using a two-wave survey of 306 German public employees, Asseburg (2018) concluded that public service motivation is a predictor of work–family conflict, and job crafting partially mediated the conflicts.

A more prominent connection between job crafting and public administration arises in research on street-level bureaucrats, which originated with an influential book by Michael Lipsky (2010), *Street-Level Bureaucracy: Dilemmas of the Individual in Public Services*. Lipsky coined the term "street-level bureaucrats" to refer to public employees, such as police officers, teachers, and welfare case workers, who interacted directly with citizens and service recipients. His overarching contention is that street-level bureaucrats influence policy implementation through at least two mechanisms, their exercise of discretion and the relationships they develop with citizen clients. These two mechanisms, discretion and relationships with citizen clients, are a bridge between research on street-level bureaucracy and job crafting, a point that becomes clear later.

Contributions to the street-level bureaucracy literature often come in the form of narratives about street-level workers (Maynard-Moody, Williams, and Musheno 2003; Riccucci 2005; Zarychta, Grillos and Andersson 2020). The narratives offer a naturalistic picture of what transpires in the jobs of street-level bureaucrats (Maynard-Moody and Musheno 2000), which ties their stories to job crafting by identifying the processes by which jobs are modified and the outcomes of the modifications. Steven Maynard-Moody and Michael Musheno (2003), for instance, share the stories of cops, teachers, and counselors that illuminate how these street-level workers make their jobs not only more rewarding but also easier and safer.

One study, focusing on early childhood education caregivers, represents a formal intersection of research about street-level workers and job crafting. Carrie Leana, Eileen Applebaum, and Iryna Shevchuk (2009) surveyed 232 teachers and aides in 62 childcare centers in Pennsylvania and New Jersey. They were interested in how individual and collaborative job crafting affected a variety of outcomes, including turnover intention, job satisfaction and commitment, and quality of care. The form of job crafting they studied was "task crafting" because the interventions involved altering work practices. Leana, Applebaum, and Shevchuk found that both individual and collaborative job crafting influenced outcomes of interest. Their exploration of both individual and collaborative job crafting is especially relevant for public organizations where individual accountability is important, but mission success can often depend on teamwork, in services like early childhood education, policing, and teaching.

4.4.1 Job Crafting to Increase Meaningfulness

Job crafting, as a strategy for infusing meaning into work, originates from the positive psychology movement. Rather than designing jobs for employees that reinforce the meaning of their work, job crafting relies on the initiatives of employees to craft their work to add meaning. Job crafting gives the employee discretion in how they frame their work, physically, socially, and cognitively. Employees have an opportunity to build their job responsibilities around their strengths and simultaneously enhance the meaning of what they do.

Job crafting gives individuals who pursue public service an opportunity to proactively shape the meaning of their work (Buchanan 1975; Perry and Porter 1982; Perry and Vandenabeele 2008). It gives them the tools to change their work to fit their identity. Job crafting is not a monolithic technique, but covers three general avenues by which employees may craft their jobs (Wrzesniewski and Dutton 2001; Berg, Dutton, and Wrzesniewski 2013). They are:

1. *Task crafting* involves changing job tasks in ways that will infuse the job with more meaning. The changes to tasks could involve jettisoning tasks, adding tasks that are particularly appealing, or changing the way tasks are performed.
2. *Relational crafting* focuses on changing the social relationships of work. It may include developing new relationships and reframing existing relationships, all with the purpose of making work more meaningful.
3. *Cognitive crafting* involves changing how people think about their jobs, which means reframing begins with an individual's perceptions of the work. Employees may seek to alter their perceptions of the purpose of work, and they can reframe their job to better fit their identity.

Figure 4.1 (Berg, Dutton, and Wrzesniewski 2008) provides a schematic summarizing the overall job-crafting model according to motivations for job crafting, the techniques described earlier, and individual outcomes associated with job-crafting interventions.

Box 4.1 summarizes a process for implementing job crafting. The process involves four steps. Step 1, "rethink your job – creatively," involves thinking about the job holistically, taking stock of tasks involved in the work, and reflecting about possibilities. Step 2, "diagram your day," gets down to a detailed analysis of processes surrounding the job to gain insights into what is done and how job tasks might be reconfigured. The next step, "identify job loves and

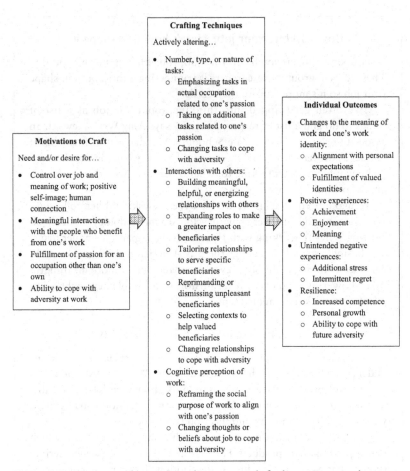

Crafting Techniques

Actively altering...

- Number, type, or nature of tasks:
  - Emphasizing tasks in actual occupation related to one's passion
  - Taking on additional tasks related to one's passion
  - Changing tasks to cope with adversity
- Interactions with others:
  - Building meaningful, helpful, or energizing relationships with others
  - Expanding roles to make a greater impact on beneficiaries
  - Tailoring relationships to serve specific beneficiaries
  - Reprimanding or dismissing unpleasant beneficiaries
  - Selecting contexts to help valued beneficiaries
  - Changing relationships to cope with adversity
- Cognitive perception of work:
  - Reframing the social purpose of work to align with one's passion
  - Changing thoughts or beliefs about job to cope with adversity

Motivations to Craft

Need and/or desire for...

- Control over job and meaning of work; positive self-image; human connection
- Meaningful interactions with the people who benefit from one's work
- Fulfillment of passion for an occupation other than one's own
- Ability to cope with adversity at work

Individual Outcomes

- Changes to the meaning of work and one's work identity:
  - Alignment with personal expectations
  - Fulfillment of valued identities
- Positive experiences:
  - Achievement
  - Enjoyment
  - Meaning
- Unintended negative experiences:
  - Additional stress
  - Intermittent regret
- Resilience:
  - Increased competence
  - Personal growth
  - Ability to cope with future adversity

Figure 4.1 Summary of key job crafting research findings. Berg et al. (2008) http://positiveorgs.bus.umich.edu/wp-content/uploads/What-is-Job-Crafting-and-Why-Does-it-Matter1.pdf. Accessed on August 15, 2020.

hates," is an opportunity for the employee to connect the analysis of step 2 with his or her emotional connections to the work. This part of the process gives employees the ability to rediscover the passions and motives that attract them to the work. Step 4, "put your ideas into action," is all about implementation, making change happen. This part of the process entails consultations with others who may be consequential for job changes to happen, including supervisors and coworkers.

Box 4.1 Hate your job? Here's how to reshape it

Once upon a time, if you hated your job, you either quit or bit your lip. These days, a group of researchers is trumpeting a third option: shape your job so it's more fruitful than futile.

"We often get trapped into thinking about our job as a list of things to do and a list of responsibilities," says Amy Wrzesniewski, an associate professor at the Yale School of Management. "But what if you set aside that mind-set?" If you could adjust what you do, she says, "who would you start talking to, what other tasks would you take on, and who would you work with?"

To make livelihoods more lively, Wrzesniewski and her colleagues Jane Dutton and Justin Berg have developed a methodology they call job crafting. They're working with *Fortune* 500 companies, smaller firms, and business schools to change the way Americans think about work. The idea is to make all jobs – even mundane ones – more meaningful by empowering employees to brainstorm and implement subtle but significant workplace adjustments.

Step 1: Rethink Your Job – Creatively

"The default some people wake up to is dragging themselves to work and facing a list of things they have to do," says Wrzesniewski. So in the job-crafting process, the first step is to think about your job holistically. You first analyze how much time, energy, and attention you devote to your various tasks. Then you reflect on that allocation.

Take, for example, a maintenance technician at Burt's Bees, which makes personal-care products. He was interested in process engineering, though that wasn't part of his job description. To alter the scope of his day-to-day activities, the technician asked a supervisor if he could spend some time studying an idea he had for making the firm's manufacturing procedures more energy efficient. His ideas proved helpful, and now process engineering is part of the scope of his work.

Barbara Fredrickson, author of *Positivity* and a professor of psychology at the University of North Carolina at Chapel Hill, says it's crucial for people to pay attention to their workday emotions. "Doing so," she says, "will help you discover which aspects of your work are most life-giving – and most life-draining."

Many of us get stuck in ruts. Berg, a Ph.D. student at the Wharton School at the University of Pennsylvania who helped develop the job-crafting methodology, says we all benefit from periodically rethinking what we do. "Even in the most constraining jobs, people have a certain amount of wiggle room," he says. "Small changes can have a real impact on life at work."

Step 2: Diagram Your Day

To lay the groundwork for change, job-crafting participants assemble diagrams detailing their workday activities. The first objective is to develop new insights about what you actually do at work. Then you can dream up fresh ways to integrate what the job-crafting exercise calls your "strengths, motives and passions" into your daily routine. You convert task lists into flexible building blocks. The end result is an "after" diagram that can serve as a map for specific changes.

Ina Lockau-Vogel, a management consultant who participated in a recent job-crafting workshop, says the exercise helped her adjust her priorities. "Before, I would spend so much time reacting to requests and focusing on urgent tasks that I never had time to address the real important issues." As part of the job-crafting process, she decided on a strategy for delegating and outsourcing more of her administrative responsibilities.

In contrast to business tomes that counsel managers to influence workers through incentives, job crafting focuses on what employees themselves can do to reenvision and adjust what they do every day.

Step 3: Identify Job Loves and Hates

By reorienting how you think about your job, you free yourself up for new ideas about how to restructure your workday time and energy. Take an IT worker who hates dealing with technologically incompetent callers. He might enjoy teaching more than customer service. By spending more time instructing colleagues – and treating help-line callers as curious students of tech – the disgruntled IT person can make the most of his 9-to-5 position.

Dutton, a professor at the University of Michigan's Ross School of Business, says she has seen local auto-industry workers benefit from the job-crafting process. "They come in looking worn down, but after spending two hours on this exercise, they come away thinking about three or four things they can do differently."

"They start to recognize they have more control over their work than they realized," says Dutton, who partnered with Wrzesniewski on the original job-crafting research.

Step 4: Put Your Ideas into Action

To conclude the job-crafting process, participants list specific follow-up steps. Many plan a one-on-one meeting with a supervisor to propose new project ideas. Others connect with colleagues to talk about trading certain tasks. Berg says as long as their goals are met, many managers are happy to let employees adjust how they work.

Job crafting isn't about revenue, per se, but juicing up employee engagement may end up beefing up the bottom line. Amid salary, job, and benefit cuts, more and more workers are disgruntled. Surveys show that more than 50 percent aren't happy with what they do. Dutton, Berg, and Wrzesniewski argue that emphasizing enjoyment can boost efficiency by lowering turnover rates and jacking up productivity. Job crafting won't rid you of a lousy boss or a subpar salary, but it does offer some remedies for job dissatisfaction. If you can't ditch or switch a job, at least make it more likable.

Original report by Jeremy Caplan
TIME
December 4, 2009
http://content.time.com/time/business/article/
0,8599,1944101,00.html

4.4.2 Some Considerations for Job Crafting in the Public Sector

Although the logic and techniques of job crafting are transportable to the public sector, it is worthwhile to raise a few considerations for public employees interested in pursuing job crafting. The considerations, which may not apply to all public work, are as follows: legal compliance, consultation with supervisors, collaborative job crafting, and job crafting as a strategy to manage employees' work stressors.

4.4.2.1 Consider Legal Compliance

Work in the public sector is often embedded in public laws, regulations, and ordinances. This means that changing tasks, relationships, and perceptions of the work may have some form of association to public law. Employees considering job crafting should reflect about any implications job crafting might have for public law. An extreme example is whether American interrogators in foreign conflicts could add particular techniques, like waterboarding, to the range of techniques they could choose to interrogate prisoners. It is conceivable that an individual interrogator could conceive such task crafting as a means to increase job challenge. The option of waterboarding is, however, prohibited by US law and therefore outside the legitimate options for job crafting. Although this example is extreme, it helps make the point that job crafters should be attentive to the legal context for job crafting.

4.4.2.2 Engage Your Supervisor about Your Plans

Someone contemplating job crafting might assume the need to consult with supervisors, but the employee-initiated logic of job crafting does not require consultation. Especially in situations where hierarchical authority is typical and employees are subject to regular performance reviews, a conversation between an employee and his or her supervisor makes good sense. Among the advantages of consultation with the supervisor is that it makes it easier to sustain the results of job crafting. An employee's exchange with a supervisor also offers opportunities for the employee to get credit for taking initiative and improving upon the ideas the employee has for crafting his or her work. Yet another potential benefit of consultation relates to the prospect of adding collaborative crafting to the mix of options for job crafting.

4.4.2.3 Given the Team Environment, Explore Collaborative Job Crafting

Leana, Applebaum, and Shevchuk's (2009) study of job crafting in sixty-two childcare centers illustrates that individual and collaborative job crafting can coexist. In fact, given the ubiquity of teamwork in so many public services – among them the military, police and fire services, elementary and secondary education, and policy development – collaborative job crafting is likely to bring significant advantages. It may, for example, assure that legally essential tasks that are shed by one employee are embraced by another who finds them more challenging. Collaborative job crafting may also open more paths for innovative configurations of public services. In addition, the process of collaboration may help spread the collective passion that brings many employees to public service in the first place. Thus, collaborative job crafting merits serious consideration in public services.

4.4.2.4 Consider Job Crafting as a Strategy to Manage Employees' Work Stressors

A risk of attracting employees with high public service motivation is that these employees may be more susceptible to work strain. Strain could be a function of two factors, excessive job demands resulting from a highly motivated employee's conscientiousness or willingness to take on extra duties and a shortage of resources to help the employee cope with job demands. Some evidence exists that employees with high levels of public service motivation cope with this "dark side" (Van Loon, Vandenabeele, and Leisink 2015; Jensen, Andersen, and Holten 2019) of their dispositions, perhaps because of their inherent resilience. Bangcheng Liu, Kaifeng Yang, and Wei Yu (2015) surveyed 412 police officers in a metropolitan city in east China to investigate relationships between work stressors, employee well-being, and public service motivation. They found that public service motivation moderated the relationship between work stressors and individual well-being. Public employees with higher levels of public service motivation were apparently better able to deal with stressors in ways that offset negative effects. Dong Chul Shim, Hyun Hee Park, and Tae Ho Eom (2015) obtained similar results in a survey of 4,974 Korean street-level bureaucrats. The outcome they studied was turnover intention. Job demands were directly related to turnover intention. The job demands–turnover intention relationship was also mediated by work exhaustion. Public service motivation was found to moderate all three relationships in the causal chain from job demands to work exhaustion to turnover intention.

Although Liu et al. and Shim et al.'s findings are encouraging about a potential dark side of high public service motivation, employees and their managers can also take affirmative steps, like job crafting, to address job demands that potentially threaten employee well-being. Arnold Bakker (2015) offers several paths for employees and attentive managers, some grounded in the logic of job crafting, to mitigate possible exhaustion flowing from excessive job demands or constrained resources for coping:

> Managers should ask themselves which specific job resources they offer their employees on a daily basis.... Do employees receive feedback about their daily work activities? It may be a good idea to walk around regularly and ask employees how they are doing and whether they need support, task variety, feedback, or other job resources. Also, it may be

a good option to provide employees with sufficient job control, so that they have the daily autonomy to craft their own jobs. Simultaneously, managers should have an eye for the daily job demands – is the work to be done interesting and challenging enough? Are there daily hassles that need to be taken care of? Although high public service motivation can help public servants take care of their own daily job demands, chronic job demands are likely to lead to stress and undermine public service motivation. (p. 730)

Bakker's advice for managing long-term threats from daily exhaustion is simple, but powerful. Managers should attend on a daily basis to both job demands that are stressing employees and resources that enable employees to cope with their job demands (Caillier 2017).

4.5 Career Counseling

The concept of calling, "work that a person perceives as his purpose in life" (Hall and Chandler 2005, 160), is understudied but intersects with research on both public service motivation and job crafting. Comptroller General Elmer Staats' (1982) description of "public service," which verges on others' definitions of calling, was invoked by James Perry and Lois Wise (1990) when they developed the public service motivation construct: "In its broadest sense, 'public service' is a concept, an attitude, a sense of duty – yes, even a sense of public morality" (p. 601).

The roots of the concept of calling begin more than a century ago, often associated with Max Weber's early twentieth century contributions. J. Stuart Bunderson and Jeffrey Thompson (2009) remind us of the concept's roots in Greece and the concept's transformation by Martin Luther during religious reformation. Bunderson and Thompson's (2009) study is also noteworthy because it focused on zookeepers, whose organizations are often either owned or significantly funded by governments, functionally making many zookeepers public employees.[3] Jeffrey Thompson and Robert Christensen (2018) recently sought to bridge the literatures of public service motivation and calling. They identified similarities, but differences too, and suggested a list of research questions that would better identify how the concepts can come together.

The meaningfulness of work is the key concept around which the public service motivation and job-crafting literatures intersect. This fortuitous intersection also brings with it another tool that organizations and managers can use to strengthen public service motivation. The tool is career counseling or career guidance, counseling for choosing or changing a career (Dik and Duffy 2009; Dik, Duffy, and Eldridge 2009). Career counseling differs from several of the other interventions mentioned here because it is externally mediated rather than accessed directly from inherent features of the work.

Bryan Dik, Ryan Duffy, and Brandy Eldridge (2009) assert that "calling and vocation are valuable constructs to promote because of their theoretical relation to enhancing meaningfulness and because they have been consistently linked in research to work-related and general well-being" (p. 627). For these reasons, they offer general advice for incorporating career counseling interventions to strengthen employees' pursuit of their callings. It is worth noting that public organizations and their employees have multiple paths for access to these career counseling interventions. Large public organizations may have specialized human resource talent either dedicated to career counseling or with the competencies to lead such interventions. It is also conceivable that leaders could arrange special external resources for assisting employees in developing their sense of calling (e.g., Korn Ferry, a large consulting firm, promotes career counseling services). A public organization's managers, supervisors, leadership coaches, and mentors represent another group of resources who could facilitate career counseling. All the options mentioned earlier are avenues for strengthening calling and vocation among employees who embrace their work as their purpose in life.

What specific steps might be taken to strengthen calling as a motivator, thereby taking full advantage of meaningful work? Bryan Dik and Ryan Duffy (2009) sort their recommendations for career counseling according to a three-dimensional definition of the calling construct:

1. Transcendent summons
   ○ *Assessing relevance.* Help clients evaluate the relevance and importance of their transcendent summons by reflecting about spontaneous experiences or assessing their dispositions with open-ended questions.

o *From passive to active discernment.* Encourage clients to actively discern a transcendent summons by engaging in career decision-making tasks.

o *Incorporating religion and spirituality.* Assess the importance of religion to the client by asking open-ended questions about the role of religion or spirituality for career or life decisions.

2. Connections of work and meaning

o *Assessing current work meaning.* Counselors can assess the extent to which their clients are experiencing meaning in their work by asking open-ended questions such as, "How meaningful do you find your work activities?" or "What would make your job more meaningful?" (Dik, Duffy, and Eldridge 2009, 268).

o *Connecting meaning in work to meaning in life.* Counselors can facilitate clients' making ties between meaning in their lives and meaning within their work roles. The connection between meaning in life and work furthers the clients' assessment of calling and vocation and will be worthwhile to clients generally for helping them to extract work-related values.

o *Encourage meaning-making behaviors.* Counselors can help clients to find meaning at work by practicing well-developed meaning-making techniques. These techniques include having clients use their signature work-related strengths daily and pursue realistic career-related expectations and goals.[4]

3. Other-oriented values and goals

o *Bridging social and personal fit.* In career counseling, person–environment fit has traditionally been defined narrowly to focus on individual and job characteristics. Broadening attention to social aspects of fit increases the prospects of clients experiencing meaning that will enhance motivation and performance.

o *Broadening the scope of socially significant jobs.* The exploration of the social implications of work between a counselor and a client can help to expand understanding of how particular work (e.g., the janitor at NASA) contributes to prosocial benefits.

o *Reframing and refocusing.* Rather than clients changing jobs, the counseling process can support the client in finding ways to strengthen work's prosocial connection. Drawing from strategies proposed by Blake Ashforth and Glen Kreiner (1999), two approaches are reframing and recalibrating the work experience.

4.5.1 A Tool for Career Counselors and Employees

Michael Steger, Bryan Dik, and Ryan Duffy (2012) offer a tool for employees, career counselors, and others to systematize the pursuit of meaningful work by proposing an inventory for the meaningfulness of work. Their instrument is the Work and Meaning Inventory. The inventory of meaningful work consists of three theory-based dimensions: positive meaning, meaning making through work, and greater good motivations. The three subscales are measured using ten items (Steger, Dik, and Duffy 2012, 330):

- Positive meaning
  - I have found a meaningful career.
  - I understand how my work contributes to my life's meaning.
  - I have a good sense of what makes my job meaningful.
- Meaning making through work
  - I have discovered work that has a satisfying purpose.
  - I view my work as contributing to my personal growth.
  - My work helps me better understand myself.
  - My work helps me make sense of the world around me.
- Greater good motivations
  - My work really makes no difference to the world. (R)
  - I know my work makes a positive difference in the world.
  - The work I do serves a greater purpose.

Steger, Dik, and Duffy (2012) report good reliability and validity for the inventory of subjectively meaningful experiences. The measure correlated as expected with work-related indices and explained unique variance in job satisfaction, absence, and life satisfaction. The inventory has been used successfully by scholars (see, e.g., Tims, Derks, and Bakker 2016) and practitioners (Steger, Dik, and Shim 2019).

4.5.2 Summary

Although research and practice about career counseling have penetrated neither research on public service motivation nor the literature of public administration, the contributions of Dik and Duffy (2009), Dik, Duffy, and Eldridge (2009), and others (Seligman, Rashid, and Parks 2006; Steger, Dik, and Duffy 2012) merit attention from people interested in improving the motivational potential of public service. The counseling techniques that Dik and colleagues propose have applicability well beyond the boundaries of calling and vocation. Wider diffusion and application of the techniques could be a valuable part of the tool box public organizations use to reinforce public service motivation across their workforce.

4.6 Conclusion

This chapter offers two broad arguments. The first is that public institutions occupy a special status in most societies because of their "publicness," and that status means that much of the work allocated to public institutions by their societies is inherently meaningful. The social usefulness of public work is a distinct competitive advantage for recruiting and motivating people. Curiously, the public sector's competitive advantage is often camouflaged in other attributes – bureaucratic rules, corruption, and the stereotyped laziness and self-interest of bureaucrats (Brehm and Gates 1997). Public managers need to consider proactive ways to overcome these impediments to realizing the competitive advantage of public work.

The second broad argument is that public organizations and managers can draw upon a variety of tools to leverage the meaningfulness of public work. The tools have been developed over decades, but represent powerful resources to leverage the meaningfulness of public work. Interestingly, the tools put responsibility into the hands of a variety of people with a stake in meaningful work – from organizations, to leaders and managers, to employees themselves, to specialized personnel like career counselors. One of the tools, work design, uses methods developed during the last fifty years to infuse work with meaning. The nature of work design tools has evolved since the 1960s, but manifestations from job enrichment (Herzberg 1968), to job design (Hackman and Oldham 1976, 1980), to relational job design (Grant 2007) offer organizations and their leaders and managers an important tool kit to reinforce meaningfulness. In cases where barriers may make work design difficult, employees themselves can alter the meaning of their work through self-persuasion. And in other situations where the organization may not take the lead on work design, employees themselves can embrace work design by becoming job crafters. Finally, career counseling offers avenues for discerning career dispositions and strengths, connections work and meaning, and discovering other-oriented values and goals.

Notes

1 Recent research by Andrew Carton (2018) indicates the story is indeed grounded in an exchange between President Kennedy and a janitor at Cape Canaveral. Carton's research is considered explicitly in Chapter 8 in the context of leader behavior.
2 Heslin, Latham, and Van de Walle (2005), citing the research of Pratkanis and Aronson (2001) as their source, write that "self-persuasion is the most effective persuasion tactic, because the resulting message comes from a source that people almost always consider credible, trustworthy, respected, and liked, namely, themselves" (p. 850).
3 According to the Association of Zoos and Aquariums, 47 percent of the funding for zoos is provided by government, meaning many zoos are government entities or highly dependent on government support; Bunderson and Thompson (2009) report that, according to the U.S. Bureau of Labor Statistics, there were 4,680 "nonfarm animal caretakers" (i.e., zookeepers) working at 210 zoos and aquariums in the United States in 2004.
4 Dik, Duffy, and Eldridge (2009) describe the techniques for meaning-making behaviors in terms that are familiar to public service motivation and public administration scholars. They credit Seligman, Rashid, and Parks (2006) for the two techniques. With respect to using strengths daily, they credit Seligman et al. for the central idea: "using one's signature strengths and talents to belong to and serve something one believes is larger than oneself" (p. 777). Regarding realistic career-related expectations, Dik et al. again cite Seligman et al. (2006) for recommending "satisficing instead of maximizing" (p. 782).

5 | Creating a Supportive Work Environment

Developing public organizations that effectively pursue their missions and the public interest depends on many building blocks falling into place (Rainey and Steinbauer 1999). Chapter 3 focused on prospective members of the organization and how better to match their predispositions with the incentives public organizations offer. In Chapter 4, the work itself became the focus, with the goal being assuring meaningful work for employees. This chapter turns to a third of the building blocks, work environments within public organizations. The work environment is a product of many variables (Perry and Porter 1982, 91), but foremost among them are coworkers, supervisors, and organizational policies that affect the workplace. We know from past research that work environments are important factors in public employee motivation (Perry and Porter 1982) and public service motivation (Christensen, Paarlberg, and Perry 2017).

Creating a work environment that supports public service motivation is likely to produce several positive consequences for public organizations:

- A supportive work environment is likely to reinforce public values employees bring to the organization, motivating their retention and work effort.
- A supportive work environment creates conditions for fulfillment of employees' basic psychological needs that reinforces their public service motivation and pursuit of public values.
- A supportive work environment promotes fulfillment of basic psychological needs, facilitating autonomous motivation by stimulating member identification and integration.

5.1 How Public Institutional Arrangements Sustain Supportive Work Environments

One finding from the research about public service motivation puzzled me when I first encountered it: Supportive work environments are antecedents of high public service motivation. Robert Christensen, Laurie Paarlberg, and James Perry (2017) identified thirty studies published between 2008 and 2015 in which the authors concluded that an important implication of the research was that supportive work environments sustain and enhance high public service motivation. Nineteen of the thirty studies addressed the practical implications of work environments in some depth. The volume of direct research and inferences about work environments testifies to scholarly interest in improving public work experiences. But the inferences authors drew about the practical implications of their research largely leave the "why" question unanswered.

The answer to the "why" question has come into clearer focus for me in the period since Christensen, Paarlberg, and Perry (2017) appeared. Understanding the micro-level results – how a supportive work environment nurtures public service motivation – begins at the macro-level with an understanding of effective public institutions. Carl Dahlström and Victor Lapuente's (2017) *Organizing Leviathan: Politicians, Bureaucrats, and the Making of Good Government* brings the role of modern public institutions into focus. In their book, they make the case for the core processes that sustain good government. Dahlström and Lapuente write: "The main idea in this book is that if the organization of the state apparatus, or the Leviathan in the book's title, divides public officials into two distinct groups, the possibilities for abuse and opportunism by public officials are diminished because these two groups have different career incentives" (p. 13). Dahlström and Lapuente contend that separating political and bureaucratic careers puts the two groups in positions to respond to different accountability regimes characterized by distinct incentives. The distinct incentive systems for politicians put them in a position where they are accountable to electors. The distinct systems for bureaucrats, typically formal civil service systems and other public laws, position them to be accountable to professional peers. The distinct incentives for politicians and bureaucrats stimulate mutual monitoring between the groups and put bureaucrats in positions to speak truth to power (Tonon 2008).

The distinct rule systems and incentives for bureaucrats and politicians that Dahlström and Lapuente describe are the ultimate foundation for the findings referred to at the beginning of this section that supportive work environments are antecedents of high public service motivation. The distinct careers for bureaucrats and politicians create conditions to nurture public service motivation. Connecting macro-rules, specifically the distinction between career systems for bureaucrats and politicians, with micro-environments, that is, work environments in public organizations, mirrors earlier arguments about institutions (Kiser and Ostrom 1982) and civil service systems (Bekke, Perry, and Toonen 1996). The types of constitution-level rules identified by Dahlström and Lapuente create conditions for supportive work environments.

Dahlström and Lapuente marshal extensive comparative evidence for their arguments about the value of separating political and bureaucratic careers and incentive systems. Their case is further strengthened by recent survey research about developing countries. Jan-Hinrik Meyer-Sahling, Christian Schuster, and Kim Sass Mikkelsen (2018) surveyed 23,000 civil servants from 10 countries to identify civil service management practices that influenced civil servant attitudes and behaviors. The ten countries, distributed across four continents, are Albania, Bangladesh, Brazil, Chile, Estonia, Ghana, Kosovo, Malawi, Nepal, and Uganda. The first lesson Meyer-Sahling, Schuster, and Mikkelsen (2018) draw from the survey research is to depoliticize civil service management. They write: "The data shows that such politicization of civil service management functions adversely affects the work motivation, job satisfaction, public service motivation, performance and integrity of civil servants. It also shows that certain formally meritocratic civil service management practices – such as oral and written exams to recruit civil servants or public advertisements for positions – curb politicization" (p. 18).

Effective constitutional rules separating civil servants (bureaucrats) from politicians establish two conditions that nurture public service motivation: creating an environment for common pool resources and promoting basic psychological needs of employees. These two facets of public work environments are discussed next.

5.1.1 Civil Service Rules Create an Environment for Common Pool Resources

Although "bureaucracy" and "bureaucrats" are maligned today, especially since the rise of the New Public Management (Boruvka and Perry 2019), Max Weber developed the concepts as exemplars of efficient and effective organization and staffing. The bureaucracy ideal type represented technical efficiency and rationality. Elise Boruvka and James Perry (2019) summarize the attributes of bureaucrats as:

- their selection for their office based on merit rather than attachments to political superiors;
- adherence to rules for their office with dedication and integrity;
- acting in accordance with the political and normative order in which bureaucracy is embedded; and
- serving as stewards for constitutional principles, the rule of law, and professional standards (Verkuil 2017).

The structure of bureaucracies and the attributes of bureaucrats are often characterized in sweeping terms. Johan Olsen (2006), for example, writes: "An ideal bureaucratic structure is assumed to contribute to unity and coordination, precision and speed, predictability, obedience and loyalty, impartiality, reduction of friction and of material and personal costs, knowledge of files and an institutionalized memory, and continuity across changes in government" (p. 8). Unity, coordination, loyalty, impartiality, and continuity are admirable qualities. Bruno Frey and Margit Osterloh (2005) elevate Olsen's argument by claiming that the qualities he describes are common pool resources produced by the institutional arrangements governing bureaucracy. According to Frey and Osterloh, the institutional arrangements associated with Max Weber's model of bureaucracy are superior to the organizing principles of agency theory. The "goods" that Olsen describes – from unity to continuity across changes in government – are collective goods that flow to everyone in and affected by bureaucracy.

Recent research about effects of social capital echoes the common pool argument. Alexander Kroll, Leisha Dehart-Davis, and Dominick Vogel (2019), who cite earlier UK local government research (Andrews 2010), observe that higher levels of social capital reinforce employee commitment and engagement. They define social capital as "a collective resource made up of collaboration, trust, and a sense of mission among members within organizations" (p. 1), which captures the same sense of internal climate associated with Olsen's bureaucratic ideal and Frey and Osterloh's common pool resources. Thus, the work environment described in recent social capital research describes conditions associated historically with public institutional arrangements.

Although the scholarship referred to earlier points to the importance of institutional arrangements associated with bureaucracy and social capital as foundations for an environment supportive of public service motivation, the environment flowing from the antecedents is not guaranteed. Institutional arrangements are consequential, but do not make positive outcomes automatic. Human agency within public organizations still plays a critical role in realizing positive flows between structure and outcomes. Inputs from organizational members, especially their motivational makeup, and people up and down the organizational hierarchy loom large in effecting positive outcomes.

5.1.2 Civil Service Rules Can Promote Basic Psychological Needs

In Chapter 2, I discussed self-determination theory. A key feature of the theory is the importance of three basic psychological needs that are essential to individual well-being and, in turn, self-determination. Ironically, the buffering of bureaucratic careers from political careers (Dahlström and Lapuente 2017) creates conditions for the realization of the three basic psychological needs. Although traditional bureaucracies are often depicted as limiting and even oppressive (Goodsell 2004), they can also liberate employees to achieve basic psychological needs. Thus, the goods associated with an ideal bureaucratic structure do not accrue by chance, but are rather the result of giving employees, among other emergent dynamics, the space to fulfill basic psychological needs.

5.1.2.1 Competence
A brief review of the history of civil service systems makes the connection between foundational institutional arrangements and basic psychological needs at the center of self-determination theory explicit. Two of the basic psychological needs, competence and autonomy, are firmly rooted in institutional arrangements governing civil service in many countries. The first of the three needs is competence, which

involves the mastery of skills that give individuals belief in their ability to achieve goals. In the language of civil service systems, competence typically translates to "merit," meaning that individuals are selected and advanced for competence in their jobs (Ingraham 2006). A fifty-two country comparative study (Dahlström, Lapuente, and Teorell 2012) of meritocratic recruitment found that one indicator of quality of government – corruption – was lower in governments that practiced meritocratic recruitment. Other variables such as competitive salaries and internal promotion had no significant influence on corruption.

Former Secretary of the Treasury Paul O'Neill recounts how satisfying his basic psychological need for competence made a big difference early in his career (Perry 2017). O'Neill was a career civil servant when George Shultz, then Director of the newly created Office of Management and Budget (OMB) in the Executive Office of the President, asked O'Neill to give up his career status to take on the role of assistant director of OMB. O'Neill accepted the assistant director appointment and his opportunity to satisfy his basic psychological need for competence likely was a factor in his decision. As O'Neill recalled in an interview years later: "George really appreciated people who were prepared and could contribute to complex problems. As such I had the great pleasure of working with him on some really important things."

The limits of O'Neill's competence were likely tested many times as one of Shultz's deputies, but an occasion he remembers well involved forced busing. He describes the situation:

> In 1972 or so, the country was going through a crisis because the Supreme Court had ordered forced busing in order to achieve integration in the public school domain. George was given the assignment by the president to figure out how to do this in a way that didn't create strife and riots in the streets. George engaged me and a few other people at the Office of Management and Budget to help him achieve this. I had developed knowledge about flexible use of funds across the federal domain, but not with this particular question in mind. However, when it was necessary to find funds to support the creation of local leadership groups to work behind the scenes on this question of desegregating the schools, I knew where the money was. I hadn't consciously prepared for this time, but that knowledge accumulation I had gained, along with the timing of everything, really made a huge difference. (p. 132)

5.1.2.2 Autonomy

The second basic psychological need, autonomy, is also identified with the institutional arrangements of civil service systems in many countries. In most of these systems, political neutrality or similar terminology signals that civil servants are granted a high degree of autonomy. In a classic article in American public administration, Herbert Kaufman (1969) describes politically neutral competence as one of the three values that at different times have animated the design of the machinery of American government. Richard Mulgan (2007), describing the Australian public service, identifies a similar political neutrality in a parliamentary system. Both the Australian and Canadian governance systems inherited their forms of political neutrality from their British Empire origins, which imprinted many governance systems because of its extensive colonial reach and history.

Autonomy is an important influence on bureaucratic behavior and performance, not only in developed English-speaking democracies like Australia, Canada, and the United States but also in developing countries, too. Merilee Grindle (1997) studied twenty-nine organizations in six developing countries to identify factors that might account for organizations performing relatively well in unfavorable contexts where overall public sector performance was poor. Grindle identified autonomy in personnel matters as a factor that differentiated higher performing organizations from poor performers. "Autonomy in personnel matters does not necessarily assure good performance; rather, it provides a facilitating context in which effective managers and management practices can encourage performance-oriented norms and behaviors" (p. 491). Grindle inferred that autonomy, as a facilitating condition, supported development of organizational cultures conducive to higher performance. Although she did not specifically link autonomy to individual psychological factors, the context she identified may also enhance prospects for employees to fulfill their basic psychological need for autonomy.

Recent research by Erin McDonnell (2017, 2020) in Ghana extends Grindle's research by providing more details about both antecedents and outcomes associated with autonomy in developing countries. Based upon her research in Ghana and historical comparisons with the United States, China, Kenya, and Nigeria, McDonnell (2017) develops the construct of bureaucratic interstices as niches in bureaucracies within poorly performing states that exhibit characteristics such as autonomy that are at odds with traditional Weberian bureaucracy but simultaneously support bureaucracy-like culture and behavior. McDonnell observes: "… bureaucratic interstices potentially serve as sites within which individuals gain lived exposure to the benefits of Weberian-style bureaucracy, thereby augmenting the corps of bureaucratically experienced and oriented individuals, that scarcest of all bureaucratic resources" (pp. 493–494). Among the distinctive characteristics of bureaucratic interstices are high levels of autonomy, enticements beyond salary, pride and positive identification with the niche, and adaptive redundancy. Although McDonnell does not connect these distinctive characteristics directly to either common pool resources or fulfillment of members' basic psychological need for autonomy, her description of bureaucratic interstices suggests that enhancement of bureaucratic performance could be influenced by these factors.

The most direct evidence about individual benefits of autonomy in a developing country comes from Imran Rasul and Daniel Rogger's (2015) research on the Nigerian bureaucracy. They coded variations in management practices across more than 4,000 projects. They found that civil servant autonomy was positively correlated with job performance. This evidence is again not a direct assessment of whether autonomy serves the basic psychological needs of Nigerian civil servants, but it is again suggestive of a relationship.

David Grant's lifelong commitment to public service is an object lesson about fulfilling an individual's need for autonomy. Grant started in the federal government as a twenty-three-year-old intern who fully expected to jump to the private sector after his three-year procurement internship. One of his third-year assignments was negotiating a $75 million contract for digitization of mobile communications systems. His detailed recounting of what transpired as a result of this assignment appears in Box 5.1. In the midst of intensive week-long negotiations at Ft. Monmouth, Grant experienced a revelation. He and the Captain who joined him in the negotiations discovered they had much more latitude shaping the terms of an agreement than their GTE counterparts. Despite being the youngest person in the negotiations, he had the authority to evaluate, negotiate, and finalize the contract. What difference did this make to him? As he remembers: "It occurred to me that I preferred to be in that position than to be one of the support team members, performing research, etc. for the manager or even be the contracts manager who didn't have the same level of authority as I did." David Grant's realization at a "moment in time" was the beginning of a thirty-five-year career in the U.S. federal government.

Box 5.1 An intern's career-changing moment in time[a]

I was a contract specialist at the Communications-Electronics Command at Ft. Monmouth, NJ. This was a three-year internship consisting of multiple rotations through various organizations within the Office of Procurement. The purpose of these rotations was to expose interns to as much of the life cycle of procurement as possible during this three-year period.

My goal was to work through the internship and look for work in the private sector ... hopefully at a higher salary.

During the third year of my internship I was assigned to the Multi Service Communication Systems (MSCS) Branch. This branch acquired communication equipment for the Army, Air Force and Marine Corps.

I was given the chance to negotiate and award a $75M digitization of the mobile communications systems that rode on Jeeps and in backpacks. These units communicated with the newly deployed digital echelons above corps network also awarded in our Branch.

This project was on a critical timeline because the larger network was already in process of being transitioned from analog to digital and there was an upcoming biannual NATO Reforger Exercise. These mobile communication devices were necessary for US Troops to participate in the upcoming exercise with their NATO counterparts.

We requested GTE to submit their proposal for the upgraded systems, services to install, deploy and train the troops. We received and evaluated their proposal and found some issues that needed to be negotiated. We hosted the GTE team at Ft. Monmouth for a weeklong negotiation session. I led the Government side which consisted of myself and an Army Captain who was the technical expert. The GTE team was led by a 20 year+ GTE veteran and a small team of younger contracting, pricing and technical staff.

We met each day to discuss questions that either the Captain or I had about the technical, contract or price issues in the proposal. The GTE team was eager to resolve any question we had on technical issues. They were more reserved about discussing contract terms (e.g. delivery times, training or support terms, and particularly pricing questions). By mid-week I noticed that the GTE Contracts Manager/team would ask for a formal break and a separate room for them to call back to their HQ to get input regarding any movement on contract terms or pricing reductions.

By mid-week the Captain and I discussed that it was apparent that the GTE team was not fully empowered to negotiate a complete deal on site. Whereas he and I apparently had a much wider latitude to agree to terms, conditions, and schedules. In fact, when it came to pricing the effort, we discovered that the GTE manager had very little room to negotiate. They constantly had to break and call their HQ for room to move on their pricing. The Captain and I were at least 20–25 years younger than their Manager ... much closer in age to his support team. But it appeared we had more authority to negotiate and close the deal.

It was an eye-opening moment for my career. I was aware of what similar positions in industry like the manager and team made for salaries because I had access to cost and pricing data that showed us their actual costs, overhead, G&A and profit. Of course, I didn't know what any of the specific individuals made but I knew the neighborhood so to speak. I knew I was the youngest person in the room and that everyone in that room likely made significantly more than I did, but I had more authority than anyone in the room.

I watched the Contracts Manager consistently ask his team for updates, research, spreadsheets, etc. The Captain and I had to do all that work ourselves as we didn't have a support staff. But the bottom line was that I knew our requirement, terms and conditions, estimated pricing as well as the corresponding portions of the GTE proposal as well or better than anyone else in the room. And I had been given the authority to evaluate, negotiate and finalize the deal.

It occurred to me that I preferred to be in that position than to be one of the support team members, performing research, etc. for the manager or even be the contracts manager who didn't have the same level of authority as I did.

I decided after that project was finished that if I stayed in a bit longer and gained even more experience on larger and more complex programs I might be even more valuable to my organization or to the private sector when I finally reached the point of exploring that option.

I ended up staying in government for almost 35 years.

[a] The details in the textbox are from a personal communication with David Grant, August 26, 2019.

5.1.2.3 Relatedness

Although the third basic psychological need, relatedness, is not as obviously situated in language used to describe civil service rules or principles as are competence and autonomy, public institutions are inherently about connections to others and belonging, about communal interests and access. Work environment behaviors and emotions associated with relatedness – being heard, trust, friendship, caring, belonging – are supported by both the values and rules inherent in many public institutional arrangements. Two public executives, one an engineer from Europe and the other a military officer from the United States, serve to illustrate relatedness.

Jean-Jacques Dordain led the European Space Agency (ESA), an organization he joined in 1986, for twelve years as a director general and retired in 2015 (Lambright 2016). Although ESA is Europe's counterpart to the National Aeronautics and Space Administration (NASA), it is a cooperative venture that grew from thirteen members in 1986 to twenty-two when Dordain retired. Dordain's twelve years at the apex of an international cooperative venture gave him both a deep appreciation for relationships and opportunities to experience fulfillment of his need for relatedness. As a director general, Dordain's "strategy was proactive – to devise a European space policy within which the EU [European Union] and ESA could be partners rather than having a hierarchical relationship" (Lambright 2016, 508).

Dordain placed sensitivity to social relationships at the core of his success in leading ESA as a cooperative venture. What he says about personal relationships provides insights into his philosophy and motivation, "No recipe can replace people, and this is the reason why cooperation is not only a collection of recipes. It must become a culture, and even, beyond a culture, it must become an identity" (Lambright 2016, 510).

One of Dordain's biggest challenges involved Galileo, Europe's global positioning system. He initially encountered funding delays from member states who sought to use their contributions to leverage proportional access to facilities. He surmounted this hurdle by reflecting on his role in the context of ESA relationships: "My role is not to maintain a war between [ESA] member states. My role is to make the program succeed" (Lambright 2016, 509). A later hurdle involved not ESA member states, but the European Commission (EC), the executive for the EU. W. Henry Lambright (2016) describes this episode:

> The EC threatened ESA and the industrial consortium building Galileo with penalties.... In a press conference, Dordain made it clear ESA was not giving in to the EC, which essentially summoned ESA to its headquarters

to answer questions. He took the high road, stating, "We are not interested in who is to blame [for Galileo's problems] – we want to get things done." Dordain admitted that "cooperation is not easy, it is slow. EU and ESA cultures are different, but that's not a reason not to work together.... Indeed, it is very important that we create this link, bringing space infrastructure into the political sphere. It makes life more complicated but we have to do it." (p. 509)

Thad Allen attained the rank of admiral, ending his thirty-nine-year military career as Commandant of the U.S. Coast Guard. As a military officer, he knew hierarchy and could recite the chain of command from the lowest rank to Commander in Chief. But late in his career, he encountered special challenges, first as commander of onsite relief efforts for Hurricane Katrina in New Orleans in 2005, a role into which he was thrust after Secretary of Homeland Security Michael Chertoff removed Federal Emergency Management Agency Director Michael D. Brown just days after the hurricane struck. Within five years, he became national incident commander for the Deepwater Horizon oil spill, the largest in US history.

The unique nature of the Hurricane Katrina and Deepwater Horizon crises placed a premium on Admiral Allen's capacity to understand and value the social space, his relationship to the people affected, and their relationships with others. Although he stepped into his roles in the two crises from a military command, his priority was to establish "unity of effort" rather than "unity of command." Reflecting about the aftermath of a major crisis like Katrina, Allen observed about the distinction: "... chain of command doesn't exist. You have to aggregate everybody's capabilities to achieve a single purpose, taking into account the fact that they have distinct authorities and responsibilities. That's creating unity of effort rather than unity of command, and it's a much more complex management challenge" (Berinato 2010).

Allen's instinct immediately following the press conference that announced his appointment as commander for onsite relief efforts after Katrina was to gather everyone together – all 4,000 people assigned to him. Unfortunately, no facility could accommodate all 4,000. He eventually was able to gather 2,000 into a Dillard's department store warehouse in Baton Rouge.

What Allen did when he had gathered everyone together is equally revealing about his relational perspective. "I got up on a desk, with a loudspeaker, and told everybody that I was giving one order: They were to treat anybody they came into contact with who had been affected by the storm like a member of their own family. Their mother, father, brother, sister, whatever."

Like the macro-attributes of common pool resources or social capital discussed in the preceding section, the micro-attributes of need fulfillment do not flow automatically from public institutional arrangements. Institutional arrangements affirm the design, but not the realization of basic psychological needs. Critiques of bureaucracy often start with observations about the detachment of bureaucratic rules and norms from an understanding of human behavior derived from cognitive evaluation theory (i.e., fulfillment of basic psychological needs for competence, autonomy and relatedness). Bruce Buchanan (1974) describes, for example, how bureaucratic risk aversion produces restraints on the initial job challenges assigned to new recruits, which in turn dampens recruit organizational commitment, ultimately resulting in long-term diminished work effort or turnover. Achieving the promise of public institutional arrangements requires vigilance by members and leaders that eliminates barriers to basic psychological need fulfillment made possible by rules favoring competence, autonomy, and relatedness.

5.1.3 Summary

Public institutional arrangements establish conditions conducive for creating common pool resources and fulfilling basic psychological needs. The outcomes achievable from conditions advantaged by institutional arrangements that separate career from political incentives are not automatic. The achievement of positive outcomes requires understanding of and explicit attention to dynamics associated with the ends pursued.

5.2 Strategies for Reinforcing Supportive Work Environments

As emphasized in the introduction to this chapter, institutional arrangements in many governments and public organizations create favorable contexts for fulfillment of members' basic psychological needs. Despite what flows routinely from organic common pool resources, meritocratic norms, and buffering of career incentives, however, more can be done to facilitate development of intrinsically motivated behavior through a variety of developmental tools available to public organizations. Among these tools are establishing robust learning and growth opportunities, developing norms that balance job security and performance, and nurturing public service motivation to reinforce ties between organizations and their employees.

5.2.1 Robust Learning and Growth Opportunities

Public organizations have many tools at their disposal for establishing robust learning and growth opportunities. Three that offer high value for creating a supportive work environment are learning and development across the career, developing leaders up and down the hierarchy, and promoting subjective career success.

5.2.1.1 Learning and Development throughout the Career

The concept of development across one's career is firmly established in many government organizations. We take for granted, for example, that the military services in the United States and other countries develop their members from the day they enter service until the day they separate. During the course of military careers, various tactics are used to promote cognitive and experiential learning, ranging from frequent job rotation, increasing the challenge and responsibility of successive assignments, and exposing members to roles and functions outside their specialization (Jans and Frazer-Jans 2004).

Despite successes in some parts of the public sector, employee development across their careers is not universal. The reliance of government organizations on tax revenues means that economic downturns are often met with budget cuts, and training and development resources are often among the first expenditures to be cut. These cuts are doubly problematic because of the importance of training and development both for the quality of services delivered and the value employees place on such opportunities. In a 2018 Boston Consulting Group survey of 366,000 people worldwide, respondents ranked "learning and training opportunities" and "career development" fourth and fifth among twenty-six workplace satisfaction factors (Roediger et al. 2019). Given the relative importance of learning and development for most employees, meeting their expectations is consequential for fulfilling their basic needs for competence and growth, which are vital for energizing and sustaining employee public service motivation.

One jurisdiction that has successfully implemented learning and development throughout the careers of their employees is the Shanghai school system (World Bank 2016), which is recognized as one of the highest performing districts in the world. Responsibilities for professional development are distributed widely, among schools as an entity, principals, professional colleagues, and the teachers themselves.

> Shanghai designs professional development activities to be collaborative and to focus on instructional improvement. School principals are responsible for creating targeted teacher training plans based on each teacher's evaluation results. Professional development is often a substantial part of schools' operational expenditure. The city pairs weak and inexperienced teachers with high performing and experienced ones. Important platforms for teacher professional development and performance evaluation – teaching-research groups and lesson observations – are also practiced universally in schools. Teachers are expected to be researchers who would evaluate and modify their own pedagogy in relation to student outcomes. The city requires new teachers to complete at least 360 hours of professional development in their first five years of service, and an additional 540 hours to be considered for a senior rank.

The Boston Consulting Group's report, *Building the Government Workforce of the Future* (Roediger et al. 2019), offers examples of innovative programs that have the potential for measurably facilitating learning and development throughout the career. The examples include:

- *Tailored career paths for developing specialized skills.* The rapid rise of new specialities such as cybersecurity, artificial intelligence, and data analytics demand creative responses, particularly when competition for talent is intense and targeted skills are in short supply. The Boston Consulting Group describes a UK-tailored career path program: "The UK Civil Service developed 12 cross-government functions in areas such as analysis, project delivery, and digital. Each function has a unique career track and learning curriculum, as well as a dedicated team leader focused on developing capabilities and sharing best practices" (Roediger et al. 2019). The tailored career paths permit employees to work across agencies and departments while building unique skill sets.

- *Learning pacts.* Voluntary individual development plans are tools common in government to facilitate employees in achieving their development goals. They are agreements between employees and supervisors that set expectations for learning objectives and competencies. A learning pact is a formal agreement between employers and employees to commit to training and development for current roles and future roles anticipated by changing circumstances. Learning pacts mirror individual learning accounts, a base amount of resources set aside for an employee to use for learning and development, which have existed in the U.S. federal government since 2000 (U.S. Office of Personnel Management 2019b). While individual learning accounts may be used to develop knowledge, skills, and abilities that relate directly to an employee's official duties, learning pacts are likely to cover employees collectively for a wider array of uses.
- *Choice of assignments.* Traditional job rotation training and development often put employees on paths identified and directed by the organization. A modern variant is when agencies give employees a choice over how and where they contribute. Canada has introduced a demonstration, Canada's Free Agents (Agents Libre du Canada), that offers staff the ability to select projects that match their interests. The program permits employees to contribute in ways that are meaningful (see, too, the discussion in Chapter 4 about methods to enhance the meaningfulness of work), simultaneously increasing prospects for retaining talented employees.

Nicole Ogrysko (2019) reports similar innovations in the U.S. federal civil service are impeded by an outdated civil service framework, but progress is being made even in the absence of comprehensive civil service reform. One illustration is an automated career path tool in the Department of Interior, which is described in Box 5.2.

Evidence from experiments in developing countries indicates that transfers, one way of giving employees a choice of assignments, can make a significant difference for employee performance. Abhijit Banerjee et al. (2014) conducted randomized trials in a sample of 162 police stations serving almost 8 million people in Rajasthan, India. In the second of two sets of experiments, they offered

---

**Box 5.2 An automated career path tool in
the U.S. Department of Interior[a]**

Interior employees, on average, stay with the department for fourteen years. Employees want to stay with the agency, but they're often seeking new or different career opportunities, said Jennifer Ackerman, Interior's deputy chief human capital officer.

The tool shows possible career paths for twenty mission critical occupations and four "high-density" occupations, more than 50 percent of the Interior workforce, she said.

"What we wanted to show is how do you get from A to B in a non-linear fashion?" she said. "Sometimes people are intent on [being a] park ranger. They didn't get there by starting out as just a GS-4. It's non-linear in a lot of cases."

The site quizzes employees on their competencies and shows them potential opportunities based on the results. It links back to USAJobs. gov and shows possible detail opportunities within the department.

"This is 1.0. Eventually we want to get to ... 11.0," Ackerman said. "The first day that we launched it, we had over 9,000 hits. It was the most hits we had in over two years on DOI Careers."

Interior launched the career mapping tool after conducting a "values survey" of its employees. Feedback showed Interior employees placed an especially high value on working in an environment that valued respect – and workplace flexibilities.

[a] *Source:* Ogrysko (2019).

---

incentives to police officers to carry out sobriety traffic checkpoints, linking good performance with transfers from reserve barracks to desirable police station postings. The incentives produced large effects on performance, suggesting desirable transfers, even in hierarchical and highly bureaucratic settings, are attractive growth opportunities.

5.2.1.2 Leader Development Up and Down the Hierarchy
Just as public organizations signal inclusive messages about growth opportunities for all staff, many leadership development programs have become more inclusive to attract candidates at all levels of the

organizational hierarchy. The US-based Partnership for Public Service's (2019) Public Service Leadership Model reflects a developmental perspective that envisions activities at many levels of the organizational hierarchy. The four levels of the Partnership's model, from lowest to highest level, are as follows:

1. *Emerging leader*, typically GS-7 to GS-11, which includes team or work group members, aspiring supervisor, and developing technical expert.
2. *Leader of teams or projects*, GS-12 and GS-13, which includes team or work group leaders, new supervisors, and technical experts.
3. *Leader of leaders*, GS-14 and GS-15, encompassing roles such as large-team leaders and technical leaders in the field.
4. *Leader of organizations*, senior executive servants and political appointees, encompassing executives and enterprise leaders, and interagency and intra-agency conveners.

This multitiered leadership development model is also prominent in many successful agency-based leadership development programs (Abner et al. 2019).

5.2.1.3 Promoting Subjective Career Success

Douglas Hall and Dawn Chandler (2005) identify a particular case of development across a career that touches on concepts introduced in Chapter 4, which related public service motivation to calling (Thompson and Christensen 2018). The developmental model Hall and Chandler present begins with a distinction between objective and subjective careers. The subjective career reflects an individual's vantage point. The subjective perspective emphasizes how individuals perceive their contributions and assessments. The objective career is the career from an external observer's viewpoint focused on tangible aspects of career, such as promotions and income. Hall and Chandler argue that the subjective career takes on special salience when an individual has a sense of calling. They posit that individuals who succeed in pursuing their calling or basic purpose in life will exhibit greater subjective career success. These outcomes, in turn, influence two outcomes, self-confidence and identity change, that Hall and Chandler call meta-competencies. The significance of the meta-competencies is that they drive a continuous cycle of adaptive, self-directed career performance.

5.2.2 Develop Norms that Balance Job Security and Performance

A defining attribute of civil service systems in many countries is job security (Hur and Perry 2016). Job security rules are one fundamental element behind neutral competence (Kaufman 1969), discussed earlier in this chapter as a foundation for the autonomy granted to many civil servants. Job security, which is typically classified as an extrinsic reward in the motivation and human resource literature, can serve several purposes. One is to buffer bureaucrats from sanctions by political principals who disagree with or seek to control bureaucratic decisions (Dahlström and Lapuente 2017). This purpose tends to sustain membership in the organization, but may have the unintended consequence of converting job security into an incentive for individuals for whom security is a powerful need. Thus, job security rules serve a second purpose, as a reward for satisfying needs that are of varying importance across the workforce. In addition, job security creates incentives for bureaucrats to invest in acquiring expertise because of their expectations for longer tenure (Gailmard and Patty 2007). Individuals who expect to be employed long term can develop their competences for future work assignments and opportunities in the organization.

During the last forty years, job security has been attacked for two primary reasons. One is that the autonomy accorded public employees because of job security reduces their responsiveness to political principals. Although there may be instances when constrained political responsiveness may do a disservice to the public interest, the rules that limit the responsiveness of public employees are intentionally designed into the collective action situation. Thus, critiques of job security as politically unresponsive usually depend on ideology rather than a broader assessment of performance criteria such as efficiency and effectiveness. The responsiveness critique was at the root of the U.S. Civil Service Reform Act of 1978 and similar reforms executed in other countries in the 1980s.

A more recent critique of job security involves issues of employee performance. The critique is two-pronged, one prospective and the other retrospective. The prospective prong is that the threat of job loss because of an employee's performance deficiencies removes leverage for motivating employees. The threat of job loss, often associated with at-will employment policies, is considered a motivator surrendered by supervisors and the organization by employee-centered job security practices. The retrospective prong is that job security accords employees protections that may make it difficult to remove them when performance falls short of satisfactory.

Some of the ideas presented earlier in the book begin to mitigate rationales behind the performance critique of job security. Selecting for high public service motivation is one way of screening out prospective employees whose primary motivation is need for security. A more discriminating selection process also increases the prospects of screening out poor performers who may be trying to conceal either their motivational orientation or characteristics of their competency profile. The idea presented in Chapter 3 to scrutinize more closely probationary employees, for example, essentially extending the selection process, is one way to screen-out prospects who might be poor organizational fits – for either performance or other reasons – prior to giving them career status.

Recent research suggests that the critiques of job security may be either exaggerated or, more simply, wrong. Hyunkang Hur (2019) conducted a meta-analysis that emphasizes job security's role in enhancing employee attitudes and job performance. Hur's meta-analysis consisted of thirty-seven studies covering forty-five independent samples. He expected a curvilinear relationship between job security and employee outcomes such as job satisfaction and organizational commitment, with poor outcomes at low and high levels of job security. Hur found that job security generally has positive consequences for employees' work attitudes. Across the studies, the correlations for job satisfaction were 0.327 and for organizational commitment were 0.253. The findings indicate that the relationship between job security and employee work attitudes is positive rather than curvilinear, as Hur hypothesized. Thus, contrary to trends toward at-will employment, Hur concluded that "job security is worth retaining in some form in the public sector" (p. 1).

Hur's meta-analysis is supported by other recent empirical research. Chang-qin Lu et al. (2017) conducted research using Chinese subjects that related job security to the job demands model (Bakker 2015). They investigated the moderating effect of job security on the relationship between job demands and job performance across three separate studies using both cross-sectional and time-lagged designs. All three studies found that job demands significantly improved employee performance in the context of higher job security, but achieved the opposite result when job security was low. The authors concluded that job security improved employees' performance in stressful contexts.

5.2.2.1 Balancing Performance and Property Rights Protections

The research reviewed immediately above suggests that the critique of job security as a barrier both to accountability and high performance may be overstated. In fact, given Hur's (2019) meta-analytic findings about job security and employees' attitudes and the extensive case Dahlstrom and Lapuente make that rules typical of modern civil service systems simultaneously increase government effectiveness and reduce corruption, the case against job security may be dead wrong. The proposals presented later are intended to sustain traditional job security, but simultaneously address legitimate concerns about potential protections of employees who may be performing unsatisfactorily.

A growing body of research by Hur (2019), Hyunkang Hur and James Perry (2016, 2020), and others (Bartol et al. 2009; Kraimer et al. 2005) indicates that abandoning public job security arrangements in favor of at-will systems is ill-advised. Modestly changing traditional property-rights rules might better assure a balance between job security and performance, if for no other reasons than such change would signal to prospective employees and attentive stakeholders that performance is valued, perhaps on par with protections for employees. Several modest adjustments of traditional property-rights rules might serve to create better balance with performance.

- *Use medium-term employment contracts* (e.g., ten to fifteen years). In recent years, some governments have eliminated job security altogether (i.e., transitioned to at-will employment) and others have turned to short-term (three to five years), renewable contracts. Hur's meta-analysis and other job security research suggest another, different alternative that may optimize traditional benefits of job security and simultaneously offer public employers opportunities to counteract stakeholder concerns about performance and responsiveness. Hur and Perry (2016) concluded that "granting high job security for the short- and medium-term (but not long-term) may be a means to maximize employee job satisfaction and organizational commitment" (p. 277). Their inference was based on meta-analytic results that "associations between job security, job satisfaction, and organizational commitment were more positive for new and medium-term employees, but level off over time" (p. 277). Although the idea of medium-term employment contracts is, to some extent, speculative, it is consistent with evidence about the effects of job security and therefore merits more research and experimentation.

- *Extend probationary periods.* The length of probationary periods, usually one year, appears to be more a product of tradition than of systematic analysis of the appropriate term to sample and observe an employee's readiness for particular work assignments. Changing traditional practices and considering longer options, two years for example, have already occurred in some governments (Lunney 2016) and are under active discussion elsewhere (Wagner 2019).
- *Manage employee receptivity to change.* Offering training and development opportunities for employees (Aguinis and Kraiger 2009) could permit them to increase their productivity in the organization, enhance their chances of being employed, and provide the security of being able to find a new job quickly (Wilthagen and Tros 2004). Affective job insecurity may also be mitigated by effective career counseling and quality out-placement services (Hur and Perry 2016).

5.2.2.2 Improving the Effectiveness of Performance Management Systems

Governments have struggled to find effective and sustainable performance management systems, but research evidence about what works is abundant and well documented (National Research Council 1991; U.S. Merit Systems Protection Board 2018). Meyer-Sahling, Schuster, and Mikkelsen (2018) identify that performance management is critical for effectiveness in developing just as in developed countries. Another lesson they drew from their survey of 23,000 civil servants in 10 developing countries is that managers and leaders must "ensure that performance matters in civil service management" (p. 36). They write: "The evidence thus underscores the importance of ensuring both that performance matters in civil service management decisions, and that formal performance management systems are designed and implemented well to achieve this end" (p. 36).

Performance management is a set of activities that facilitate effective and efficient achievement of organizational goals. For many years, performance management in government was considered the equivalent of performance reviews or evaluations. Performance management, however, is a more encompassing, higher-level process than the individual performance reviews that are usually conducted annually and are likely part of the performance management system. The elements of an effective performance management system include:

1. *A mission and vision statement.* A repeated emphasis in this book is the central importance of an organization's mission for articulating a path for the efforts of all organization's members. The mission must be prominent and reinforced regularly and routinely across the organization.
2. *Goals, performance plans, and performance information.* The organization and its members need to visualize progress toward achieving their mission. Indicators can be quantitative, qualitative, and symbolic, providing for both ongoing and public critical assessment of progress.
3. *Regular, constructive feedback*, which likely separates feedback to employees and their units from administrative uses of the feedback. Every organizational member involved in delivering feedback should be trained for their conversations with those receiving feedback.
4. *Formal developmental reviews.* Government organizations typically allocate too much attention to formal reviews that categorize employees on a five-point scale for administrative purposes. The administrative role of such reviews typically overwhelms the developmental function. The administrative information simultaneously fails to meet organizational needs because it discriminates poorly for the uses to which it is put (e.g., contingent pay, recognition, promotion, reductions in force). Public organizations need to develop distinct systems for different human resource management decisions that have appropriate discriminatory power for the purposes for which they are used.
5. *Regular, frequent coaching.* Coaching is a developmental resource to promote and sustain employee growth and competence (Katz 2018b). It supports employees and creates a culture of mutual support rather than adversarial exchanges.
6. *Performance recognition.* Recognizing employee performance brings multiple dividends. It signals to employees and other stakeholders that high performance is valued, a priority for the

organization. For recognition recipients, the result is a pat on the back, a thank you for a job well done. Recognition need not require creation of pay-for-performance systems, but instead low-powered incentives (see Chapter 6 for more details about incentives).

5.2.2.3 Improving Performance Appraisals

Although the performance management system is far broader than the individual appraisal alone, performance appraisals remain a vital part of performance management, particularly in government organizations. Practices associated with the individual performance appraisal are gradually changing. Attributes emerging from the transformation of performance appraisals are summarized in Box 5.3. Two of the more novel practices emerging in the transformation of performance appraisal are the increasing role of technology and a focus on culture. The shift toward more explicit attention to public service, which is considered in Section 5.2.2.4, is consistent with a focus on culture.

A major reason for shortfalls in the positive results expected from performance appraisals involves conflicts between the roles for which they are used.[1] The foremost conflict is between the administrative role of performance appraisal and its role in developing people through their work (Meyer, Kay, and French 1965). Scholars and practitioners have repeatedly documented this conflict. Performance appraisals have traditionally been seen as a means for the parties to the performance appraisal, usually a supervisor and a subordinate, to meet and exchange information about recent performance and future goals and ways to improve performance. The exchange of information about an employee's recent performance creates opportunities to reinforce what the employee has done well, what can be improved, and how the employee, with coaching and support from the supervisor, can actualize improvements. The developmental process presumes free and open flow of information between supervisor and subordinate and a common objective.

In contrast, the administrative role of performance appraisal is largely about control and distribution of scarce resources. The folly of using the same appraisal for employee development and pay adjustment was articulated by Herbert Meyer, Emanuel Kay, and John French (1965) more than fifty years ago: "It seems foolish to have a manager serving in the self-conflicting role as a counselor (helping a man to

Box 5.3 Transformations in performance appraisal

1. *A shift in feedback frequency.* Organizations are abandoning the annual performance review. In its place are systems that allow for real-time, frequent feedback by managers, coworkers, and customers. Software platforms allow for immediate feedback, constructive criticism, and actionable insights. These data can be aggregated and quantified to enable big-picture conversations and analysis about employees and groups.
2. *Better conversations.* Shifting away from the annual review requires managers to have more disciplined approaches to how they speak with employees about performance. Frequent feedback works best when managers can help employees see their roles and impact on goals.
3. *Bottom up.* Establishing goals can shift from a top-down approach to one that begins with employees. Once organizational goals are established, employees can take ownership of individual goal setting by setting priorities that align with bigger objectives.
4. *Better manager training.* Effective performance management in the new paradigm will rely on managers extensively. That means those managers need additional training and leadership development to help their employees succeed. This training can include how to help employees orient their goals around corporate strategy, coaching employees about career paths and opportunities, and committing to regular feedback mechanisms.
5. *Technology role.* Companies today are using powerful technologies to integrate performance management with other core HR programs. This enterprise approach allows for quantification, analysis, and impact to be determined more quickly. Platforms allow companies and their employees to interact, learn from each other, leave feedback, find mentors, and solve problems.
6. *Focus on culture.* Performance management is evolving beyond meeting basic business goals. Today's complex workforces require focusing portions of performance management on employee impact on workplace culture and climate.

improve his performance) when, at the same time, he is presiding as a judge over the same employee's salary action case" (p. 127). Appraisals for administrative purposes typically put employees in defensive positions where they are inclined to withhold information, magnify their achievements, and minimize and defend their shortfalls. At the same time, supervisors find themselves "justifying" their assessments. The ideal of the developmental appraisal where information flows freely and the focus is on goal-directed exchanges can quickly deteriorate into self-serving exchanges between adversaries.

Although conflicts may be difficult to eliminate because of legal and regulatory constraints on public organizations and their managers, workarounds are available to mitigate the conflicts. The most direct way is to augment developmental reviews with separate ratings and rankings for administrative purposes (National Research Council 1991). When organizations rely on a single annual performance review, which typically rates employees on an adjectival scale from outstanding to unsatisfactory, conflicts between developmental and administrative uses of the appraisal are inevitable.

5.2.2.4 Public Service as Criteria in Performance Management and Appraisal Systems

An element of the bureaucratic ideal type referred to at the beginning of this chapter is values. "Bureaucrats are generally expected to act within the political and normative order in which bureaucracy is embedded" (Boruvka and Perry 2020, 8). Many of the values consequential for the political and normative order are not readily captured in metrics related to job or mission performance. But public servants are stewards for constitutional principles, the rule of law, and professional standards. Suzanne Piotrowski and David Rosenbloom (2002) refer to these values as "nonmission-based values." They contend that "results-oriented" reforms in the spirit of New Public Management can reduce employee attentiveness to important governance values. Thus, public service values – especially democratic-constitutional values – should be integrated into organizational performance management and individual performance appraisal systems.

The argument that public service and associated values should be incorporated into performance management and appraisal systems is consistent with generic research about high performance. It is consistent, for example, with the principle from high-performance research, first introduced in Chapter 3, that employees should be selected for person–organization fit, not just the job (Bowen, Ledford, and Nathan 1991). Bowen and his colleagues contend a necessary element in making a transition from selecting for jobs to selecting for person–organization fit is to conduct an organizational analysis, in addition to job analysis, to assess the overall work environment. If both person–job and person–organization fit are relevant for selection, then they must be integrated into performance management and appraisal. This inference, which is consistent with David Bowen, Gerald Ledford, and Barry Nathan's (1991) call for reinforcing person–organization fit through training and organization design, is also consistent with generic research on job performance (Welbourne, Johnson, and Erez 1998; Viswesvaran and Ones 2000). Theresa Welbourne, Diane Johnson, and Amir Erez, for instance, advance a role-based performance scale, based on role and identity theory, that captures trends moving away from job-based toward competency-based models, which focus on skills related to a person's current and future jobs (Lawler 1994; Milkovich and Boudreau 1997).

Piotrowski and Rosenbloom (2002) contend that using a balanced scorecard in performance plans could enhance attention to democratic-constitutional values. Some public organizations have long used a form of balanced scorecard to reconcile technical and value expectations. Most branches of the US military services use systems of performance ratings that include not only technical proficiency but also conduct. The U.S. Navy and Marine Corps issues annual fitness reports that include "the adoption of core values in his/her life" (Parkyn 2006, 231). Parkyn describes the consequence of these core values in the U.S. Marines: "Marines who hold common values and beliefs can trust one another, communicate with one another, and harmonize with one another in the most challenging of circumstances. A service ethos – a shared set of core values – facilitates the trust, communications, and harmony – the oneness – that becomes cohesion" (p. 218).

In a study of civilian employees at a U.S. Navy installation, Laurie Paarlberg and James Perry (2007) observed that managers in high performing work units often focused on developing performance appraisals with principled goals, such as honesty, teamwork, commitment to the customer, and being a good steward of the installation's resources.

In the Flemish government, four core values have been defined – collaboration, continuous improvement, client orientation, and reliability – which are part of the competency framework and are found in the competency profiles of all public servants (Brans and Hondeghem, 2005).

5.2.2.5 Performance-based Reductions-in-Force

Another step toward more balance between job security and performance is to base reductions-in-force (RIF) on performance rather than seniority or other, nonperformance criteria. Reductions-in-force involve elimination of programs and/or employees because of change in policy or decline in demand. The criteria used for making RIF decisions include factors such as length of service, membership in a protected class, type of appointment, and performance. A reason for criticism of job security rules in recent years is that many view them as protection for poor performers (Hur and Perry 2016). A recent proposal from the Partnership for Public Service and The Volcker Alliance (2018) argues for making performance the most important criterion for RIF.

5.2.3 Nurture Public Service Motivation to Reinforce Ties between Organization and Employee

Bradley Wright and Sanjay Pandey (2008) articulate a fundamental public management principle that affirms much of the preceding discussion about supportive work environments. They write: "It [public service motivation] must be nurtured through communication and performance feedback that highlights how the organization's values and goals coincide with those of employee[s]" (p. 515). Wright and Pandey's principle is supported by experimental research on public service motivation and prosocial behavior. Marc Esteve et al. (2016) investigated the relationship between public service motivation and prosocial behavior using a student sample of 263. Not only did they identify a positive relationship between the two constructs but they also found that the behavior of group members moderated the relationship. Esteve et al. (2016) write: "We find that the prosocial behavior of high-PSM people depends on whether these people are in a setting in which other people are more or less prosocial. Indeed, our results show that high-PSM people will adjust their behavior to the social context. That is, they act prosocially if they are dealing with prosocial individuals, but they do not act in favor of others if those others do not show prosocial behavior" (p. 183). A more recent study of collective public service motivation by Jessica Breaugh, Kerstin Alfes, and Adrian Ritz (2019) in 131 teams in Switzerland reinforces Esteve et al.'s findings. Team-level motivation scores, which

Breaugh, Alfes, and Ritz (2019) term public service motivation climate, indirectly affect team effectiveness through team identification, and the relationship is strengthened in strong public service motivation climates. Thus, the collective public service motivation of colleagues in two studies suggests that work environment makes a difference.

In what ways can public managers and their organizations nurture public service motivation? The research suggests several avenues. One is satisfying basic psychological needs, which was highlighted earlier in this chapter. Aside from theoretical support discussed in Chapter 2 and inherent advantages of public institutional arrangements considered in this chapter, several empirical studies provide further evidence. Wouter Vandenabeele (2014) analyzed survey responses of more than 3,000 civil servants from Flemish state central ministries. He looked at two dependent variables, leadership promotion of public values and individual public service motivation. He found that basic psychological need satisfaction moderated the relationship between the two variables. Thus, an organization's attention to the basic psychological needs satisfaction of members elevates both the efficacy of leaders' promotion of public values and members' public service motivation.

Lutz Kaiser (2014) gathered a cross-sectional survey sample of 498 public employees in a German city in North Rhine-Westphalia, achieving results consistent with Vandenabeele (2014). He inferred that satisfaction of basic psychological needs of autonomy and competence is a source for intrinsic motivation that permits individuals to internalize public service values that are part of their autonomous identity. Kaiser writes: "Further results strongly recommend ... putting up-to-date human resource management tools into action. Notably, a modern management toolbox of HR-management should include devices to allow for self-determination at the workplace, like the transferability of competence and autonomy" (p. 14).

5.3 Unraveling Consensus: When Value Systems Collide

A consistent theme across Chapters 2–4 is the importance of "fit" – between the person and the job, between the person and the organization, between the organization's identity and the individual's values and passions, and between the individual's identity and work environment supportiveness. Fit is not permanent, however, not forever. One of my first personal encounters with the impermanence of fit was when I was evaluating the Civil Service Reform Act of 1978 in the late 1970s and early 1980s. One of our field sites was the California state office of the U.S. Department of Agriculture Farmers Home Administration (FmHA), whose mission was issuing credit for rural development. The transition from the Carter to the Reagan Administration was like the difference between night and day. During the Carter Administration, FmHA was assessed by the number of loans issued and the dollar value of loans accessible to rural communities, with the standards for excellence being larger numbers of loans for larger dollar volumes. The Reagan Administration reversed course and excellence was immediately equated with fewer numbers of loans for lesser dollar values. Almost overnight, the standards for excellence became starkly different.

The FmHA anecdote calls attention to what sometimes happens when the political winds shift, as can happen in public contexts when political regimes change, public support for missions deteriorate, and core organizational technologies become obsolete. Organizational members may find themselves, individually and collectively, in situations that are foreign to them. Although the story in Chapter 3 about the U.S. Bureau of Prisons (BOP) did not extend to the decline of the strong culture John DiIulio documented from the BOP's early decades, a variety of developments in the 1990s and early 2000s no doubt influenced its deterioration as a place for "principled agents" (DiIulio 1994). The popular media offers examples about other public organizations experiencing an unraveling similar to what occurred in BOP over an extended period. Here are two examples, one from the United States and the other from India:

- John Feeley, a career foreign service officer became Ambassador to Panama in 2016. He spent virtually all of his thirty-five-year foreign-service career engaged with Latin America, developing Spanish-language skills and knowledge of the region, its people, and culture (Anderson 2018). Like many other Foreign Service careerists who have left the U.S. State Department since 2017, his departure in March 2018 was not about policy. Instead, it was about the values Feeley brought to his public service and the values he then perceived represented by those leading the US government. John Feeley (2018) articulated the role values and policy played in his decision to resign in a *Washington Post* op-ed:

Now that I am no longer oath-bound to support the president and his policies, several points warrant clarification. I did not resign over any policy decisions regarding my remit in Panama, or – as was incorrectly alleged in the media – due to the president's denigrating comments about countries that participate in the visa diversity lottery. I resigned because the traditional core values of the United States, as manifested in the president's National Security Strategy and his foreign policies, have been warped and betrayed. I could no longer represent him personally and remain faithful to my beliefs about what makes America truly great.

- On August 21, 2019, Kannan Gopinathan, a member of the Indian Administrative Service since 2012, resigned to protest changes to civil liberties in Kashmir (Jose 2019). Gopinathan was joined soon thereafter, on September 6, by K Sasikanth Senthil, who became an Indian Administrative Service officer in 2009. Senthil associated his departure not with personal circumstances or specific policies, but shifting values: "Many of us enter the civil services following certain ideals and values, and when those ideals are questioned it becomes difficult to continue.... I never faced any personal issues during my career as a civil servant. I quit to make a larger point on the direction in which the country has been moving of late" (Jose 2019). Gopinathan and Senthil have reportedly been joined by many others in their actions in opposition to the ruling party (Munsi 2019).

The loss of human capital from departures of public servants such as John Feeley, Kannan Gopinathan, and K. Sasikanth Senthil, when multiplied across an organization, takes an enormous toll on effectiveness. Jon Lee Anderson (2018) describes the toll in his essay that puts Feeley's departure into the larger context of developments in the U.S. State Department:

The U.S. diplomat in the region told me that it would take a long, concerted effort to restore the effectiveness of American diplomacy. "We're into multiple years of repair needed already – say, five," he said. "It's bad." As the country works to mend relationships with allies, it will face severe shortages of experts in the working details of global affairs, and of experienced mentors for new recruits. At the State Department, the diplomat added, "we don't have arms. We don't have a huge budget. All we have to compete with is the credibility of our senior leadership. If you don't have those things, you're dealing from a position of weakness. And the way to repair it is by putting people forward who can tackle problems—people like John." He went on, "This is happening at a very dangerous time for our country. Some people liken it to an own goal. I'd say it's more like a self-inflicted Pearl Harbor."

Describing the erosion of capacity as "a self-inflicted Pearl Harbor" is an extreme characterization, but it serves to drive home the point how unraveling consensus surrounding values can eviscerate an organization.

Can such drastic outcomes in public organizations be managed or avoided? Can counterweights be developed to mitigate upheavals like those in the U.S. Foreign Service and the Indian Administrative Service? Can options for employees or stakeholders who support them be reweighted to enhance voice and loyalty as options over exit (Hirschman 1970)? These are difficult questions for which I have no easy answers. Let me suggest some considerations that help me in thinking about these questions.

First, as regrettable as the human toll of the types of value reversals referred to earlier may be, they are difficult to predict and, for many political systems, infrequent. If the Reagan and Trump presidencies are benchmarks for significant political upheavals in the United States, for example, then they are separated by forty years – not a lifetime but a substantial period nonetheless. Even in a parliamentary system like the United Kingdom, Prime Minister Margaret Thatcher's tenure may stand as the primary radical shift in value systems since World War II.

Second, large-scale changes in public organizations are often accompanied by electoral processes that shape value transformations and by mechanisms for amplifying the voices of dissenters. The point here is that value transformations are seldom the arbitrary choices of a misguided leader alone, but they reflect changes arising from popular support. Many public organizations also provide formal mechanisms for members to express their reservations – their dissent – so deep reservations about changes in direction may receive a hearing (O'Leary 2020). Although mechanisms for considering dissent may be able to address cleavages around policy differences within a community of policy professionals, they may not be effective mechanisms for addressing deep-seated, fundamental differences over values.

Finally, reexamination and occasional upheaval of value systems underlying governance and public policies can be a healthy and necessary process in democratic governments. The workings of democratic processes must take priority over the specialized knowledge and interests of public servants, some of whom may be central to the policy or implementation process. We should regret the loss of human capital that departures of public servants represent, but these losses must be weighed within the larger, long-term health of democratic processes. Of course, "who governs" varies across political regimes. Authoritarian systems may weight input from stakeholders differently. By the same token, even authoritarian systems are attentive, in the long run, to the sources and maintenance of their legitimacy.

5.4 Conclusion

Empirical research indicates that a supportive work environment is important for creating an atmosphere for reinforcing and sustaining public service motivation. The foundations for a supportive work environment are the institutional arrangements that create distinct career incentives for politicians and bureaucrats. The rules that separate civil servants from politicians establish two conditions that nurture public service motivation: creating an environment for common pool resources and promoting basic psychological needs of employees.

Despite what flows routinely from organic common pool resources, meritocratic norms, and buffering of career incentives, however, more can be done to facilitate development of intrinsically motivated behavior through a variety of developmental tools available to public organizations. Among these tools are establishing robust learning and growth opportunities, developing norms that balance job security and performance, and nurturing public service motivation to reinforce ties between organization and employee.

This chapter identified several ways in which public organizations can establish robust learning and growth opportunities. Probably the most significant step is providing learning and development throughout the career. Such career-long learning is typical for military careers, but tactics similar to how the military promotes cognitive and experiential learning could be extended broadly across the public workforce. Leader development programs could similarly become more inclusive, to open opportunities across the hierarchy. Finally, more attention could be given to developing subjective career success, which is important for individuals who succeed in pursuing their calling or basic purpose in life. Achieving subjective career success is a foundation for employee self-confidence and identity, which drives a continuous cycle of adaptive, self-directed career performance.

As important as job security rules are for maintaining a buffer between politicians and bureaucrats, security must be balanced by prospects for high performance. One way of accomplishing the balance is by defining rules that give equal deference to property rights and performance. Public organizations may be able to affirmatively influence performance by improving the effectiveness of their performance management systems and improving a central element in those systems, performance appraisals. Performance management and appraisal systems can also incorporate public service values and expectations directly into these processes. In addition, performance can be elevated as a criterion in decisions such as RIF.

A final step considered for developing intrinsically motivated behavior is for public organizations to nurture public service motivation. Communicating to employees through both routine and special organizational processes about how the organization's values and goals converge with those of employees can go a long way in fostering and sustaining public service motivation.

Note

1 Conflicts between the roles for which performance appraisals are used is not the only factor that may affect their effectiveness. Christensen et al. (2013) used a mixed experimental design to investigate relationships between public service motivation and performance appraisals with a sample of South Korean MPA and MBA students. One of their findings was that a rater's public service motivation moderated ratings for both task and nontask behaviors. Based upon their findings, they offered several suggestions for additional research.

6 | Aligning Compensation Systems and Public Service Motivation

Many people consider compensation policy, which focuses on extrinsic rewards, independent from public service motivation. The reality is that extrinsic and intrinsic rewards are inextricably intertwined. Compensation and public service motivation have intersected frequently in research, particularly research on pay-for-performance and contingent pay. Although intersections between contingent compensation and public service motivation are most prominent, many areas of compensation policy are highly relevant for public service motivation. This chapter highlights intersections between compensation policy and public service motivation, assesses inferences that professionals can draw from research for compensation policy and practice, and identifies compensation strategies that align compensation policy with public service motivation.

Aligning compensation policies with public service motivation promotes several positives for public organizations, in particular:

- Clear and coherent compensation policies signal to prospective employees the relative importance of different types of rewards, increasing the likelihood for a better fit of people and incentives.
- Motives are more likely to be aligned with autonomous rather than controlled incentives.
- Well-designed compensation systems increase prospects that intrinsic and public service motivation will be crowded in rather than crowded out.
- Aligned compensation policies help to reconcile employee interests, public expectations about appropriate compensation, and budgetary constraints.

The chapter proceeds in three stages. I begin by addressing some overarching questions, namely, what behaviors are important for effective organizations and what are effective compensation systems.

149

The presentation next turns to a discussion of components of compensation systems and what research says about what is important and how public service motivation is affected by the components. Eight specific compensation strategies are presented that support institutional arrangements that create conditions to enhance prosocial, intrinsic incentives important for collective goods and reinforcing public service motivation. The chapter concludes with an assessment of the implications of pursuing the proposed strategies.

6.1   Motivation and Effective Compensation Systems

At the outset, it will be helpful to discuss the criteria for assessing effectiveness to provide benchmarks for the ends public managers are seeking to achieve. Two parallel sets of criteria are relevant, one involving motivation and the other involving compensation systems. With regard to motivation, three concepts, that is, membership, reliable role behaviors, and innovative and spontaneous activity, encompass the behaviors required by effective organizations (Katz 1964). These concepts were discussed in greater length at the beginning of Chapter 2.

These three classes of behavior, not surprisingly, figure prominently in discussions of effective compensation. A leading compensation text (Milkovich and Newman 1999) identifies four strategic policies: (1) internal consistency, (2) external competitiveness, (3) employee contributions, and (4) administration.[1] Some of the compensation effectiveness criteria are obviously connected with behaviors required by effective organizations. Incentives, for instance, call to mind organizational efforts to stimulate innovative and spontaneous activity. The ability to attract excellent candidates and external competitiveness is the key consideration related to membership behaviors. Internal consistency is essential for reliable role behaviors. Compensation policy and strategy are therefore highly important for realizing effective organizational behaviors.

When Lois Wise and I first wrote about public service motivation (Perry and Wise 1990), we understood that compensation and public service motivation were intertwined. One of the three propositions we introduced was "Public organizations that attract members with high levels of public service motivation are likely to be less dependent on utilitarian incentives to manage individual performance effectively"

(Perry and Wise 1990, 371). Reasoning from predisposition-opportunity theory (Knoke and Wright-Isak 1982), which posits that individuals seek to match their predispositions with incentives offered by organizations, effective incentives are those that are directly contingent on the predispositions individuals bring to the organization. Individuals motivated by money, for instance, are more likely to respond to pure utilitarian incentive systems, which rely on utilitarian incentives alone rather than normative or affectual incentives (see Table 2.2). Organizations that attract members using normative and affectual incentives can rely on other types of incentive systems, such as pure normative, pure affectual, or service systems that eschew utilitarian incentives.

A discussion of compensation system design reminds us that civil service systems are mixed-motive systems that balance logics of consequentiality and appropriateness (March and Olsen 1989). Financial incentive systems typically rest on the assumption that individuals are self-interested and employee self-interest and organizational goals are best aligned through the distribution of extrinsic rewards (Deckop, Mangel, and Cirka 1999; Ferraro, Pfeffer, and Sutton 2005; Ghosal 2005). Theories about public service motivation, however, begin with alternative assumptions about human nature. Laurie Paarlberg, James L. Perry, and Annie Hondeghem (2008) address the human nature assumptions:

> "…theories about public service motivation assume that individuals are 'internally motivated' by intrinsic rewards of public service (Perry and Wise 1990). A growing body of research on motivation suggests that while some individuals are self-interested and motivated by individualistic, rational, and material incentives, others are motivated by experiences and identities that they receive from being 'other motivated,' such as the ability to make social contributions or the social acceptance of complying with normative values." (p. 279)

Aside from big picture questions about linkages between compensation design and employee behavior, a very practical consideration for public-sector compensation systems is the source of financing. Because public employee compensation is typically supported wholly from taxes and other public funding instruments, public officials confront real budget constraints because of the nature of their funding and public expectations about appropriate compensation for public servants. Any design of public-compensation systems must recognize this constraint.

6.2   Compensation Structures Affecting Motivation and Compensation System Effectiveness

Compensation comes in many forms. George Milkovich and Jerry M. Newman (1999) identify at least four main forms: base pay, merit pay, incentives, and benefits and services. Although we may have hunches about how these forms motivate particular behaviors, research on public service motivation is not so long-lived and expansive that it can be tied to each of the forms for guidance about compensation design. The discussion of lessons below focuses on several forms of compensation about which we have research: total compensation, base pay, mobility systems, and financial incentives.

The general model that underlies this chapter appears in Figure 6.1. It posits that the facets of compensation affect different mediating variables. One set of mediating variables affected by compensation is an organization's status on factors salient to employees, indicators such as the competitiveness of its base pay relative to competitors (i.e., comparators), dispersion of wages across members, and rules for advancement. These mediating variables may affect other mediators such as market competitiveness and intrinsic motivation. Finally, the mediating variables, in turn, influence motivational outcomes salient for organizational effectiveness, i.e., membership, reliable role behavior, and innovative and spontaneous activity.

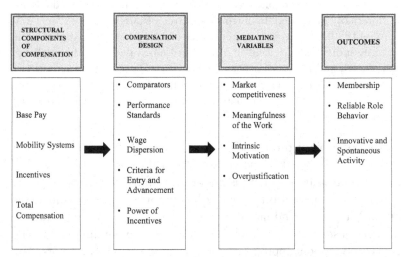

Figure 6.1 General model for compensation design and outcomes.

6.2.1 Theoretical Role of Compensation Structures

Compensation serves a variety of roles, but foremost among them is signaling in job markets (Spence 1973). One facet of signaling involves base pay – which conveys information to applicants on how important money is in the overall scheme of rewards and how important the job is to the organization's effectiveness. The immediate function of signaling is to reduce information asymmetry between an organization and prospective employees (Connelly et al. 2011). Signaling is conveyed by many facets of the job market other than base pay, including total compensation, job security rules, and promotion in organizations (Spence 1973; Celani and Singh 2011).

As a framework, signaling has the advantage that it speaks to information conveyed not only to individuals in the job market but also to all attentive stakeholders. In the corporate sector, signaling conveys information to stakeholders like potential investors and stockholders. In government, taxpayers, voters, and citizens are key stakeholders. As noted later with regard to beliefs about the generosity of public compensation, these stakeholders have keen interests in public compensation decisions because of their effects on public outlays and public performance. Given the sensitivity of various stakeholders in public-sector compensation, it is important to take into account how institutional arrangements for public-sector compensation affect not only prospective employees but also taxpayers and other stakeholders.

The subject of signaling has seldom been addressed with respect to job markets for government or public-service organizations. One exception is Bruno Frey and Margit Osterloh's (2005) comparison of corporate and bureaucratic compensation structures, which they ironically invoke in a search for institutional arrangements to reduce corporate scandals such as excessive management compensation and fraudulent accounts. Frey and Osterloh contend that institutional arrangements associated with Max Weber's model of bureaucracy are superior to the agency theory approach used by corporations. The hallmarks of corporate institutional arrangements, that is, markets and pay-for-performance, operate effectively in particular types of situations. "When interdependencies between actors are simple and easily contractual, these institutional settings work efficiently" (p. 106), write Frey and Osterloh (2005).

Frey and Osterloh (2005) demonstrate that the alternative to agency theory is bureaucracy because its institutional arrangements create common pool resources – collective goods – that rely on intrinsically motivated behaviors rather than the extrinsic rewards associated with the individual contracts of agency theory. They write: "Individuals derive utility from the activity itself or because they wish to comply to given normative standards for their own sake. The extent of intrinsically motivated behavior systematically depends on conditions that can be shaped by appropriate institutions" (p. 106).

In regard to the question of aligning compensation and motivations, the takeaway from Frey and Osterloh (2005) is that the institutional arrangements associated with compensation must be structured to support public service motivation. This means that the design of the compensation system *affirmatively* supports attraction of public-service-motivated staff; encourages reliable role behavior driven by public interests without gaming, self-serving, or shirking; and rewards innovative and spontaneous activity. It also means that the compensation system crowds in prosocial behaviors and avoids crowding out autonomously motivated public-service behaviors. The institutional arrangements that Frey and Osterloh (2005) write about are supported by a wealth of other research (see, e.g., Deci and Ryan 1985; Perry 1986; Olsen 2006; Perry and Vandenabeele 2008; Banuri and Keefer 2015).

6.2.2   Total Compensation

Total compensation is everything an organization provides an employee in exchange for working. It includes base pay, incentives, benefits, and perks. "Total compensation strategy" was a centerpiece of a prominent book about pay in the early 1990s, Jay Schuster and Patricia Zingheim's (1992) *The New Pay*. One theme they emphasized is that compensation strategy is often programmatic, looking to individual components (e.g., base pay, variable pay) of compensation programs, and instead needs to be considered holistically in relation to an organization's goals and mission. Schuster and Zingheim (1992) make a case for strategically tying all aspects of compensation to organizational mission and favored making variable pay, rather than base pay, a larger share of total compensation and making it the centerpiece of compensation strategy. My use of total compensation is in some ways consistent, but also more traditional – focusing attention on the total value of compensation for employees and the total cost of compensation for government organizations and the potential influences on employee motivation.

Although evidence about the total compensation of public-sector employees and how it compares to that of private sector workers is sparse, several studies suggest government employees may receive higher total compensation than their private counterparts. Frederico Finan, Benjamin Olken, and Rohini Pande (2017) examined survey microdata from thirty-four countries to develop stylized facts about comparative compensation in the public and private sectors. Nineteen of the countries were classified by the World Bank as low- or lower middle-income countries. The authors concluded that the public sector is substantially different than the private sector on many variables, among them the level of wages, fringe benefits, composition of the labor force, and tenure. In many countries, public-sector employees received a significant wage premium relative to private-sector employees, as reflected in Table 6.1. Finan, Olken, and Pande (2017) found that the wage gap was the largest among low-income countries. The results of public–private comparisons on health benefits and pensions are more mixed than for wages, and the available data are far less complete in providing a picture of comparative differences, as shown in Table 6.1.

The evidence about potential total compensation premiums for public-sector employees in more developed countries, as implied by the findings from Finan, Olken, and Pande (2017), is contested and leads to less obvious inferences. Research by Alexander Danzer and Peter Dolton (2011) about total rewards in the United Kingdom, for example, indicates differences by gender. Total rewards is defined by Danzer and Dolton as a comprehensive measure that includes pay, pensions, and other benefits. Danzer and Dolton (2011) compare the present value of all payments over a lifetime for highly educated workers in the public and private sectors. They found that lifetime total reward payments for men are equal, but that women experience an advantage during their careers. Matt Dickson, Fabien Postel-Vinay, and Hélène Turon (2014) arrive at different conclusions based on their analysis of five continental European countries, Germany, the Netherlands, France, Italy, and Spain. They arrived at their estimates of public–private comparative lifetime values of

Table 6.1 *Comparisons of parity between public and private sector pay, health benefits, and pensions in thirty-four countries*[a]

Country	Log pay, fully specified model	Health benefits	Pension
Albania	No premium	–	–
Argentina	Positive premium	Positive premium	Positive premium
Armenia	No premium	–	–
Bolivia	No premium	–	–
Bosnia and Herzegovina	Negative premium	Positive premium	Positive premium
Bulgaria	Negative premium	Negative premium	Negative premium
Colombia	No premium	–	–
Egypt	Negative premium	Positive premium	–
Georgia	Positive premium	–	–
Ghana	Positive premium	–	–
India	Positive premium	Positive premium	Positive premium
Indonesia	Positive premium	Positive premium	Positive premium
Iraq	Negative premium	Positive premium	Positive premium
Kenya	Positive premium	–	–
Korea, Republic of	No premium	–	–
Laos	Negative premium	–	–
Malawi	Positive premium	–	–
Mexico	Positive premium	Positive premium	Positive premium
Nicaragua	No premium	Positive premium	Negative premium
Niger	No premium	Positive premium	Positive premium
Nigeria	Positive premium	–	Positive premium
Pakistan	Positive premium	–	–
Panama	Positive premium	–	–
Peru	Positive premium	No premium	–
Serbia	Positive premium	Positive premium	Positive premium
South Africa	Positive premium	Positive premium	Positive premium
Sri Lanka	Positive premium	–	–
Tajikistan	Negative premium	–	–

Table 6.1 (*cont.*)

Country	Log pay, fully specified model	Health benefits	Pension
Tanzania	Positive premium	–	–
Timor-Leste	No premium	–	–
Uganda	No premium	No premium	No premium
United Kingdom	No premium	–	–
United States	Positive premium	Positive premium	Positive premium
Vietnam	No premium	–	–

a Data are for differing years for each country, varying from 2004 to 2014. See Appendix in the study by Finan, Olken and Pande (2017, 509–511), for year and source. Positive premium denotes the public sector is significantly better than the private sector. Negative premium denotes the private sector is significantly better than the public sector.

employment using data from the European Community Household Panel for the period 1994–2001. Although Dickson et al.'s concept of lifetime values – the present discounted sum of future income flows – is similar to that of Danze and Dolton's (2011) concept of total rewards, the method they use to estimate income flows does not rely on wage levels, but instead takes into account differences in earnings mobility, earnings volatility, and job loss risk. Their estimates of premia vary across the five countries. They estimate positive lifetime premiums in the public sector for France, Spain, and Italy. The lifetime premiums at the top in the Netherlands and Germany are negative. Thus, the public–private comparisons for total compensation among wealthy European countries, unlike low-income countries, are heterogeneous.

For a variety of reasons, the total cost of compensation has not factored significantly into compensation policy or strategy for government organizations (Risher and Reese 2016). One reason is technical. The methods for public–private salary comparisons have been widely criticized (see the discussion later regarding base pay). Seeking metrics for a more complex compensation portfolio, including items such as benefits and pensions, is likely to generate even more contentious disagreements about design and methodology for comparisons.

A second reason is related to politics and policy development. Changing any piece of the compensation package in government organizations may require sign-off by internal and affected stakeholders and formal approval by appropriate legislative bodies. Public employee compensation is often the result of decisions made in different forums, including collective bargaining and legislatures. Current pay, for instance, is often a product of local decisions, perhaps the result of collective bargaining, but deferred compensation decisions are often made by legislative bodies, sometimes far removed from the decision forum for current pay. Thus, public officials are challenged to rationalize total compensation across forums that function according to different decision rules and processes. These technical and decision-forum challenges aside, total compensation deserves serious attention because of its consequences for public organizations.

Little research has taken up the relationship between total compensation and public service motivation, but a group of scholars in Denmark (Andersen, Eriksson, Kristensen and Pedersen 2012) have approached the issue in a novel way. Andersen et al. developed vignettes in which they offered varied respondents' different compensation packages with items such as wages, health-care packages, working-time flexibility, and bonuses. Given variations across the vignettes, the authors assessed how compensation packages should be structured to appeal to employees with high public service motivation. Although the research does not test directly the influence of total compensation, it supports the logic and importance of considering compensation holistically – as a package – with respect to public service motivation.

6.2.2.1   Total Compensation Strategy

Schuster and Zingheim's (1992) idea of thinking about compensation holistically and linking all compensation components strategically to organizational goals is a worthy aspiration for public organizations. This leads me to argue that as a foundation for compensation strategy, total compensation is the appropriate benchmark for external, market comparisons.

> Strategy 1: Use total compensation as the benchmark for market comparisons.

Pursuing a total compensation strategy will be a significant departure for many public-sector organizations. Government organizations that use total compensation as the benchmark for their outlays are likely to realize at least two benefits. First, using total compensation as the standard for outlays will help to control the ratio of extrinsic to intrinsic rewards. The goal is to avoid making extrinsic rewards so large that they become behavioral drivers – for membership or other outcomes – that crowd out public service motivation, thereby sustaining public service as a defining value of government institutions (Perry and Buckwalter 2010).

Second, and a dividend beyond the motivational implications, is that using total compensation as a benchmark may generate economies because it constrains excessive expenditures. Controlling costs is a direct budgetary benefit.

An indirect benefit of using total compensation as the standard for market comparisons is what it signals to citizens and their representatives about employee compensation, which may help to change the discourse about public compensation. Public employees are often painted as self-aggrandizing beneficiaries of excessive pay, benefits, and/or pensions. Howard Risher and Adam Reese (2016) observe, "Compensation has been a lightning rod for the critics of government" (p. 1). They summarize a series of reports, albeit from conservative foundations, that make a case that US public employees are generously compensated:

- In 2014, the American Enterprise Institute published, "Overpaid or Underpaid? A State-by-state Ranking of Public-Employee Compensation" (Biggs and Richwine 2014), which concluded that state employee total compensation imposed a "modest penalty" for public service in only one state, Virginia.
- The Cato Institute has frequently published evidence about generous pensions and benefits and high annual salary increases.
- A Heritage Foundation report, using data from the American Time Use Survey, indicates government employees work as much as a month less per year when compared to similar private-sector employees (Richwine 2012).

It is unlikely that criticisms of public compensation will be curbed completely, but the total compensation standard could reduce signals sent to taxpayers and change the discourse about both public-sector compensation and public service.

What are some of the attributes of an effective total compensation strategy in government? They would likely include the following:

- Total compensation associated with employee wages and salaries, benefits, and pensions would collectively closely match total compensation in the private sector for similarly situated occupations and organizations; and

- No component of employee rewards would deviate significantly from market norms, calling prospective employees' attention to it.

Following their survey of ten developing countries, Meyer-Sahling, Jan-Hinrik, Christian Schuster, and Kim Sass Mikkelsen (2018) suggested an alternative way to answer the question posed at the beginning of this paragraph. The fourth lesson they drew from their survey of 23,000 civil servants is "Pay enough to retain (more) motivated staff" (p. 49). Their answer provides a good rule of thumb to guide both total compensation and the subject of the next section, base pay.

6.2.3 Base Pay

As the discussion mentioned earlier indicates, total compensation is a portfolio of rewards, and among the most important of these rewards for employees is base pay. Base pay is the cash compensation that an employer pays for the work performed and is typically tied to the value of the work or skills (Milkovich and Newman 1999). Public organizations have a variety of choices about base pay strategies. Most of these strategies begin with some form of comparison to market wages, which serves as a useful starting point. Three comparators considered here are alternative wage, efficiency wage, and public-service-motivation-adjusted wage.

6.2.3.1 Alternative Wage

Alan Krueger (1988b) refers to one strategic option as the *alternative wage*, which involves a comparison between public- and private-sector wages for the same position or occupation, controlling for age, education, and other variables that might affect comparability. Although Krueger's research (1988a, 1988b) is dated, his results remain instructive for thinking about issues germane to aligning base pay with public-service-motivation research and theory. One issue raised by Krueger, which is an ongoing source of controversy (see, e.g., an exchange between Biggs and Richwine [2012] and Condrey, Facer, and Lorens [2012] in *Public Administration Review*), involves methods for identifying comparability of alternative wages. Krueger raised the issue of sensitivity of comparisons to whether estimates are based on cross-sectional or longitudinal datasets, whether nonwage compensation is included, and related factors. It is worth noting that the legitimacy of alternative wage comparisons rests on acceptance of the validity of estimation methods. Thus, it is important for public officials to gain acceptance of wage comparison methods as a foundation for executing and gaining acceptance of its base pay strategies.

Krueger's (1988b) findings about queuing for federal jobs have several implications for public-sector wage setting. His analysis showed that an increase in the wages of federal workers leads to an increase in the number and average quality of applicants for federal jobs. He concluded that because job application rates appear to reflect economic incentives, job application data could be used for adjusting wages. This would broaden the evidence used to identify alternative wages beyond wage data alone. Krueger suggests how job applications might be used in wage setting: "If the number of job applications for a given job opening falls below or rises above a certain level, wages could be adjusted accordingly to minimize costs" (p. 578). In addition to suggesting a change in policy tied directly to his application queuing analysis, Krueger suggested another option would be an examination of the rate at which workers turn down job offers, which is an additional indicator of the generosity and competitiveness of compensation. Krueger's third option anticipated the recent turn toward performance management, which is assessing the effect of differences in application rates on the performance of government agencies rather than making comparisons with private-sector employers.

6.2.3.2 Efficiency Wage

Another strategic option for base pay raised in both the economics (Gerhart and Rynes 2003) and public administration literatures (Davis and Gabris 2008; Taylor and Taylor 2010) is efficiency wages. Efficiency wage theory posits that paying employees wage premiums encourages maximum effort, thereby realizing increased effectiveness. The generalization that paying employees premiums maximizes effort, like all "good things," has limits (Solow 1979). Two questions arise immediately about efficiency wages in public jurisdictions: (1) Are they effective? (2) Are they sustainable given the budget constraints of most public organizations?

Empirical research about the effectiveness of efficiency wages comes largely from research in the private sector. In a meta-analysis of seventy-five estimates of the efficiency-wage effect, Eric Peach and T. D. Stanley (2009) found a strong efficiency-wage effect. The results of the meta-analysis are consistent with foundational research on the efficiency-wage effect (Krueger and Summers 1988; Stiglitz 2002).

The sustainability of efficiency wages in government is at least as much a question of public norms as is effectiveness. In one of the few studies of efficiency wages in government, Trenton Davis and Gerald T. Gabris (2008) found that efficiency-wage rates were a significant predictor of increased reputational service quality, a subjective measure representing assessments of professional administrators about the quality of services provided in surrounding communities. The Davis and Gabris (2008) study is limited, however, confined to a small geographic area near Chicago and reliant on inferences from reputational surveys and anecdotes rather than more robust evidence, such as applicant quality, productivity, and organizational performance.

6.2.3.3 Public-Service-Motivation-Adjusted Wage

A third way to think about base pay that is germane to the concept of public service motivation is what Jeannette Taylor and Ranald Taylor (2009) term the public-service-motivation-adjusted wage. By this they mean setting base pay at a level that encourages high effort without undermining public service motivation. The public-service-motivation-adjusted wage has some affinity with the "reservation pay premium" that reflects an applicant's willingness to accept lower pay for jobs with higher social responsibility (Frank 1996). Based on a study of fifteen diverse countries (e.g., Bulgaria, Israel, Russia, Taiwan, and the United States), Taylor and Taylor (2010) concluded that public service motivation "… is a more cost-effective way to raise government employees' effort than wages" (p. 81). They also found that efficiency wages differed widely across countries, with some countries paying better than the market rate and others well below. In addition, the public-service-motivation dividend varied across countries. Government workers in the United States and Israel were more likely to raise their effort as a result of public service motivation than public employees in France and Japan. Thus, the public-service-motivation-adjusted wage has effects similar to efficiency wages with respect to effort levels, but the power of such effects is likely to vary across countries. Of course, we do not know why such effects vary across countries and whether they can be influenced by more strategic attention to levers influenced by public service motivation.

Studies from other fields reinforce Taylor and Taylor's findings (Fehrler and Kosfeld 2014; Banuri and Keefer 2016; Burbano 2016). Two experimental studies are highlighted here. In two randomized field experiments, Vanessa Burbano (2016) recently replicated Frank's findings about the reservation pay premium. Burbano manipulated information recruits to short-term jobs received about the employer's social responsibility. Information about employers' social responsibility lowered prospective workers' wage bids. The lower bids were even more pronounced for the highest performers. Overall, the results confirmed the willingness of workers to give up pecuniary benefits for nonpecuniary benefits. The other experiment, which involved 1,700 students seeking entry to the private and public sectors and the Indonesian Ministry of Finance, is reported by Sheheryar Banuri and Philip Keefer (2016). They investigated the interaction between prosocial motivation and wages in prosocial organizations and arrived at three conclusions. They found that high pay attracts less prosocially motivated workers, but workers with greater prosocial motivation exhibited higher effort. They also found that prospective entrants to the Indonesian Ministry of Finance were higher in prosocial motivation than a comparison group of general workers.

At least one high-quality study arrived at different results from research that suggests prospective employees are willing to sacrifice pecuniary for nonpecuniary benefits. Ernesto Dal Bó, Frederico Finan, and Martín A. Rossi (2013) studied recruitment for positions across municipalities in Mexico. Salaries were randomized across recruitment sites, job offers were also randomized, and screening used exams validated to measure intellectual ability, motivation, and personality. The randomization of salaries and job offers permitted Dal Bó and colleagues to assess the effects of financial incentives on the size and quality of the labor pool and the influence of job attributes such as the attractiveness of the municipality on filling vacancies. They found a positive relationship between higher wages and applicant quality as measured by IQ and public service motivation. Higher wage offers were also positively related to acceptance rates, both in general and for less attractive municipalities.

Dal Bó, Finan, and Rossi (2013) study identifies one potential downside to adjusting compensation based on a job's appeal to high public-service-motivation individuals – the reservation pay premium may not exist. Another potential downside of adjusting wages to reflect the attractiveness of the work to high public-service-motivation individuals is that "calculating" the worth of the compensation-public service tradeoff will, over time, serve to crowd out intrinsic motivation associated with the work. Thus, this option for setting base pay ought to be exercised with caution. Policymakers might be better off using pay comparisons augmented by indicators like job application queues and other measures of the attractiveness of jobs relative to the labor market and adjusting base pay according to fluctuations in the other indicators.

6.2.3.4 Base-Pay Design Strategy

The general research is presently of greater utility for base-pay design than is the research on public service motivation. Specific research on public service motivation by Taylor and Taylor (2010) offers insights that deserve to be incorporated into how we think about setting base pay. The research summarized above leads to two strategies that are important for setting base pay:

> Strategy 2. Compensation strategy should incorporate an assessment of alternative, efficiency and public-service-motivation-adjusted wages into setting base pay.

The three standards for base pay are likely to lead to different choices about where to set base pay, but a comparison of options is useful. Assessing base pay for each option would make tradeoffs among them transparent. The comparisons would permit assessments of differences in overall costs, efficiency, and likely motivational impacts.

> Strategy 3. Pay comparability assessments should use salary surveys and complement them with a variety of additional indicators, including job application queues, offer turn-down rates, quit rates and other measures of the attractiveness of jobs relative to the labor market.

Base pay in government, particularly in the United States, is widely criticized for being overly generous, with flaws in salary-survey methods coming in for the lion's share of criticism (Biggs and Richwine 2014). Complementing salary surveys with other indicators will permit governments to triangulate what is an externally competitive wage. Indicators such as job application queues and turndown rates also provide insights into adjustments that could be made in pay rates. Grounding base pay firmly in different conceptions of appropriate wages (e.g., alternative and efficiency wages) and behavioral outcomes (e.g., application queues and quit rates) assures that base pay is accurately weighted in any determination of compensation, whether it is assessed independently or as a component of total compensation.

6.2.4 Mobility Systems

Another dimension of compensation structure is the rate at which individuals ascend the pay ladder, both the slope of the salary line and the rate at which individuals traverse the pay ladder, and prospects for career advancement. An alternative way of expressing and thinking about this dimension of compensation structure is defined as mobility systems, a concept developed in both the career and personnel economics literatures. One of the first scholars to address mobility systems was Ralph Turner (1960), who identified two mobility systems, contest and sponsored, in a comparison of teachers in the United States and the United Kingdom.

Contest mobility, which Turner (1960) associated with the American system of education, is distinguished by its emphasis on opportunity, where no policies cut off anyone's prospects for elite status or, conversely, for elites to move downward. As James E. Rosenbaum (1984) explains: "In a selection system which follows the contest mobility norms, selections are delayed and individuals are allowed complete freedom for mobility through most of their careers" (p. 16).

Sponsored mobility, which is indicative of UK education norms, favors efficiency in contrast to opportunity. Individuals are selected for elite positions very early in their careers and are not permitted to deviate from these early assignments under sponsored mobility norms. Early selection permits organizations to focus specialized training and socialization on those selected for future elite status.

Rosenbaum (1979, 1984) identified yet a third model of mobility, which he called the tournament model. "In the *tournament mobility model*, careers are conceptualized as a sequence of competitions, each of which has implications for an individual's mobility chances in all subsequent selections" (Rosenbaum 1984, 42). Although Rosenbaum was the first to present the tournament model, economists Edward Lazear and Sherwin Rosen (1981) formalized it and showed how pay raises are associated with promotions. The tournament model contends that individuals are promoted not on their absolute performance but on their ranking relative to others. The compensation for winners of the tournament does not necessarily serve to motivate individuals working at that level, but motivates all of those below that level who are seeking promotion. Increasing pay dispersion between organizational levels increases the incentive to put forth effort.

The tournament mobility model may have unintended consequences if it is not effectively managed (Lazear and Shaw 2007). Although large pay spreads may induce high effort, they may also create ultracompetition that promotes an unpleasant work environment. Teamwork, especially among the executive teams who recognize the potential zero-sum nature of the tournament, could suffer from passive forms of noncooperation that supports the failure of others or active sabotage of coworkers.

In their sweeping analysis of variable pay introduced earlier in this chapter, Frey and Osterloh (2005) provide theoretical and empirical support for resolving the mobility system question. The title of their article conveys the solution, "Yes, Managers Should Be Paid Like Bureaucrats." The argument is that high-powered incentive compensation like that associated with tournament models generates a variety of undesirable consequences – short-term focus, crowding-out prosocial behaviors, incentives for fraudulent accounts, and underinvestment by selfish team members in firm-specific resources. The solution to these undesirable consequences is not to improve current pay practices in the corporate sector but to emulate some features of bureaucracy. The two most prominent features are conceiving the organization as a bundle of common pool resources, which are collective goods that "generate a joint surplus not attributable to single actors" (Frey and Osterloh 2005, 106). The other feature of bureaucracy is the cultivation of prosocial intrinsic incentives, which Frey and Osterloh contend is essential for the production of collective goods.

6.2.4.1 Pay for Ability, Skills, and Performance
Another facet of mobility involves the criteria used for entry and movement up the pay line. The options have proliferated in recent years. I touch on three here: pay-for-ability, skill-based pay, and pay-for-performance.

Beginning with the advent of modern civil service systems, governments have relied heavily on *pay-for-ability systems*. Ability is typically tied to examinations that formally measure ability. Examinations are the measure of ability or "merit," but rewards are associated with jobs. Progression through a pay range occurs over time, but is largely dependent on initial qualification via the examination. Effort or performance comes into play only if the job incumbent's performance and behavior fall below minimum standards.

Skill-based pay does not follow the job, but instead ties compensation to the portfolio of skills a person commands. Although skill-based pay is tied to skills employees possess rather than the job they do, pay is often contingent on the use of the skills in their work. Skill-based pay is consistent with and reinforces a logic introduced in Chapter 3 – hiring for the organization rather than the job (Bowen, Ledford, and Nathan 1991). Among the reasons organizations may tie pay to skills is to increase flexibility, encourage skill acquisition, improve customer service, facilitate more complex problem solving (Zingheim and Schuster 2002), and build the organization's culture (Bowen, Ledford and Nathan 1991).

Pay-for-performance explicitly links pay to measured performance. Traditional merit pay schemes rely on supervisory judgments of performance. Some schemes developed more recently use objective indicators to measure performance. A substantial body of research has been conducted since 1980 assessing the efficacy of pay-for-performance schemes (Perry, Engbers, and Jun 2009), and other research has looked at crowding effects (see the discussion later), but little research has directly compared these different criteria for mobility. Banuri and Keefer (2015) conducted an experiment to examine the effects of pecuniary compensation on the ability and motivation of individuals in organizations with prosocial missions. Their experiment compared three pay systems – flat pay, pay-for-ability, and high-powered pay-for-performance. The flat pay system was unrelated to ability or effort. Pay-for-ability, which Banuri and Keefer refer to as a Weberian system, is independent of effort. The experiment used a sample of future public-sector workers in Indonesia. All three pay schemes attracted motivated workers into tasks with a prosocial mission, but the flat pay scheme also attracted low-ability workers. In the short run, pay-for-performance generated higher effort than the other two systems, a difference driven wholly by effects on unmotivated workers. After controlling for selection effects, the levels of effort for the prosocial task from subjects under the pay-for-ability and pay-for-performance schemes were statistically equivalent. Given the higher cost for the pay-for-performance scheme, pay-for-ability was more efficient for generating effort. In response to the question they pose in the title to their paper, Was Weber Right?, Banuri and Keefer answer with a qualified yes. Although the experiment indicates that pay-for-performance and pay-for-ability yield essentially equivalent results for attraction to the prosocial task and effort, they caution about uncertainties associated with effectively measuring performance in the pay-for-performance scheme, which potentially gives an advantage to pay-for-ability schemes.

6.2.4.2 Mobility Design Strategy

As research illustrates, overall form (contest, sponsored, and tournament) and criteria (e.g., ability, skills, and performance) for mobility have important strategic consequences for individual and organizational outcomes. The research leads to three strategies important for designing compensation systems that are consistent with public service motivation.

> Strategy 4. As a compensation strategy, the contest model is best suited for public organizations; the sponsored and tournament mobility models may merit selective use.

Aside from the issue of whether the mobility models are consistent with social norms, the contest mobility model has advantages over the other models in public contexts. It creates rules and an environment to retain talent. The contest model creates an environment to sustain common-pool resources – norms that everyone shares a common responsibility for the organization's success. These norms are likely to be difficult to sustain under either the sponsored model, which relegates some staff to lesser opportunities early in their tenure, or the tournament model, which places competitors for the top rank in zero-sum competition with one another. The contest model is also likely to be more efficient than, for instance, the tournament model that may require high payoffs for staff who achieve the highest rank and, therefore, the contest model is more sustainable under conditions of constrained budgets. It also creates an environment for sustaining and nurturing public service motivation (see Chapter 5).

Despite my broad endorsement of the contest model, selecting an optimal model depends on the situation. A case can be made for using tournament mobility models, for instance, in industries where the public enterprises replicate similar enterprises in the private sector (e.g., hospitals and financial institutions) and/or where significant flows of talent cross public and private organizational boundaries. Similarly, the costs to develop talent may be so high that candidates may need to be selected well in advance of their attaining a position.

> Strategy 5. As a compensation strategy, public organizations should pursue more pronounced wage dispersion among high-skill occupations and executives, seeking to create incentives for retention and promotion but simultaneously avoiding tournament-like fixation on high salaries.

Although tournament models may not be appropriate for general adoption in government settings, they do call attention to a common problem with compensation system design. The problem involves internal dispersion of pay. A pay dispersion problem in public settings that receives frequent attention is salary or wage compression. The International Monetary Fund (IMF) (Clements et al. 2010) identifies wage compression ratios, defined as the ratio of the highest salary to the lowest, as one of three primary indicators by which wage levels can be assessed.[2] The IMF observes that the compression ratio is an indicator of the adequacy of pay and highly skilled workers are likely underpaid and unskilled workers are likely overpaid when the compression ratio is low. The IMF also points to evidence that low compression ratios are associated with corruption.

Research by George J. Borjas (2003) indicates that internal dispersion in pay is an important design feature, independent of the form of mobility systems. His research also reinforces earlier research by Lawrence Katz and Alan Krueger (1991), which found that government personnel policies yield an inflexible internal wage structure "that is insensitive to labor market conditions and an overall rate of pay growth that appears quite sensitive to economic conditions" (p. 33). Borjas' research found that since 1970, relative to the private sector, the distribution of wages in the public sector has compressed significantly. This differential evolution of wage structures has significantly influenced the sorting of workers across sectors. The consequence of the relative wage compression, according to Borjas, is that the public sector has had increasingly more difficulty attracting and retaining high-skill workers. Given historical patterns of underpaying managers and executives, relative wage compression is likely pronounced at the top of the public-sector pay range. Borjas' findings are supported by other labor economics research. Edward Lazear (1999), a pioneer in personnel economics research, was among the first to model and investigate relationships among pay growth, promotions, and performance. Lazear contends that promotions effectively discriminate the growth in pay between high and low performers. The lesson from Borjas' research is that public decision-makers can constrain pay given the nature of public institutions, but when pushed to extremes such frugality impedes attracting and retaining high-quality staff, even among those willing to endure personal sacrifice for public service.

> Strategy 6. Ability, skills and performance collectively are strategic criteria for assessing eligibility for entry and advancement.

Although Weberian pay-for-ability (Banuri and Keefer 2015) is a staple of traditional civil service systems, it is not the only criterion for entry and advancement. The complexity of public work and the rapidly changing environments in which governments operate are reasons for considering alternative criteria. Skill-based pay is another option. As Banuri and Keefer (2015) caution, pay-for-performance schemes are accompanied by measurement challenges that diminish their attractiveness. As argued in the next section, pay-for-performance schemes may also undermine public service motivation.

One way to recognize performance is to build it more robustly into promotional and career advancement processes. Assessments surrounding promotions are more episodic, thorough and holistic, and therefore may be more valid than annual performance reviews that serve both developmental and administrative functions. The strategic direction in Strategy 5, pursuing more pronounced wage dispersion among high-skill occupations and executives, can provide strong recognition for performance and avoid unintended consequences associated with the tournament mobility model.

6.2.5 Incentives

When a merit pay scheme was introduced into the U.S. federal government in 1979, a common reaction was: It's about time! It did not take long, however, before government managers and scholars began to understand the reasons for the long wait. Merit pay simply did not work. After many trials in the United States and other countries (Lah and Perry 2008; Bellé and Cantarelli 2015), the reasons for the failure of variable or contingent pay schemes in the public sector have become clearer.

Although theory lagged, we now have a growing body of scholarly research that makes sense of why incentives in the public sector frequently fail. Two streams of research, which were introduced in Chapter 2, are worth reiterating here: self-determination theory and motivation-crowding theory.

Self-determination theory (Deci and Ryan 1985), rooted in social psychology, particularly the pioneering research by Edward Deci on intrinsic motivation, dates to the early 1970s (Deci 1971). Deci, joined later by his colleague Richard Ryan, distinguished between two broad types of motivation, autonomous and controlled. Autonomous motivations are those that individuals choose willingly, of their own volition, and are grounded in interest, enjoyment, and value. Controlled motivation elicits behavior to gain a reward or avoid a punishment based on external demand or pressure. These two types of human motivation are influenced by the state of an individual's psychological needs. All human beings have a set of basic psychological needs, encompassing competence, relatedness, and autonomy. Individuals whose basic human needs are satisfied will be autonomously motivated.

Much of Deci and Ryan's research has shown the effects of imposing forms of controlled motivation (e.g., monetary incentives) on individuals who are autonomously motivated. At least nine meta-analyses (Deci, Koestner, and Ryan 1999; Cerasoli, Nicklin, and Ford 2014) summarize the consistent findings of this research. One line of explanations is associated with cognitive-evaluation theory. Another line of research has developed around what psychologists have come to call the overjustification effect (Tang and Hall 1995), which describes situations in which individuals' intrinsic motivation in an activity declines because they are induced to engage in that activity as an explicit means to some extrinsic goal. Frey and Osterloh (2005) put the overjustification effect into more common parlance: "doing one's duty without extra pay is not enough."

Motivation-crowding theory (Frey 1997; Frey and Jegen 2001) has a direct relationship to Deci and Ryan's research, and offers an economic theory and interpretation for why extrinsic rewards "crowd out" intrinsic motivation. Patrick Francois (2000), drawing upon a long-running stream of public administration research (Rainey 1982, 1983; Perry and Wise 1990; Denhardt 1993; Rainey and Steinbauer 1999) and recent research in economics (Frey 1997), develops an argument that public organizations can outperform private firms. He argues that public workers driven by public service motivation, i.e., caring about public outcomes they personally value, can be expected to put forth more effort than workers in a private firm, and they will do so more efficiently because they are prepared to perform the work at lower compensation. Thus, the effort they expend is also more efficient, eliminating a need for high-powered incentives. Although an optimal design for financial incentives is hard to specify in general, the evidence suggests compensation systems that offer low-powered incentive pay are most effective for rewarding public service (Burgess and Ratto 2003; Ashraf, Bandiera, and Jack 2014). Nava Ashraf, Oriana Bandiera, and Scott S. Lee (2014) report how even nonmonetary awards incentivized performance in a health worker training program in Zambia. They found that employer recognition and social visibility, two awards consistent with the identification motive in self-determination theory, increased performance while social comparisons, a control-oriented motive, reduced performance, especially among low-ability trainees. Ashraf and colleagues' findings are consistent with prior research by Michael Kosfeld and Susanne Neckermann (2011), which studied the impact of status and social recognition on the performance of a sample of Swiss students in a field experiment.

6.2.5.1 Crowding-out

The most common context in which scholars and practitioners have expressed concern about the phenomenon of crowding-out public service motivation, is the use of contingent pay schemes, like merit pay or pay-for-performance, in public organizations. As argued in the studies above (Frey 1997; Francois 2000; Perry, Engbers, and Jun 2009), extrinsic rewards may be less potent than public-service motivation. Extrinsic rewards may also be less persistent than public service or prosocial motivations (Grant 2008a; Perry, Engbers, and Jun 2009).

Public-sector research that investigates the crowding-out phenomenon is extensive. Among the public-sector studies of crowding-out are

- British higher education and National Health Service – Yannis Georgellis, Elisabetta Iossa, and Vurain Tabvuma (2011);

- Swiss cantons – David Giauque, Simon Anderfuhren-Biget, and Frédéric Varone (2013) found that pay-for-performance negatively influences public-service motivation and concluded, "The current trend in public HRM management, which mainly consists of proposing pay for performance, is not capable of reaching the desired ends, which are, namely, to increase the motivation of civil servants and of organizational performance" (p. 141); and
- Danish school teachers – Christian B. Jacobsen, Johan Hvitved, and Lotte B. Andersen (2014).

At least a couple of cautions about the injunction to avoid performance-related pay, as distinct from performance-sensitive pay adjustments linked to promotions, deserve mention. First, almost all the evidence accumulated about performance-related pay focuses on individual rather than group-, team-, or organization-level incentive systems. The amount of evidence about group incentive plans, such as profit sharing and gain sharing, is limited, even if the scope of research is extended to the private sector. Research in public education offers some examples that school-level incentive systems may trigger supportive interactions among teachers that lead to enhanced teacher performance (Kelley 1999). What may distinguish effective from ineffective school-level programs is that money is a secondary consideration and professional development, playing to the intrinsic rewards that brought teachers to their work in the first place, is paramount. This interpretation is consistent with research in the United States which points to professional development as a powerful incentive and reward (Hawley 1985; Desimone et al. 2002).

The design of incentive systems is likely consequential for their efficacy in the public sector, but other research suggests context is also important. Research syntheses indicate that the effectiveness of incentive pay is related to the type of public service and employees' organizational role. In their synthesis of sixty-eight public-sector studies between 1977 and 2008, James L. Perry, Trent Engbers, and So Yun Jun (2009) suggested that the efficacy of outcomes may vary by public-service industry. Incentives in medical services exhibited the highest success rate. These results contrasted with the regulatory and financial sectors, where performance pay usually failed and was viewed as "divisive" (p. 44). Results for public education and public safety occupied a middle ground between medical services and the regulatory and financial sectors.

A second factor affecting pay incentive efficacy is related to whether covered employees are managers or nonmanagers. Perry, Engbers, and Jun observed that "research on non-managers accounts for a disproportionate share of positive performance results" (p. 44). Although the differences in success rates between nonmanagers and managers were modest, 20 percent compared to 14 percent, Perry et al. suggested the differences may reflect that the job responsibilities of nonmanagerial employees may be more concrete and more measurable.

The volume of research and the elapsed time since the last major research syntheses (Perry, Engbers, and Jun 2009; Hasnain, Manning, and Pierskalla 2014) and meta-analysis (Weibel, Rost, and Osterloh 2010) mean that revisiting research findings about the efficacy of performance-pay incentives in public organizations may be appropriate. Rather than a sector-wide research synthesis, one focused on specific public services, like public education, may be more appropriate. Little more than a decade ago, Michael Podgursky and Matthew Springer (2007) expressed optimism about the probable positive effects of teacher performance pay. Research like that by Karthik Muralidharan and Venkatesh Sundararaman (2011) adds to the views expressed by Podgursky and Springer. Muralidharan and Sundararaman conducted a randomized evaluation using a representative sample of government rural primary schools in Andhra Pradesh, a state in India. After two years, students in incentive schools performed significantly better in math and language tests. The authors report no evidence of adverse consequences. Although this is just one study, it suggests a need for continued experimentation and evaluation.

The research referred to immediately above suggests that designers of public incentive systems must be open to variations in program design, like group-based incentive systems, and how financial incentives are juxtaposed relative to other rewards like professional development that may reinforce public service motivation by strengthening the collective and common-pool culture of the organization. This relates closely to another potential outcome of incentive systems, crowding-in.

6.2.5.2 Crowding-in

Crowding-in public service motivation seems much less common than crowding-out, but the literature offers some suggestive examples.

One is a study of six school districts by David Cohen and Richard Murnane (1985); Murnane and Cohen (1986). Each of the districts had used merit pay for at least six years. Cohen and Murnane found that merit pay programs were most successful when teachers were already performing at a high level. In these schools, it was unclear what value the merit pay program added. One prospect is that merit pay reinforced existing values that supported quality teaching. At the same time, the challenge for principals to make fine distinctions between "exceptional" and "outstanding" teachers led to questioning whether the programs should be sustained. Each district pursued strategies to mitigate these types of conflicts, transforming incentives from high-power to low-power. Among the strategies was providing extra pay for extra work rather than for higher performance, keeping rewards small and distributing them widely, and making participation voluntary.

6.2.5.3 Incentive Design Strategy

Research on incentives and variable pay provides several strategies for maximizing the utility of compensation systems for motivational results in the public sector. Two strategies consistent with this logic are discussed next.

> Strategy 7. When designing incentives, government organizations should emphasize low-powered rather than high-powered incentives.

Recent experimental research, much of it focused on developing countries, points to two primary threats to employee motivation in public services where high-powered incentives are introduced (Banerjee et al. 2014; Finan, Olken, and Pande 2017). These threats have also been documented in developed countries (Perry 1986; Frey 1997; Burgess and Ratto 2003; Perry, Engbers and Jun 2009; Bellé and Cantarelli 2015). One threat is the reduction of prosocial motivation, which has long been identified by social psychologists (Tang and Hall 1995) and, more recently, economists (Frey 1997; Frey and Jegen 2001) as a negative consequence of high-powered financial incentives. Erika Deserranno's (2019) experimental research on new health-promoter positions in Uganda offers an example of potential unintended consequences of high-powered financial incentives. She found that more lucrative positions discouraged agents with strong prosocial preferences from applying for health-promoter positions. Although higher financial incentives increased the probability of filling a vacancy, the signals they sent reduced the ability to recruit the most socially motivated agents, who tended to stay longer and perform better.

The second motivational threat associated with high-powered incentives is an increase in multitasking problems, where employees focus on incentivized tasks rather than on nonincentivized tasks (March and Simon 1958; Perry 1986; Holmstrom and Milgrom 1987). Finan, Olken, and Pande observe that multitasking problems may be especially pronounced in the public sector because of the coupling of coercive powers with the difficulty of measuring outcomes. They write: "While multitasking is an issue in many contexts, it can be particularly severe in public sector contexts where agents wield substantial authority (e.g., police and judges), and it is hard to find an objective measure of the "truth" on which to incentivize them" (p. 471).

These two motivational threats from high-powered incentives, i.e., reduction of prosocial motivation and multitasking, do not take such incentives off the table as a motivational option, but they stand as a strong caution for public organizations considering such options. In their review of experimental studies in developing countries, Finan, Olken, and Pande (2017) frame the caution for public-service leaders considering high-powered incentives:

> The literature has begun to identify some of these tradeoffs, but much more research is needed to better understand in which settings these issues are most likely to arise. For example, task complexity might provide such a setting. The multitasking concerns associated with performance pay are more likely to arise when bureaucrats are tasked with complex jobs. At the same time, complex jobs are more difficult to monitor. Whether the benefits of lower monitoring costs outweigh the costs associated with multitasking is an interesting question with important implications for how bureaucracies should be organized. (p. 508)

Finan et al.'s observation that situations can be discovered where monitoring offsets multitasking problems to make high-powered incentives appropriate and workable is one incentive strategy option for the public sector. Scholars who have studied public-service motivation have arrived at an alternate option for the public sector (Burgess and Ratto 2003; Miller and Whitford 2007; Perry, Engbers and Jun 2009) – relying on low-powered incentives as an alternative superior to high-powered incentives. Low-powered incentives have some immediate advantages. Intrinsic motivation can be sustained in the presence of low-powered incentives (e.g., Stazyk 2013). Low-powered incentives are also more likely to be sustainable in budget-constrained institutions that characterize the public sector (Ashraf, Bandiera, and Jack 2014; Ashraf, Bandiera, and Lee 2014).

> Strategy 8. Government organizations should avoid incentives that crowd out public service motivation, i.e., prosocial, intrinsic, autonomous motivations. Conversely, they should seek opportunities to crowd in prosocial, intrinsic, autonomous motivations.

In some respects, this strategy is a corollary of the preceding strategy. Strategy 7 addresses the incentive side of the motivational equation. Strategy 8 addresses employee motives, focusing on the extent to which employees possess some form of public service motivation along the continuum of controlled to autonomous motivation. Strategy 8 is consistent with self-determination and motivation crowding theories reviewed above and in Chapter 2. Empirical evidence in developing contexts supports Strategy 8. Recent research in developing contexts also supports the strategy. Imran Rasul and Daniel Rogger (2015), for example, conducted an extensive review of project performance in the Nigerian bureaucracy, focusing on variations in management practices across more than 4,000 projects. They found that civil servant autonomy was positively correlated with job performance, but financial incentives and monitoring were negatively correlated with performance. Rasul and Rogger's specific results support general findings (Grindle 1997; McDonnell 2017) that autonomy is associated with unexpectedly high levels of performance in bureaucracies in developing countries where poor performance is the norm and good performance is the exception. These results coincide, too, with the theory and evidence presented in Chapter 5 about autonomy, employee motivation, and performance.

6.2.6 *Position Classification*

An important compensation design issue is how pay is structured to assure consistency and fairness in the allocation of pay across positions and occupations within an organization. In public organizations, this aspect of compensation design has traditionally been associated with position classification, which groups jobs for assigning them to an appropriate pay range. Managers and compensation experts invoke position classification in conversations about many of the concepts in the last two sections, involving questions ranging from wage dispersion, to criteria for entry and movement up the pay line, to incentives. Unfortunately, neither research on compensation in general nor on public service motivation specifically provides clear and strong guidance about behavioral consequences and tradeoffs associated with variations in position classification systems.

The lack of research is surprising in light of the longevity of most government position-classification systems and the extent to which they have been criticized in recent years. Traditional systems have been criticized for job titles and classifications that proliferate to unwieldy levels, rigidity associated with a need to maintain fine distinctions between grades, the inability of organizations and their managers to use them, and the impediments classification poses for both market-based and performance pay (Partnership for Public Service and Grant Thornton 2010; Stier 2011; Partnership for Public Service and The Volcker Alliance 2018).

Given the extensive criticisms of traditional position classification systems, many governments have sought alternatives. The alternative that has received the most attention and scrutiny is paybanding or broadbanding. These changes involve collapsing several pay grades into a smaller number of grades or pay bands with significantly larger pay ranges. No rigorous evaluations have been conducted to assess the effects of broadbanding against organizational or compensation performance criteria, but reports from both practitioners and scholars are mixed. Edwin Arnold and Clyde Scott (2002) analyzed broadbanding in the private sector against a set of criteria to assess compensation systems, among them internal equity, external competitiveness, employee motivation, and ease-of-administration. They concluded, "The impact of broad banding on the achievement of pay system effectiveness may be far more negative than anticipated" (p. 7).

The literature about experiences in public organizations is similarly cautious about embracing broadbanding as a solution to the shortcomings of traditional classification systems, but on the whole may be more positive.[3] Interviews with sixty-eight U.S. federal chief human capital officers and human resource leaders, both political appointees and civil servants, offered a generally positive assessment of broadbanding (Partnership for Public Service and Grant Thornton 2010). The interviewees had a positive view of broadbanding as an alternative to the traditional 15-grade classification system. One reason for the attractiveness of the broadband systems was that managers have greater authority over pay within bands and initial pay for new hires. The sentiments from the sixty-eight interviews coincide with conclusions in a subsequent analysis by James Thompson and Rob Seidner (2009). Among the lessons they draw based on classification demonstration projects dating as far back as the early 1980s are that broadbanding systems benefit employee recruitment and managerial accountability, changes are often not radical, and implementation needs to be carefully managed and monitored.

Cortney Whalen and Mary Guy (2008) examined trends in the American states and discovered that only twelve states had converted fully to a broadband system, four adopted it on a limited basis, eighteen states considered but rejected adoption, and sixteen had not considered it. Based upon a more intensive look at three states, Whalen and Guy concluded that broadbanding did not achieve its promise because it was not accompanied by other, complementary administrative changes, especially providing more budgetary and managerial discretion. Todd Jordan and Paul Battaglio (2014) conducted a systematic review of public personnel reform research across five themes: decentralization, performance-based pay, declassification, deregulation, and privatization. They discovered that only two articles, less than 1 percent of the 238 articles they identified, focused on broadbanding as a central theme, and they were US-based rather than international. Both Jordan and Battaglio (2014) and a subsequent review by Gene Brewer and J. Edward Kellough (2016) concluded that empirical evidence linking personnel reforms with results, particularly with respect to broadbanding, was deficient. Brewer and Kellough (2016) observed: "Even under the best of circumstances, it is not clear that a broad-banding system for job classification will make public organizations more productive" (p. 184). None of the international studies Brewer and Kellough identified in their systematic review addressed broadbanding.

To summarize, research about broadbanding is sparse and provides no clear path about its efficacy as an alternative to traditional position classification. At the same time, research suggests possible benefits from broadbanding – ranging from greater flexibility, to greater managerial control and accountability, to higher employee motivation – that constitute a set of outcomes that might be assessed in future research. Some of the outcomes, like effects on employee motivation, are consequential for research on public service motivation, but no research has yet made any connections between broadbanding and public service motivation.

6.3 Conclusion

This chapter synthesized research on compensation and motivation to identify strategies for designing public-sector compensation systems to optimize outcomes. It looked at four aspects of compensation structure – total compensation, base pay, mobility systems, and incentives – and identified eight strategies that are likely to increase compensation effectiveness and, in turn, motivation and organizational outcomes. Many of the strategies stem from public service motivation research findings, thereby strengthening alignment between research and compensation design.

The strategies presented in this chapter improve public-sector compensation practice in government in several ways. First, strategies align compensation practices with other features of motivation in institutions for which public service, prosocial, other-oriented action is central, creating more internal coherence for overall compensation policies. In aligning compensation practices with public service institutions, the strategies also affirm a principle from the high-performance literature first introduced in Chapter 3: hiring for the organization rather than the job (Bowen, Ledford and Nathan 1991). The benefits of greater coherence and alignment transcend the policies themselves because they produce employee behaviors that sustain organizational effectiveness – greater member attraction and retention, reliable role behavior, and innovative and spontaneous activity.

A second advantage is that the proposed strategies are likely to be perceived as fairer by stakeholders. Although the chapter did not dwell on this facet of the proposed strategies, public-sector compensation in most countries gets attention from a variety of stakeholders, among them public employees and their representatives, businesses, taxpayers, and citizens. In light of the "public" status of public employee compensation, stakeholder preferences about compensation are likely to have consequences for the legitimacy of governance institutions.

Increasing the perceived fairness of public-sector compensation policies and practices is likely to bring positive consequences. The total compensation strategy, for example, is likely to be perceived as fairer in societies where public employees are viewed as either over-compensated or compensated in ways that favor one type of compensation (e.g., pensions) over another (e.g., base pay) (Reilly 2012). The category of stakeholders that is likely to find the proposed strategies least satisfactory may be those who work in what in the United States are called "blue-collar jobs" because their lifetime total compensation may be exceeded by that of their private counterparts (Reilly 2012). The goal of the strategies proposed in this chapter is putting "public service" at the center of employee-organizational exchanges. Achieving the goal may affect stakeholders differently, but the ultimate test of effectiveness of the proposed strategies is restoring the health of public-service institutions.

A third advantage of the proposed strategies is reducing costs and increasing efficiency and effectiveness of public-sector compensation. Aligning public compensation with public service motivation is likely to reduce pressure on budgets and therefore help government organizations live with budget constraints. Of course, projecting reduced costs as an advantage of the proposed strategies assumes their successful implementation, which is not a foregone conclusion.

The strategies in this chapter do not address some key issues important for comprehensive reforms. One is the issue of internal consistency. Most of the strategies presented in the chapter deal with either external competitiveness or employee contribution. Policymakers will need to assess the implications of the strategies for the internal consistency of compensation systems and redesign systems to accommodate changes. One reform of traditional position classification, broadbanding, was discussed in the chapter, but little robust research has investigated the effects of broadbanding and no research has looked at its relationship to public service motivation. A second issue that I did not address is the role of unions and collective bargaining in wage determination. Although collective action is an important influence on wage determination (see, e.g., Krueger and Summers 1988; Zweimüller and Barth 1994), its influence varies across countries, therefore making it difficult to isolate general influences, especially involving public service motivation, for which we have no direct research evidence. Like issues of internal consistency and public service motivation, collective action and public service motivation await more strategic research.

A final, related key issue to which policymakers and public leaders need to give attention is the change process itself. It is likely, in many settings, that employees and their representatives will be involved intimately in the change process. Given the far-reaching consequences of public-sector compensation systems, the change process should probably include stakeholders across the society, incorporating groups in addition to employees and their representatives.

Notes

1 In the *Handbook of Public Administration,* 2nd ed, Charles Pounian and Jeffrey Fuller (1996), consultants for the Hay Group, an organization with a long track record in government compensation, identify nine characteristics of successful compensation policy: (1) a clearly defined philosophy, (2) cultural alignment, (3) the ability to attract excellent candidates, (4) incentives, (5) internal equity, (6) external competitiveness, (7) support for sound administration, (8) clarity, and (9) legal compliance. Although this list of criteria is more comprehensive, Milkovich and Newman's criteria capture the primary compensation effectiveness criteria that are germane to this chapter.

2 Another of the three wage-level indicators is "average government wages as a share of comparator private sector wages" (Clements et al. 2010, 2). This indicator is among the options implied in the discussion of base pay earlier in this chapter. The third wage-level indicator, "average government wage as a share of GDP per capita" (p. 2), also has merit for public jurisdictions assessing their wage levels.

3 In the U.S. federal government, experimentation with alternative position classification systems began in the late 1970s as a result of Title VI of the Civil Service Reform Act of 1978. Subsequent evaluations of alternative systems were unable to arrive at firm conclusions about their efficacy because of limitations in the design and execution of the evaluations. Because of limitations in these evaluations, I do not dwell on them here. For more detail about the early U.S. federal government experience, their evaluation, and optimistic projections about their influence, see Risher and Schay (1994).

7 | Providing Opportunities for Newcomers to Learn Public Service Values

Chapter 3 emphasized the importance of recruiting and attracting staff with high public service motivation. One obvious reason for targeting high public service motivation candidates is the prospect that staff will fit the public organization's mission and values. Even with careful targeting of prospects, however, it is unlikely that all staff who join a public enterprise will arrive steeped in the value propositions associated with their organization's mission and their roles in it. For this and other reasons, therefore, public organizations need programs to integrate and engage staff who either may be newcomers to public service values or merit further orientation to the social setting.

Although transforming new staff – organizational outsiders – to where they are knowledgeable and committed to the public enterprise's core values may be a challenging task, it is achievable. We know from accumulating research that public service motivation is dynamic, changing over time in response to organizational and individual stimuli (Perry 2000; Moynihan and Pandey 2007; Bellé 2013; Oberfield 2014; Pedersen 2015; Vogel and Kroll 2016). We also know a good deal about the socialization process and how organizational members come to learn about their environments, history, and values. Thus, public managers can take heart that prospects for long-term success in establishing a unified culture are feasible.

Socializing staff to public service values is likely to produce several positive consequences for public organizations:

- Creating greater integration of staff and organizational public service values increases member–organization fit, thereby increasing commitment, retention, and work effort.
- Socialization expands prospects that members will act based on their identification with what the organization does and their embrace of its values, increasing the autonomy of member behavior.

- Greater integration increases employee mission valence and ultimately the work effort of employees.

This chapter explores further the dynamics behind these positive consequences and what public organizations can do to achieve them. I begin with a brief review of the logic for socializing employees. Following the discussion of socialization dynamics, two strategies for developing a rich and coherent social milieu are discussed. The first of these strategies is onboarding, which involves an organization's activities to integrate new staff early in their tenure. The second strategy is mentoring, which connects new and continuing members with established members to promote their integration and learning about the organization.

7.1   Rationales for Socializing Employees

The theme of employees adapting to and learning about their organizations after accepting a position is deeply embedded in both organizational behavior and public service motivation theory and empirical research (Brief and Motowidlo 1986; Chatman 1991). The theories and empirical research presented in Chapter 2 make the point. Although the "matching" logic of predisposition-opportunity theory is silent about socialization because the theory focuses primarily on the pre-employment period, socialization is central to attraction–selection–attrition (ASA) theory. Organizations do their best to attract members whose personalities are congruent with the organization's goals, structures, and culture. Mismatches are resolved either by member adaptation to their context or by people leaving the organization. The reliance on socialization is not high, but noticeable. Person-fit theory and research are more open to improved matching through socialization.

7.1.1   Socialization and Organizational Outcomes

The role of socialization for establishing an employee–organization match is prominent in the generic organization behavior literature, too. Jennifer Chatman's (1991) study of the early careers of auditors in eight large US public accounting firms was one of the first to investigate how employee values became congruent with those of the organization. Chatman found that person–organization fit resulted from several mechanisms. Selection, choices made before an individual joins an organization, was one of them. Another was socialization, what happens to an individual after he or she becomes a member of an organization. As a result of the research, Chatman arrived at several generalizations, including that employee fit with the organization's values was a positive result of socialization intensity. She also found that employees whose values were more congruent with the organization's adjusted more quickly and were more satisfied and remained with the organization longer.

Chatman's findings converge with research on organizational commitment. In a study of forty-five firms, David Caldwell, Jennifer Chatman, and Charles O'Reilly (1990) found that normative commitment, which is based on internalization and identification, was facilitated by rigorous recruitment and selection procedures and a clear and strong organizational value system. In earlier research, Bruce Buchanan (1974), studying five public bureaucracies and three private firms, found that social interaction with peers and superiors strengthened peer group cohesion and group attitudes toward the organization.

7.1.2   Socialization and Public Service Motivation Research

The general theoretical orientation to socialization was introduced into research on public service motivation by James L. Perry (2000). Perry's process theory was intended to integrate the macrocontext into motivation theory. A central focus of the theory was the sociohistorical context of public service motivation to facilitate understanding of the environmental variables that shape individual preferences and motives. Among the early sources of socialization are institutions such as the family, churches, and schools (Bandura 1977, 1986; Colby and Damon 1992), whose influences correlate with public service motivation (Perry 1997). Social influences from prework settings are joined later in life by socialization in work settings.

Perry's theory received support from subsequent research on public service motivation. Wouter Vandenabeele (2011) studied more than 3,500 state civil servants in Flanders, Belgium, to investigate whether institutions play a role in the development of public service motivation. Following the general logic set out by Perry (2000), Vandenabeele assessed the role of prominent institutional antecedents – organizations for which one works, family, and political affiliation. He found that "being exposed to public values by coworkers and direct supervisors seems to socialize individuals into internalizing public values themselves, thus engendering a higher degree of public service motivation. Both supervisors and coworkers seem to have an effect on the internalization of public service motivation" (pp. 100–101). Anne Mette Kjeldsen and Christian Bøtcher Jacobsen (2013) and Kjeldsen (2014), in studies of Danish workers, found that postentry shifts in the public service motivation profiles of public employees were influenced by the interplay between work tasks and sector. They concluded a socialization effect existed, but workers' postentry changes were the result of newcomers being affected by the complex interplay between both the task and the sector.

Bradley E. Wright and Sanjay K. Pandey (2008) studied seven US public organizations in two adjacent northeastern states, using survey data collected from managerial and professional employees in 2005. The sample included respondents from four local government organizations and three state government organizations. Based on their study, Wright and Pandey concluded that scholars and practitioners should be cautious regarding claims about the effects of public service motivation because neither higher employee satisfaction nor commitment flows automatically from work in public organizations. Their research suggests a need for continuous attention to employee needs and values, that is, continuous attention to socialization. Among their guidance to leaders and managers is to:

- communicate how the organization's values and goals converge with the employees;
- communicate how the employee's work contributes to the organization and society;
- help employees understand that value conflicts they encounter in their work reflect competing responsibilities of public service; and
- provide rationales for policies so that employees understand them and how they can coexist with performance expectations in their jobs (p. 515).

Leonard Bright's (2016) research involving students in MPA programs also supports relationships between socialization in higher education and public service motivation. Based on a sample of about 500 students in 26 master's degree programs in the United States, Bright concluded that aspects of the degree programs, such as student participation in service learning and characteristics of the professional community and organizations in which students participated were significantly related to public service motivation. Although this is a cross-sectional study of a student population, it affirms the general logic of the effects of socialization on public service motivation and values. Jennifer Waterhouse, Erica French, and Naomi Puchala (2014) studied a small sample of students in Queensland, Australia, who were enrolled as a cohort in a graduate program and transitioning to full-time public service. Their research used a longitudinal, mixed-method design, including surveys and interviews. The results were equivocal about the effects of socialization on public service motivation, indicating both positive and negative influences of socialization.

Empirical research does point to potential negative effects of socializing experiences that may diminish public service motivation over time. Donald Moynihan and Sanjay Pandey (2007) surveyed health and human service managers in the fifty states. Their goal was to test predictions based on Perry's sociohistorical model. Their most surprising finding was that the length of organizational membership was negatively related to public service motivation. Red tape was also negatively related to public service motivation, but this finding was predicted. Moynihan and Pandey interpreted the negative relationships for red tape and tenure, together with positive relationships for hierarchical authority and reform efforts, as strongly supporting the significant influence of organizational institutions. Their findings overall support the sociohistorical model. Public service motivation was also strongly and positively related to the level of education and membership in professional organizations. Moynihan and Pandey concluded that public organizations have both opportunities and responsibility for creating a climate where employees feel they are contributing to the public good.

The initial research about socialization and public service motivation sought to identify empirical relationships, but more recent research has taken a more proactive stance. It poses the question: How might organizational socialization help to bring new employees onboard so they perform well, are integrated into the organization, and committed to the mission and values of the agency? Deneen Hatmaker (2015) presents a case: "Insofar as organizations and institutions can influence public service motivation ..., organizational socialization tactics may be especially timely and effective mechanisms for instilling or increasing newcomers' public service motivation" (p. 1147).

What are the most effective ways for public organizations to create a climate where employees feel they are contributing to the public good? Many of the ideas suggested throughout this book clearly contribute to that goal. Other ideas may be drawn directly from research about organizational socialization (Hatmaker and Park 2014; Hatmaker 2015). A study of state agencies in New York by Deneen Hatmaker and Hyun Hee Park is informative about strategies public organizations might pursue to socialize staff to public values and public service. Their studies link distinct streams of research on organizational socialization and social networks. Their research acknowledges that organizations explicitly intervene to assist newcomers in adapting to their settings, usually through mechanisms like orientation and mentoring. This organization-level perspective, however, is but one lens through which employee socialization can be understood. Hatmaker and Park write, "At the same time, newcomers engage in their own proactive efforts to seek information and establish ties with experienced organizational members who have access to valued resources" (p. 718). They arrive at several conclusions about employee social networks and how they change over time that have implications for what organizations do to socialize newcomers.

Although Hatmaker and Park's findings about social networks are too detailed and complex to summarize here, the implications they draw are straightforward. The most prominent is that public organizations should develop both formal and informal mentoring programs. Their social network analysis suggests that traditional one-to-one mentor–protégé relationships may not be sufficient for newcomer integration. They argue instead for formal mentoring to be augmented by developmental networks (Higgins and Kram 2001) in which multiple mentors, many of which may be informal, provide access to different types of resources and support. Paul O'Neill, who ultimately became the CEO of Alcoa and Secretary of the Treasury, shared a poignant example of the type of informal mentoring envisioned by Deneen Hatmaker and Hyun Hee Park (2014): "When I was very young, working as a construction engineer in Alaska, there was a laborer who was working on the same job where I was doing the engineering. He taught me how to shovel. He was a mentor. Maybe not in the conventional sense, but he was a mentor. He taught me something that was really important to me for 60 years now" (Perry 2017, 132).

Another implication from Hatmaker and Park's (2014) research, an extension of informal, developmental networks, is for public organizations to foster interactions between newcomers and experienced organizational members. Hatmaker and Park acknowledge Moynihan and Pandey's (2007) study as the origin for the idea of creating mechanisms to foster informal social networks. Among the mechanisms Hatmaker and Park identify for fostering informal social networks are special events (e.g., lunch and learn sessions, celebration of group, or individual successes), informal social gatherings, and office designs that encourage interactions. A third implication, more speculative than the other two but worthy of mention here, is rewarding core advisors of newcomers. Core advisors are experienced organizational members who are proximate in an employee's social network, serve as a source of resources, and likely know one another. Core advisors may play central roles in helping employees learn cultural and social aspects of their new job. Hatmaker and Park raise the issue about rewards for core advisors both because of their centrality for an employee's integration, and because their "organic" roles may be overlooked and unrecognized, unlike formal mentors whose contributions may be reviewed by the organization. If Hatmaker and Park's hunch is correct, then explicit attention to core advisors as good organizational citizens may add value for the organization.

7.2 Strategies for Socializing Staff to Public Service

Organizational socialization is the sum of the processes "by which employees learn about and adapt to new jobs, roles, and the culture of the workplace" (Klein and Weaver 2000, 47). The process for new employees typically begins when they are hired, the juncture at which employees may be most eager – and anxious – to learn appropriate behaviors and "fit in" (Cooper-Thomas and Anderson 2002; Cooper-Thomas, Van Vianen, and Anderson 2004; Parkyn 2006). Generic organizational socialization research is extensive and varied, but more attentive to private- than public-sector settings and phenomena. Despite a dominant empirical focus on the private sector, its theoretical content (Van Maanen and Schein 1979; Fisher 1986; Ostroff and Kozlowski 1992; Wanous 1992; Saks and Ashforth 1997) is rich and a number of empirical studies shed light on the phenomena important in the public sector (see, e.g., Buchanan 1974; Van Maanen 1975; Maynard Moody and Musheno 2009).

Two organizational socialization strategies, which surfaced in the research reviewed in the preceding section, are candidates for both instilling and reinforcing public service motivation. Strategically designed onboarding and mentoring programs can go a long way toward integrating newcomers with the public service values that define a public organization.

7.2.1   Designing Onboarding to Align Organizational and Employee Public Service Values

An individual's early experiences in an organization are a critical time for conveying to the individual the organization's identity (Dutton, Dukerich, and Harquail 1994) and framing and reinforcing the psychological contract that binds individuals to their employers. A means used increasingly by organizations for shaping an individual's early experiences is onboarding, which Paarlberg and Lavigna (2010) contend is important for shaping person–organization fit by helping to align an employee's values, skills, and goals with the organization's goals, values, and culture.

Before proceeding down the path of making a case for specific onboarding practices, it is helpful to define what onboarding is. "Onboarding is the process of integrating and acculturating new employees into the organization and providing them with the tools, resources and knowledge to become successful and productive" (Booz Allen Hamilton 2008, 2). Onboarding is distinct from orientation. Orientation has traditionally been associated with activities to which an employee is exposed in the first day or week of work, activities such as meeting the new boss and work associates, completing forms, and learning about benefits. In contrast, onboarding is strategic, longer-term, focused on integrating employees into their new social systems and enhancing their capacity to perform at high levels.

Onboarding has received significant attention in the last decade, as reports from organizations such as the Partnership for Public Service (Booz Allen Hamilton 2008), Society for Human Resource Management (Bauer 2010), and Govloop (2017) attest. Fortunately, the structure and prescriptions of the models are highly consistent. The Partnership for Public Service model for public organizations, developed by Booz Allen Hamilton and widely diffused since 2008 (Lavigna 2009), is summarized in Figure 7.1.

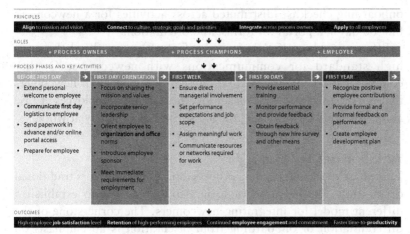

Figure 7.1   Onboarding model. Booz Allen Hamilton (2008). https://ourpublicservice.org/wp-content/uploads/2008/05/c04bbbb3d5c41dfd b39f779dbc8003da-1403634756.pdf, p.6.

7.2.1.1   Before First Day

At one time or another, virtually all of us have experienced an uninspiring first day in a new job. We arrive. We sit around waiting to meet people. We are paraded from office to office to complete routine paperwork. If we arrive with high aspirations, then these experiences can lower our expectations quickly and lead us to begin wondering whether the excitement we brought was misplaced.

Modern technology can alter these traditional patterns. Sending paperwork in advance or giving new employees online portal access can go a long way to remove the routineness and drudgery of uninspiring first days.

Another way technology can begin to integrate newcomers is by conveying clear messages about mission, vision, and values and providing useful resources that employees can access before the first day on the job. The U.S. National Institutes of Health (NIH) offers a useful picture of what can be accomplished with technology. The NIH onboarding webpage, https://hr.nih.gov/working-nih/onboarding, provides a wealth of videos and slides, which use the voices and images of employees to convey to newcomers not only the wide-ranging work NIH does, but also the missions, values, and vision it represents. In addition to videos and slides, the website contains a comprehensive set of links to benefits, community resources, NIH resources, an onboarding checklist (distributed across activities for a newcomer's first 60 days), a portal for forms, and orientation.

Effective onboarding before the first day can also help set a high standard for communications with newcomers. Quality communications before the first day can establish with newcomers that the organization "has its act together" and set employees at ease about the flood of forms and the logistics of the first day at work.

7.2.1.2 First Day/Orientation

This phase of the onboarding process most closely mirrors traditional orientation. At the same time, it also strikes out to establish a different model for integrating newcomers. The cornerstone of the differentiation of onboarding from orientation is an emphasis on sharing the mission and values of the public organization. Orientation has traditionally been transactional. The Booz Allen Hamilton's (2008) report observes, "The most common or consistent onboarding activities agencies use are processing new employee paperwork, explaining employee benefits, and key administrative and security policies" (p. 2). Onboarding strategically attends to mission, values, and organizational culture. The attention given to mission and values in the first days of onboarding reinforces steps discussed elsewhere in this book, especially in Chapters 3, 7, and 8.

By the time the first day or orientation concludes, employees will have passed several key milestones. One milestone important for the newcomer is that they will have met the immediate requirements for their employment. A second milestone is that they will become socially connected to the organization with a sponsor or buddy, typically a peer within the organization, who can help them integrate and understand and navigate the organization's culture. A third milestone is exposure to senior leadership, another important component of the organization's social system. The involvement of senior leaders is important on at least two counts: "Senior leadership involvement sends a clear message that the organization is invested in the new employee. Senior leaders can support the onboarding process by finding ways to communicate and reinforce the mission and values of the organization" (p. 8). The fourth and perhaps most important milestone is that newcomers will be exposed to, and enmeshed in, conversations about the organization's mission, values, and culture.

7.2.1.3   First Week

As the first week of onboarding progresses, the process shifts from transactions-heavy orientation to "real work." The most important focus of the first week following orientation activities is engaging newcomers in meaningful work, a subject addressed at length in Chapter 4. The assignment of meaningful work will also require direct interactions between newcomers and their supervisors around the scope of the newcomer's work and performance expectations.

The first week's emphasis on assigning meaningful work creates opportunities for reinforcing the point with newcomers. Adam Grant (2008b) describes an event that public organizations might stage early in the onboarding process (the first week or month) to engage staff around expectations for employee behavior tied to mission and public service values.

> ... several students and I developed a pilot program to introduce police officers to stories about their departments making a difference in the community. Through the news media and our personal networks, we tracked down several local citizens who were grateful for the work that officers had performed. We asked the citizens to write stories about how the department's efforts had made a difference in their lives. We then shared the stories with officers and asked them to describe their reactions. One detective explained, "This experience made me realize how rare positive feedback is in this profession. We never hear from citizens who appreciate what we do. It seems that this would be good for officer morale and mental health". (p. 59)

An event of the kind described by Grant creates not only an opportunity for newcomers to hear about the good their work brings to the community but also provides a setting in which newcomers come together with long-term employees.

7.2.1.4   First Ninety Days

This is the period during which employees and their supervisors begin to develop routines so it is important for the newcomer–organization exchanges to establish positive patterns going forward. New employees should be receiving the training and resources to become effective organizational contributors. Supervisors should simultaneously be checking that the work of new employees is challenging and job demands are reaching full capacity. Frequent feedback and coaching should go hand-in-hand with managers' monitoring of newcomer performance. Thus, job challenge, development, coaching, and feedback are important elements of integrating newcomers so they become productive and committed members of their new social community.

7.2.1.5 First Year

In some respects, this period between a newcomer's first ninety days and the end of the first year of employment is an extension of routines and patterns established in the preceding period. Most employees will still be in the midst of their probationary periods so this is an important time to assess performance, build competencies and fill skills gaps, and assess employees' readiness for the next phase of their organizational careers. Formal performance reviews at the six-month and one-year mark should be part of this process. An integral element of the formal performance reviews is creating an employee development plan, which supports a continuous learning philosophy consistent with the ideas presented in Chapter 5.

Although goal setting, monitoring, and employee development are critical at the early stages of onboarding, managers need to be mindful of giving appropriate recognition as newcomers' contributions evolve and increase. Positive employee contributions deserve recognition for a variety of reasons, foremost among them that the recognition reinforces desired behavior. The organization's attention to recognition could include a congratulatory communication from a senior executive on the newcomer's anniversary. Depending on the number of newcomers to the organization, a group celebration of their success and passage to a new phase of their careers may be an effective way to reciprocate their commitment to the organization.

7.2.1.6 Roles and Responsibilities

As is evident from the tasks described above and displayed in Figure 7.1, effective onboarding requires organizations to identify and assign roles and responsibilities so the process functions as designed. Although multiple organizational units are process owners, the human resources or human capital office bears the greatest responsibility from beginning to end. Human resources is responsible for conceptualizing, planning, and coordinating onboarding. The information technology office is responsible for developing specialized onboarding software and websites, as well as supporting the technology needs of newcomers. Other units like physical plant or facilities may play similarly specialized roles. Coordination and accountability of the various roles falls to human resources.

A second key cluster of roles is process champions, who are the organization's human interface responsible for motivating newcomers and helping them to understand how their jobs support fulfillment of the agency's mission. Process champions – especially senior leadership, managers, and supervisors – animate the onboarding process through their interaction and communication with new employees. Although a new employee's manager or supervisor works within the onboarding process conceptualized and coordinated by human resources, the manager may play the single most critical role for newcomers because they are central to so many first-year activities, ranging from welcoming new employees, to communicating job responsibilities, to assigning meaningful work, to monitoring performance, and providing feedback.

The onboarding process and the roles and responsibilities embedded within it are directed to achieving high-quality outcomes for the organization – high employee job satisfaction, retention of high performers, employee engagement and commitment, and a faster time to productivity. The mediating factors for achieving these outcomes are several processes that are simultaneously integral to the onboarding process and the organization's broader interest in enhancing public service motivation. Aligning employees to the organization's mission and vision, connecting them to culture and strategic priorities, and integrating employees fully with the organization's public service ethos are integral to the onboarding process and to facilitating public service motivation (Box 7.1).

7.2.2   *Create Mentoring Partnerships to Share and Reinforce Public Service Values*

Earlier in this chapter I pointed to Hatmaker and Park's (2014) findings about social networks, which endorsed mentoring as a mechanism to enhance member socialization to organizations. What evidence do we have about the efficacy of mentoring, both in general and in public organizations, that supports embracing mentoring to reinforce public service values? The generic evidence about mentoring is extensive and

---

Box 7.1 Best practices for onboarding

✓ Implement the basics prior to the first day on the job.
✓ Make the first day on the job special.
✓ Use formal orientation programs.
✓ Develop a written onboarding plan.
✓ Make onboarding participatory.
✓ Be sure your program is consistently implemented.
✓ Ensure that the program is monitored over time.
✓ Use technology to facilitate the process.
✓ Use milestones, such as 30, 60, 90, and 120 days on the job – and up to one year post-organizational entry – to check in on employee progress.
✓ Engage stakeholders in planning.
✓ Include key stakeholder meetings as part of the program.
✓ Be crystal clear with new employees in terms of:
  • Objectives
  • Timelines
  • Roles
  • Responsibilities.

Source: Tayla N. Bauer (2010).

---

includes several meta-analyses that support its efficacy. One of the questions assessed in the meta-analyses is the effect size. The meta-analyses consistently conclude effect sizes are significant, but vary from small to large. Two meta-analyses (Allen et al. 2004; Eby et al. 2008) concluded that effect sizes were generally small, but workplace mentoring produced larger effect sizes than youth mentoring. A third meta-analysis (Underhill 2006) concluded the overall mean effect size was significant. Thus, three meta-analyses concurred about the general efficacy of mentoring.

The effects of mentoring have been studied with respect to a variety of outcomes, including behavioral, attitudinal, relational, motivational, and career outcomes (compensation, career satisfaction). The general effect sizes reported above hold across these outcomes. Like Hatmaker and Park (2014), Christina M. Underhill's (2006) meta-analysis concluded that informal mentoring produced larger and more significant effects on career outcomes than formal mentoring, thereby calling attention to the need for organizations to design formal and informal mentoring into their policies. Another revealing finding from the meta-analyses is that mentors also derive benefits from mentoring. Rajashi Ghosh and Thomas G. Reio (2013) conducted a meta-analysis that examined five types of subjective career outcomes for mentors: job satisfaction, organizational commitment, turnover intent, job performance, and career success. Mentors were more satisfied with their jobs and more committed to their organizations than nonmentors. Thus, mentoring provides reciprocal benefits and is not simply beneficial for protégés.

Mentoring research in the public sector is sparse compared to the private sector (Bozeman and Feeney 2009a, 2009b), but findings are consistent across sectors and several studies touch upon connections between mentoring and public service motivation. Lisa Ehrich and Brian Hansford (2008) identified twenty-five research-based papers published between 1991 and 2006 about outcomes of formalized mentoring programs for public sector workers. Based on their review of the twenty-five published items, Ehrich and Hansford reported that the majority of programs reported on outcomes for leaders. Reported positive outcomes far exceeded negative outcomes. The most common positive outcome in the studies was improved culture and communication. The most common negative outcomes were all related to sustaining the mentoring program itself – maintaining and attracting mentors and funding.

In two related articles, Barry Bozeman and Mark K. Feeney (2009a, 2009b) set out a general model of what affects mentoring outcomes in public organizations. At the center of their model is social capital, which they define as "the aggregation of networks of highly institutionalized and less formal relationships and acquaintances" (Bozeman and Feeney 2009b, 429). Their thesis is that development of social capital through mentoring is the result of individual investment and participations in relationships. Protégés reap social capital to the extent that their mentors introduce them to internal and external networks rich in social capital. In a subsequent article, Bozeman and Feeney integrate their social capital logic for mentoring (2009b) with a three-tier model in which public service motivation plays a key role (2009a). The first of the three tiers emphasizes mentoring to improve employees' capacity to manage the procedural complexity of government services, essentially intervening to improve human capital through the organization's social system. The first tier is instrumental for enhancing human capital and simultaneously fulfilling an individual's basic psychological need for competence (Deci and Ryan 2000). The second tier involves providing opportunities for underrepresented groups in government services. The second tier of the model recognizes that mentoring helps to advance women and minorities. The third tier of the mentoring model involves enhancing public service motivation, largely as an outgrowth of the preceding steps. Public service motivation, as an outcome of mentoring, becomes, in turn, a mediating factor for producing salient individual and organizational outcomes – job satisfaction, organizational commitment, high performance, and reliable role behavior. Bozeman and Feeney's first study provided evidence "that a broad array of public sector commitment variables was positively related to such mentoring outcome variables as satisfaction with mentoring, career advancement, and propensity for the protégé to become a mentor" (Bozeman and Feeney 2009a, 151). Their literature review, theory, and analysis led Bozeman and Feeney (2009a) to conclude, "When mentoring is an important element of the work environment, it follows that mentoring processes might well have the effect of promoting and reinforcing PSM [public service motivation] (or perhaps in the case of ineffective mentoring, suppressing it)" (p. 151).

One recent study in Korea that links mentoring to public service motivation carries some irony. Geon Lee and Do Lim Choi (2016) found that neither public service motivation nor prosocial motivation was associated with public-sector choice, contrary to their hypotheses. They offered two plausible explanations for their unexpected results. One is that high performance on the civil service qualification exam, the gosi, is so socially prestigious that doing well on the exam is itself sufficient to motivate candidates to accept government work regardless of how well aligned their predispositions are with working for government. The other explanation is that residual concerns about economic stability dating back to the 1997 Asian currency crisis have produced widespread social risk aversion, leading many university students to take the gosi and pursue careers in government, again regardless of their public or prosocial motivations. The remedy Lee and Choi (2016) propose to overcome the lower than expected public service motivation among incoming government workers is mentoring. Their view is that mentoring would help imbue employees with the organization's underlying values.

7.2.2.1 Effective Mentoring Programs for Enhancing Public Service Motivation

It is worth beginning this section with a caution. Bozeman and Feeney (2009b) remind us that the design and execution of a mentoring program is vital, "The tendency to simply assume that 'mentoring is good' and to give little thought to the particulars needs redress" (p. 444). Rather than "assuming" the value added by mentoring will automatically generate success, organizations and their leaders need to attend to ten well-known best practices (Chronus 2019), as summarized in Box 7.2.

1. *Define Your Mentoring Program Objectives and Secure Leadership Support.* Successful mentoring programs require the attention and commitment of large numbers of organizational leaders. The building blocks for such an effort must be in place, and starting with clear objectives and leadership support are vital foundations for a sustainable program.
2. *Find a Strong, Passionate Mentoring Program Manager.* Program managers are the glue and energy for thriving mentoring programs. They help broker productive relationships between mentors and protégés. They can identify opportunities and troubleshoot issues. Their role is continuously to bring the attention of busy participants and managers to the value added from effective mentoring.

Box 7.2 Mentoring program best practices

1. Define Your Mentoring Program Objectives and Secure Leadership Support
2. Find a Strong, Passionate Mentoring Program Manager
3. Build Flexibility into the Program
4. Put Your Marketing Hat On
5. Think Win-Win
6. Use Mentoring Program Best Practices to Prepare Mentors and Mentees for Success
7. Embrace the Role of Mentoring Matchmaker
8. Track, Measure, Listen & Tune
9. Bring Closure to Individual Mentoring Connections
10. Broadcast Mentoring Successes

Source: Chronus (2019).

---

3. **Build Flexibility into the Program.** Flexibility is vital for a variety of reasons. Foremost among them is variability among participants whose goals and learning styles will vary. In addition to a need for flexibility to accommodate participant variability is the fact that participants will need a variety of mentors playing different roles. Formal arrangements may be the core of a mentoring program, but a robust program will benefit from many informal contributors across the organization (Higgins and Kram 2001; Hatmaker and Park 2014). Thus, it is important to build flexibility into the program.

4. **Put Your Marketing Hat On.** Buy-in from senior executives and program leaders does not assure concerted effort across the organization. Stakeholders need to understand the benefits of the program, its strategic value for the organization, and how different organizational members can contribute.

5. **Think Win-Win.** As noted earlier in this chapter, mentoring provides reciprocal benefits and is not simply beneficial for protégés (Ghosh and Reio 2013). Leadership should seek ways to design benefits for both mentors and protégés into the program. Recognition of mentors should be one of the benefits for mentors.

6. **Use Mentoring Program Best Practices to Prepare Mentors and Mentees for Success.** This best practice returns us to the admonition above not to "assume" the goodness of the program assures its success. Mentors and protégés need to be trained for their roles and the program's goals in light of the organization's mission. Developing a professional community around learning about one another and public service values is a by-product of the training. Regular communications about best practices will help participants stay on track and maximize the program's value.

7. **Embrace the Role of Mentoring Matchmaker.** The quality of the relationship between mentor and protégé is critical for program success. Achieving a quality relationship requires input from both protégés and prospective mentors to meet their needs. This means that protégés and mentors should be given choices for a match. Protégés should also have opportunities to designate additional mentors for specific needs associated with their development and learning plans. The mentoring program manager should take the lead in securing appropriate technology support to facilitate matchmaking and tracking.

8. ***Track, Measure, Listen, & Tune.*** The program objectives that are the foundation for the program need to come into play regularly and routinely to track its outcomes. This process can be advanced by creating a logic model at the outset that articulates the causal chain behind program outcomes and success. Tracking and measuring results can be facilitated by regular surveys of participants and technology that simplifies monitoring and input.

9. ***Bring Closure to Individual Mentoring Connections.*** Mentoring relationships are not intended to be permanent (but they may promote career- and life-long relationships outside the mentoring partnership). Knowing when to close them out, however, may be less obvious. Circumstances surrounding a particular mentor–protégé pairing – for example, via retirements or promotions – may bring it to a close. But the achievement of other milestones or tangible outcomes may be junctures for closure. Protégé progress on individual development plans or plans tied to the performance appraisal process can provide other indicators that signal time for closure. Both the mentor and protégé should have input.

10. ***Broadcast Mentoring Successes.*** Celebrating success is valuable for both signaling the value of the program and inviting organizational members on the sidelines to participate. Recognizing participant contributions and celebrating successes will help to sustain the program, expand participation, and increase support.

These ten best practices collectively convey an important message about the role of mentoring in organizations. The message is that mentoring is a shared responsibility across an organization that must be well managed and needs attention from many actors – leaders, mentors, mentees, and the mentoring program manager.

In some settings, especially poor urban communities in the developed world and developing countries, mentoring may play an even larger role than in organizations in mainstream settings. India, for example, has a massive youth population that is potentially a great economic resource, but their lack of social connectedness positions them as a future burden rather than as an asset. Poor urban youth often need help identifying their interests and aptitudes before embarking on suitable career paths or they risk preparing for careers that are not viable when they acquire their skills. Carlin Carr (2013) describes the situation in India where large numbers of 28–32-year-olds now experience large-scale unemployment and alienation because they pursued careers in the information technology labor market that boomed years earlier. Carr shares the story (see Box 7.3) of how one of the young people, Shraddha, used a youth mentorship program both to get in touch with her own interests and aptitudes and to develop skills to become a police sub-inspector. Similar youth-mentoring programs are expanding in Europe as the result of a recent influx of refugees (Rhodes, Prieto-Flores and Preston 2017).

7.3 Conclusion

Public organizations have a continuous need for newcomers and current members to learn about the organization's ideology, its culture and values, and its mission. Although it would be desirable for all members to come steeped in the organization's history, ethos, and value propositions, expectations that everyone will come and remain a perfect fit with the organization are unreasonable. Organizations instead need to engage in socializing their members either because members arrive with a need to learn more about their new environment or because the environment itself may be changing and members need to adapt. Regardless of the reasons behind needs to socialize either newcomers or veterans, many employees will be more effective if they learn more about the social system of which they are part.

This chapter has focused on two primary strategies that organizations use to facilitate employee learning. Strategies discussed in other chapters, like career counseling in Chapter 4 and performance management in Chapter 5, are important influences on employee learning. This chapter added two more strategies to the mix of ways to facilitate employee learning. The two strategies are onboarding and mentoring, which are critical levers for public organizations to advance the socialization of their employees.

Onboarding is a process for strategically integrating new employees into the organization and giving them the capacity to become successful. As presented in this chapter, onboarding is a yearlong process that stretches from prior to a newcomer's first day of work to the conclusion of their first year as an organization member. Onboarding is a comprehensive process that focuses a public organization's process owners and champions on many of the strategies discussed in this book during an employee's first year. Strategies like assigning newcomers

Box 7.3 Urban youth mentoring to realize India's demographic dividend

The Promise Foundation focuses on a more "human-centred" approach that helps individuals identify interests and aptitudes and then consider suitable career paths. Skills training without the proper guidance toward career prospects and options, says Arulmani, is sure to be a short-term fix. India's youth are largely from impoverished backgrounds and often demonstrate a near-sighted view of the future. Their choices are mainly driven by a need for immediate earning but they are on a path toward chronic unemployment or under-employment. Restlessness in their dead-end situations has grave risks for a country riding on their youthful spirit and potential.

Altering the choices of India's disadvantaged youth also requires an expansion of their social networks. Their communities have few role models who can guide the next generation with professional advice. Mentorship has been a part of urban youth community programmes around the world for nearly a century, but is a fairly new intervention with children and youth in India. When Arundhuti Gupta launched Mentor Together in 2009, there were only a couple similar programmes in the country.

Mentors are required to undergo training and commit to one year of regular meetings with their mentee. Moreover, the mentor's focus is on being a nurturing presence – a stark contrast, says Gupta, to the traditional thinking that "hard skills and cognitive growth are the only important determinants of life quality and outcomes." Their formula has proven beneficial to students like Shraddha, who is in the 10th standard, and came to Mentor Together with very little direction for her future. Shraddha lost her father, and her mother lives away from her to work in the fields, so the young girl lives in a shelter home near Pune. She was matched with Swati, who volunteered to be a mentor out of a love for teaching and children. Shraddha says that her mentor, whom she affectionately calls "didi," has been discussing with her many different career options, but she decided on a police sub-inspector. Together, the pair drafted a plan, and Shraddha has enrolled herself in appropriate science and English courses to reach her college and career goals. Shraddha is one of more than 350 mentees who have been matched with a one-on-one mentor in the organization's three target cities of Bangalore, Mysore and Pune.

Source: Carr (2013).

meaningful work and connecting performance management to public service are prominent during the onboarding process. Thus, onboarding plays an out-sized role in newcomers' learning about public service values and reinforcing public service motivation.

Mentoring involves one or more relationships between experienced and less experienced organizational members to promote learning about the organization and its values. Mentoring relations may be both formal and informal. They permit newcomers to observe their coworkers and supervisors, get advice from established organizational members, and receive important cues about organizational values and expectations (Ostroff and Kozlowksi 1992; Saks and Ashforth 1997).

8 | Leading with Mission, Inspiration, and Communication

As Chapter 7 illustrated, many formal mechanisms – among them onboarding, mentoring, and performance management – are available to socialize employees in ways that draw out their public service motivation. This chapter looks at one group of employees in public organizations that has special obligations for positioning an organization to attract, nurture, and socialize employees to optimize public service motivation – their leaders.

Developing leaders who communicate and model public service values is likely to produce several positive consequences for public organizations:

- Leader stimulation of awareness and acceptance of organizational missions increases levels of autonomous motivation, specifically identification and integration, which is more powerful and persistent.
- When employees pursue goals beyond self-interest, the goals are likely to be perceived as more difficult.
- Employees are likely to be more committed to goals associated with public missions and values.

Let me begin with an example of a public leader to illustrate some ideas that surface in this chapter. The leader is Paul H. O'Neill. O'Neill had a modest start in life. He is the son of a military officer. His first job after receiving an economics degree from Fresno State was as a computer systems analyst with the Veterans Administration from 1961 to 1966. He subsequently received a master's degree in public administration and returned in 1967 to the Federal Bureau of the Budget, which was soon to become the Office of Management and Budget (OMB). He had the good fortune of receiving mentoring from George Shultz at OMB, where he was Deputy Director from 1974 to 1977. He left government for the corporate sector at the end of the Ford Administration. During the next quarter century, he was Vice

President and President of International Paper from 1977 to 1987 and Chairman and CEO of Alcoa from 1987 until his retirement in 1999. He served as U.S. Secretary of the Treasury under President George W. Bush in 2001–2002. Since 1997, when he cofounded the Pittsburgh Regional Health Initiative, he has given significant attention to issues of patient safety and quality in health care. In 2019, he received the Gerald R. Ford Award for Distinguished Public Service.

Paul O'Neill's (2012) leadership philosophy is simple and, upon first encounter, seemingly unique. His view is that leaders are responsible for establishing conditions that permit the organization to be great. He describes the conditions in the form of three questions.[1] He writes, "If a leader produces the possibility for an organization to be truly great, then the people in the organization can say yes to three questions every day" (p. 11). Note that he frames the questions from the perspective of *followers* of what he calls "real leaders," not the leader. This is one feature of O'Neill's philosophy, but it places him squarely within the scope of what is described later in this chapter as transformational and servant leadership.

O'Neill's first question is: "Am I treated with dignity and respect every day by everyone I encounter?" (p. 11). This question implicitly makes a statement about the tenor of relations among everyone in an organization. It addresses important human aspirations – dignity and respect – and it suggests that great organizations are those whose leaders seek to have these aspirations satisfied for everyone in the organization. Reaching for dignity and respect is a high bar, but the standard surfaces frequently in this chapter. O'Neill is clear that organizations often fall short of the standard. He writes, "In hospital settings, where I spend a lot of time these days, I do not believe you can find a place where the people who clean the rooms are accorded the same dignity and respect as surgeons, even though the people who clean the rooms are arguably as important as the surgeon who wields the knife" (p. 11).

O'Neill's poses a second, equally pointed question: "Am I given the things I need – education, training, encouragement, tools, financial resources – so that I can make a contribution to the organization that gives meaning to my life?" O'Neill asks this question to call attention to the meaningfulness of work more so than transactions surrounding job resources. "Quite a few places provide all of the necessary tools, equipment, and encouragement so that you can make a contribution,"

O'Neill writes, "but not a lot of organizations set out to systematically create conditions so that people can say without hesitation, 'What I do here gives meaning to my life.'" Chapter 4 introduced the importance of the meaningfulness of work. O'Neill's questions bring us back to the concept, which he deems a fundamental responsibility for leaders.

The third question is: "Am I recognized for what I do?" (p. 11). This question may be the simplest of the three, but it still requires a "yes" from employees.

O'Neill views the role of leaders as aspiring to create the conditions – and take away excuses – that enable affirmative answers to the questions he poses. During his years at Alcoa, O'Neill aspired to an injury-free workplace to show workers across the organization that people were the organization's most important asset. The aspiration was not symbolic, but real. The goal of an injury-free workplace was O'Neill's way of making real to employees that they really were the organization's most importance resource. He supported the aspiration with action (Perry 2017):

> I believed that a truly great organization would organize and conduct itself in such a way that people who worked there never got hurt at work. Then I set out to achieve it in many important ways, knowing and recognizing that cheerleading is not an effective way to actually accomplish anything. I deliberately worked from the day I got there to create a value culture and make all aspects of the value structure true for everyone. This began with the idea that people will not be hurt here and taking actions like declaring "we will not budget for safety". (p. 133)

O'Neill's record as a leader offers many examples where he took chances and charted a course less traveled. His career serves as one example of the types of tools leaders committed to mission and values draw upon: putting followers first, focusing on an ultimate goal, attending to core values, and elevating the meaningfulness of work. We now look at systematic strategies and tactics that leaders can use to make a difference and theory that explains why they work.

8.1 How Leaders Make a Difference: Theoretical Foundations

Leadership theories and research are among the most abundant in the social and behavioral sciences (Fernandez, Cho, and Perry 2010). I am therefore selective in what I draw upon here, limiting attention to leadership theories that either have received attention in research about public service motivation or have a plausible relationship to public service motivation theory.

8.1.1   Transformational Leaders as Visionaries

The most prominent leadership theory that supports the development of public service motivation is transformational leadership. Transformational leadership has its foundations in the research of historian James MacGregor Burns (1978), whose studies of American presidents revealed an important difference in how presidents stimulated action. Some presidents developed transactional relationships with their staff and supporters. The transactions involved deftness at winning legislative battles, using administrative appointments to motivate ambitious staff, and distributions of perks to stakeholders. Lyndon Johnson, for example, was known for his transactional acumen in winning in both the legislature and executive. Another group of presidents, among them Franklin Roosevelt and John Kennedy, used a different set of tools, which engaged the values and aspirations of their followers. This approach has become transformational leadership.

Bernard Bass (1990) clearly ties the dynamics of transformational leadership to the common understanding of public service motivation in his description of the construct:

> Superior leadership performance – transformational leadership – occurs when leaders broaden and elevate the interests of their employees, when they generate awareness and acceptance of the purposes and mission of the group, and when they stir their employees to look beyond their own self-interest for the good of the group. (p. 21)

The idea of stirring employees "to look beyond their own self-interest" is consistent with the other orientation associated with public service motivation. In the context of the public sector, where public interests and public good reside institutionally, "awareness and acceptance of the purposes and mission" also tie directly to public service motivation. Thus, transformational leadership, both in its origins and consequences, resonates with motivational imperatives in the public sector.

Leadership scholars identify several levers by which leaders stimulate, that is, transform, followers. Four distinctive levers of transformational leadership are

- *Idealized influence* envisions the leader as a role model, adhering to his or her espoused principles and acting ethically and with integrity.
- *Inspirational motivation* is the leader's ability to inspire confidence and a sense of purpose in followers. Articulating a clear vision and expressing commitment, optimism, and positivity are behaviors that help instill confidence and purpose.
- *Intellectual stimulation* rests on leaders challenging followers to be innovative and creative, to use their intellects in pursuit of high performance.
- *Individualized consideration*, which reflects that the leader interacts with followers not only as members of a team but also as individuals with their own gifts that must be celebrated and nurtured. Leaders customize their personal attention to the needs, desires, and developmental opportunities of each follower.

8.1.2 Transformational Leaders as Architects

Andrew Carton (2018) recently proposed an extension of the theory by suggesting that leaders may make a difference for their followers by behaving as architects rather than transformational visionaries. By architects, Carton means motivating employees "when they create a cognitive blueprint composed of a small and streamlined constellation of connections that link everyday work and the organization's ultimate aspirations and then allow employees to mentally assemble more elaborate connections around that core structure" (p. 352). Carton's reason for shifting the focus of the motivational process from inspirational to structural rhetoric rests with a paradox he identified:

> … the very properties that make ultimate aspirations meaningful are those that leave employees unable to sense how their daily responsibilities are associated with them. Employees are likely to perceive the organization's ultimate aspirations as more significant than the time-constrained goals they work toward each day – yet also severely disconnected from them. (p. 325)

The foundation for Carton's research is the anecdote introduced in Chapter 4 – a conversation between President John F. Kennedy and a janitor at Cape Canaveral. In arriving at his architect analogy, Carton drew upon archival analysis of rich descriptions of the National

Aeronautics and Space Administration (NASA)'s efforts to land a man on the moon following President Kennedy's bold call for a lunar landing before the end of the 1960s in a speech to Congress on May 25, 1961. Carton describes the transformation in terms of four leader sensegiving actions, which he defines as "a discursive tactic in which leaders outline the relationships between daily work and NASA's intermediate goals, objectives, and ultimate aspirations" (p. 335). He associates each of four sensegiving actions to President Kennedy:

1. "Kennedy reduced the number of NASA's ultimate aspirations to one" (p. 335).
2. "Kennedy shifted attention from NASA's ultimate aspiration to a concrete organizational objective" (p. 336)
3. "Kennedy communicated milestones connecting employees' day-to-day work to the concrete objective" (p. 337).
4. "Kennedy used embodied concepts to affix NASA's ultimate aspiration to the concrete objective" (p. 338).

Carton's architect analogy is more work-focused, that is, meaningfulness in the job and how to stimulate meaningfulness, than Burns' articulation of transformational leadership. Carton attributes initiation of his sensegiving actions to the person at the very pinnacle of the federal executive. Bass and others associated with transformational leadership as inspiration look not only to the person at the top of the hierarchy for inspiration in making a prosocial difference but also to others in the hierarchy and organizational ends themselves as the context for motivation. Regardless of whether the transformational leadership model emphasizes inspiration or architecture, what is ultimately important is the difference a follower can make for the society. Carton emphasizes the potential for leader contributions that magnify or complement natural processes where employees themselves complete the motivational equation.

8.1.3 Empirical Research about Transformational Leadership and Public Service and Prosocial Motivation

The theory of transformational leadership receives strong support in research assessing its validity with respect to dynamics associated with public service and prosocial motivation. In two articles involving five different studies, including a government and a university sample, Adam

Grant and David Hofmann (2011) and Adam Grant (2012) investigated relationships among transformational leadership, beneficiary contact, prosocial impact, and performance. One purpose of the research was to test what difference the source of an inspirational message had on followers. Although a leader's ideological message is intended to inspire follower performance, Grant and Hofmann argued that this is not always the case, and failures to inspire employee performance may be a consequence of suspicion surrounding the leader's motives. Thus, the research tested whether beneficiary contact could be a substitute for a leader's ideological message. Another purpose was to test the influence of beneficiary contact, an issue that was addressed in Chapter 4. A general thesis in all the studies was that transformational leadership has more influence on followers who work with beneficiaries because the beneficiary contact reinforces prosocial impact.

Nicola Bellé (2014) replicated Grant's research with a sample of 138 nurses from a public hospital in Italy. He used a randomized experimental research design to assess whether beneficiary contact and self-persuasion interventions enhanced the influence of transformational leadership. Although a treatment group exposed only to a transformational leadership manipulation performed marginally better than a control group, the beneficiary contact and self-persuasion interventions significantly elevated the performance effects of transformational leadership. Follower perceptions of prosocial impact partially mediated the relationships. The transformational leadership effects were greater for participants who self-reported higher levels of public service motivation.

A number of nonexperimental studies shed light on various facets of transformational leadership and public service motivation. Lars Tummers and Eva Knies (2013) investigated the relationship between leadership and the meaningfulness of work, an idea we first encountered in Chapter 4. Tummers and Knies surveyed public employees in three different service sectors in the Netherlands. The services were education, health care (midwives), and municipal government. Sample sizes ranged from 229 municipal and 313 education employees to 790 midwives. The theoretical lens they used was leader-member exchange theory, which Tummers and Knies identify as a relationship-based model of leadership emphasizing social interactions. They contrast this model with transactional and transformational leadership, which they categorize as leader focused. Although they distinguish among the leadership theories, the paths through which leader-member exchange influences employee meaningfulness of work are shared with other leadership theories. They include employees' psychological empowerment, their perceptions of job characteristics, and their work engagement. Tummers and Knies found that leader-member exchanges mediated the influence of the meaningfulness of work on organizational commitment, work effort, and work-to-family enrichment. The relationships were stronger for education and health care, but the research sustained the general relationship among leadership, work meaningfulness, and work outcomes.

Wouter Vandenabeele (2014) investigated a particular type of transformational leadership, promoting public values, with a large sample of state civil servants in Belgium. This research on promoting public values is directly related to research on organizational ideology. Vandenabeele concluded that leader attempts to inspire followers did indeed influence the public service motivation of followers. The relationship between leader promotion of public values and follower public service motivation was moderated by follower satisfaction with basic psychological needs, specifically autonomy and competence (see the discussion in Chapter 5 for more about the role of basic needs from self-determination theory and a supportive work environment for public service motivation).

In related research on the influence of public values, Julie Alsøe Krogsgaard, Pernille Thomsen, and Lotte Bøgh Andersen (2014) studied whether value conflicts moderated the positive associations between transformational leadership and public service motivation. Using a mixed-methods design, they surveyed a sample of employees of Danish universities preparing students for public service-oriented careers as teachers, nurses, and social workers. A survey of 968 employees, coupled with qualitative interviews, found that the relationship between the direct manager's level of transformational leadership and employees' public service motivation was more positive when value conflicts were lower. They concluded that transformational leadership may enhance follower public service motivation, but only under conditions where there is no severe value conflict.

A subsequent qualitative study in Denmark by Lotte Bøgh Andersen et al. (2018) looked at both the overall motivational logic of transformational leadership and how it affected different types of public service motivation. They found that when leaders work to clarify an organization's vision, share it with followers, and sustain it over time, employee motivations to serve society and others are strengthened. Their interviews also revealed that followers influenced by transformational leadership were less paternalistic, that is, more deferential to "good" as specified by politicians and beneficiaries than as defined by them (LeGrand 2010; Andersen, Pallesen, and Salomonsen 2013; Jensen and Andersen 2015).

Babette Bronkhorst, Bram Steijn, and Brenda Vermeeren (2015) studied employees in a Dutch municipality to assess the general relationship between transformational leadership and work motivation, which they defined as work effort and its persistence. They found both direct and indirect effects of transformational leadership. The indirect effects involved goal setting and procedural constraints. Transformational leaders set more challenging and more specific goals, which produced greater work motivation. Transformational leadership also led to reductions in perceived procedural constraints among their followers. Thus, transformational leadership directly and indirectly improved motivational outcomes.

The research by Bronkhorst et al. sheds light on two of the three motivational outcomes important for organizational effectiveness identified in Chapter 2. The third of these motivational outcomes – membership – is the object of research by Sung Min Park and Hal Rainey (2008) and Tobin Im, Jesse Campbell, and Jisu Jeong (2016). Park and Rainey (2008) analyzed responses of 6,900 U.S. federal employees to the 2000 Merit Principles Survey. They used confirmatory factor analysis to develop four independent variables: transformation-oriented leadership, public service-oriented motivation, transaction-oriented leadership, and extrinsically oriented motivation. The structural-equation model results showed that transformation-oriented leadership, defined as leadership that is encouraging, supportive, informative, and that emphasizes high standards, was associated with several outcome variables, including turnover intention, by affecting empowerment, goal clarification, and public service-oriented motivation. Transaction-oriented leadership was not related to any of the organizational outcomes. Using a representative sample of Korean local government, Im, Campbell, and Jeong (2016) reached a conclusion similar to Park and Rainey (2008): Transformational leadership significantly moderates the relationship between public service motivation and commitment. In their view, two dynamics come into play, the first of which being the socialization effects of transformational leadership by virtue of its attention to organizational values. The second dynamic is that transformational leadership stimulates individual self-concepts that transcend self-interest, which matches well with high public service motivation employees (see also Bottomley et al. 2016).

Another group of empirical studies (Wright and Pandey 2011; Wright, Moynihan, and Pandey 2012; Caillier 2015) about transformational leadership and public service motivation focuses on mission and mission valence. This research is discussed in the next section.

8.2   Leadership Strategies and Tactics for Unleashing the Power of Public Service

A comprehensive review of leadership research may discourage aspiring leaders because of the seemingly endless advice that guides leader behaviors. The theory summarized earlier is intentionally limited, in part because of its fit with the context and expectations for public servants. Leaders who pursue the transformational and sensegiving leadership strategies mentioned earlier must think about three imperatives: mission, inspiration, and communication. The boundaries between the three imperatives overlap, but their collective consequence is to elevate public service motivation.

8.2.1   Clearly Articulate Mission and Vision

Based on wisdom he acquired about organizations from his experience at American Telephone and Telegraph in the early twentieth century, Chester Barnard (1938) wrote, "... foresight, long purposes, high ideals, are the basis for the persistence of cooperation" (p. 282). Barnard learned the lesson that aligning an individual's values with the organization's ideology paid dividends for the individual and organization. Paarlberg, Perry, and Hondeghem summarize the dividends and their source: "Individuals will commit to an organization and work hard to achieve its goals when they perceive that there is a match between the organization's ideology, manifested through mission, vision and leadership practices, and the individual's values. Creating such an alignment occurs by articulating organizational mission that clearly reflects individual public service values and fostering leadership that can effectively communicate and model such values" (p. 280). Although an organization's mission exists independent of its leaders, leaders are instrumental in articulating, steering, and activating missions and visions. Research shows that two leadership tactics have been especially helpful for realizing the power of organizational missions: strengthening employee mission valence and developing lines of sight to ultimate aspirations.

8.2.1.1 Strengthen Employee Mission Valence

Mission valence is "an employee's perceptions of the attractiveness or salience of an organization's purpose or social contribution" (Wright, Moynihan, and Pandey 2012, 206). A series of studies indicate that mission valence is a critical lever for motivating employee performance, reliable role behavior, and retention. Bradley Wright and Sanjay Pandey (2011) were the first to look empirically at mission valence in a formative study of a state personnel agency in the northeast United States. They identified three antecedents that influenced mission valence: organizational goal clarity, public service motivation, and perceived impact of an employee's work. They also established that increased mission valence was tied to important human resource outcomes, specifically job satisfaction and absenteeism.

A subsequent study (Wright, Moynihan, and Pandey 2012), using a sample of senior local government managers in the United States from jurisdictions with populations of more than 50,000, replicated results for antecedents of mission valence. They found that employee public service motivation and goal clarity directly affect mission valence. More importantly, they found that leaders using levers associated with transformational leadership – offering a vision, setting a positive example, encouraging innovation, and fostering a sense of organizational pride – can influence public service motivation, which directly increases mission valence.

James Gerard Caillier (2015), relying on a web-based sample of public employees from SurveyMonkey, conducted a third study of mission valence. His response rate was 27 percent, and his analysis included 778 usable responses. Caillier studied a different mix of variables than Wright and Pandey (2011) and Bradley Wright, Donald Moynihan, and Sanjay Pandey (2012). His model included transformational leadership, public service motivation, mission valence, and employee evaluations (a self-reported measure of performance). He found that transformational leadership and public service motivation had direct, positive effects on employee evaluations. He also found that mission valence moderated the positive relationship between transformational leadership and performance, but he did not find the same moderating effect for public service motivation between transformational leadership and performance. His analysis did not include goal clarity.

The series of studies about mission valence provides clear takeaways. One is that leaders find ways to clarify and reinforce organizational and task goals. Leaders who establish a clear vision for followers are likely to increase goal clarity and importance and, in turn, mission valence. Leaders who foster a sense of organizational pride also promote increased mission valence. Finding ways to put employees in closer touch with the impact of their work, like beneficiary contact and exposure to the end results of mission accomplishment, is also likely to increase mission valence.

8.2.1.2   Develop Lines of Sight to Ultimate Aspirations

As Carton's (2018) analysis of the NASA moon mission illustrates, employee work effort toward challenging ends can be facilitated as much by architects as by inspiring transformers. Carton (2018, 351) maps out a relatively abstract process through which a leader's sensegiving enabled employee connection building. Laurie Paarlberg and James Perry's (2007) study of civilian employees and managers over a five-year period in a Department of Defense installation suggests that strategic values are motivating to employees to the extent that they reflect employees' zone of existing values. Paarlberg and Perry's research also points to an important agent who helped employees make connections between their values and strategic values – middle managers. They played a pivotal role in integrating the organization's strategic directions with values from employees' experiences.

Thomas Bateman and Barry Bruce (2012) interviewed a purposive sample of twenty-five individuals pursuing goals whose achievement spanned decades or generations, a group similar to public employees pursuing initiatives like major economic or urban redevelopments, rural health initiatives, or landing humans on Mars. Bateman and Bruce's goal was to understand the work motivation of individuals pursuing long-term goals in contrast to short-term goals, which dominate research. Their qualitative research extracted multiple layers of activity and meaning to make sense of the work motivation of individuals pursuing long-term goals. They identified two distal and two proximate stimuli for motivating long-term goals. The distal stimuli involved possible futures and possible selves. Possible futures involve societal outcomes that rise above the personal results from goal accomplishment. The second distal influence, possible selves, highlights "the possible achievement of new personal or professional states of existence as a result of goal pursuit" (p. 992). The proximate influences, task interest and near-term gratification, involve more familiar stimuli associated with task behaviors and gratification that connect short-term outcomes to long-term goals. Bateman and Bruce's qualitative research provides a compelling architecture for building work motivation for the long term, not unlike the NASA moon mission documented by Carton (2018).

In an earlier study of how organizations connected employees to strategic results, Wendy Boswell and John Boudreau (2001) introduced the idea of line of sight, which Carton (2018) drew upon in his research. Boswell and Boudreau define line of sight "as employee understanding of the organization's objectives and how to contribute to those objectives" (p. 851). They identified a variety of mechanisms that increase employees' ability to identify the line of sight. These mechanisms include:

- *Regular communication about organizational mission and goals.* A widely shared consensus about the organization's mission is a good starting point for establishing employees' line of sight to ultimate aspirations. Communication about goals and results at the program and organization level is also helpful. Communications about goals and results could be shared monthly or quarterly and be published on the web.
- *Human resource management practices.* A well-supported performance management and appraisal system that includes meaningful conversations about task and organizational goals is a strong foundation for employee line of sight. A system for recognizing contributions to organizational achievements that is visible across the organization can strengthen understanding of the organization's objectives, and how to contribute to them, and create pride in making a contribution. A robust onboarding and mentoring program can socialize employees to expectations and facilitate their learning from experienced staff.
- *Employee involvement.* Involving employees in conversations about goals and how to achieve them are valuable for making employees aware of what is happening and giving them ownership.

- *Labor–management partnerships.* In unionized settings, developing collaborative labor–management relationships can increase the likelihood of everyone pulling in the same direction.

An especially interesting and innovative example of developing lines of sight for ultimate aspirations involves the Rocky Flats Nuclear Weapons Plant. At the outset of the project in 1995, the Department of Energy estimated that the levels of contamination would take seventy years to decontaminate. Not only was the scale of the cleanup unprecedented – the first nuclear weapons production facility in the world to be closed – but Rocky Flats faced other daunting challenges. Kim Cameron (2008) summarizes several of them:

- Workers at the facility were represented by three unions, for whom "grievances were common, expectations of life-long employment were the norm, and a high degree of pride existed among the workforce regarding the skilled work they performed" (p. 2).
- The 385-acre production facility was highly secure because of the facility's sensitive mission.
- The site was highly polluted.
- The facility was the object of jurisdictional disputes among contractors, citizens, and federal and local agencies. It was raided by the FBI in 1989 and shut down immediately.

Despite the many daunting challenges, the facility was decontaminated and closed in just ten years at a cost of $6 billion dollars, $30 billion less than originally projected.

What accounts for the extraordinary performance? Kim Cameron and Marc Lavine (2006) and Cameron (2008) identify several techniques and practices that parallel those identified by Carton (2018) in his research on NASA and the Apollo moon landing. Clean-up leaders were able to create lines of sight to ultimate aspirations by sharing before-and-after renditions of the plant and symbolic acts to help employees envision their mission of closing the facility (Cameron and Lavine 2006). Among the leadership principles that directed the Rocky Flats initiative were identifying a profound purpose for the organization's activities that benefitted humans for the long term and focusing symbolism on what the organization aspires to become (Cameron 2008).

8.2.2   *Develop Leadership Styles that Inspire Followers*

An important issue for leaders is selecting an authentic leadership style and developing the personal capacities to execute it. Public managers may know what they want to achieve, for instance conveying an inspiring vision across the organization, but may not know the particulars of what they need to do for others to perceive a vision as inspiring. This demands that public managers choose a leadership style that will serve their goals and make the style their own to support their ends. Two styles that can be especially effective for inspiring followers are charismatic leadership and servant leadership.

8.2.2.1   Develop and Apply Charisma to Inspire Followers

One aspect of transformational leadership with a long history of scholarship and practice is charismatic leadership. Charismatic leaders are distinguished for their communication and rhetorical skills (Martin Luther King's communication skills, for instance, are often held up as exemplary). They also are set apart by the influence of their personality on followers, their personal attachments to followers, personal vision, and personal dedication to their moral convictions. Charismatic leaders are largely associated with the idealized influence and inspirational motivation dimensions of the transformational model.

Charismatic leader behaviors influence public service motivation through the self-concepts of followers (Shamir, House, and Arthur 1993; Perry and Vandenabeele 2008). Boas Shamir, Robert House, and Michael Arthur (1993) present a detailed model of relationships among leader behaviors, influence on followers, and motivational effects. They identify six behaviors of charismatic leaders that set the process in motion: providing ideological explanations, emphasizing collective identities, referring to history, to followers' worth and efficacy, and to collective efficacy, and expressing confidence in followers. Shamir et al. argue that the results of the motivational processes triggered by these behaviors are follower behaviors and dispositions associated with public service motivation, personal commitment to leader and mission, self-sacrificial behavior, organizational citizenship behavior, and task meaningfulness.

The aspirational descriptions of charismatic leadership and the exemplars that are frequently invoked – John F. Kennedy, Martin Luther King, and Winston Churchill – may be off-putting for anyone contemplating applying charisma. But leading scholars express confidence that charisma is not innate and can be learned. John Antonakis, Marika Fenley, and Sue Liechti (2012) make a persuasive case based upon their laboratory and field research that prospective leaders can learn and develop charisma. They identified twelve charismatic leadership tactics, nine verbal and three nonverbal, that help anyone trained in them "become more influential, trustworthy, and 'leaderlike' in the eyes of others" (p. 127). The nine verbal tactics are metaphors, similes, and analogies; stories and anecdotes; contrasts; rhetorical questions; three-part lists; expressions of moral conviction; reflections of the group's sentiments; the setting of high goals; and conveying confidence that they can be achieved (Antonakis, Fenley, and Liechti 2012, 128). The three nonverbal tactics are animated voice, facial expressions, and gestures (p. 128). Although these twelve tactics do not exhaust a leader's repertoire, Antonakis et al., based on their research, contend that they are the most consistently effective.

In explaining the twelve tactics, Antonakis, Fenley, and Liechti (2012) condense them to an extended "three-part list":

1. Connect, compare, and contrast – tactics like *metaphors, similes, analogies, stories and anecdotes, and contrasts* are helpful for engaging listeners, and relating to and remembering messages.
2. Engage and distill – tactics like *rhetorical questions* engage followers and *three-part lists* give them something easy to take away from group or individual encounters.
3. Show integrity, authority, and passion – *expressions of moral conviction, setting high goals,* and *conveying confidence that they can be achieved* demonstrate a leader's character and increased identification between leader and follower.

Experimental research by Adam Grant and John Sumanth (2009) confirms one of the premises behind Antonakis et al.'s case for charismatic leadership, which is that a leader's trustworthiness strengthens the relationship between follower prosocial motivation and performance. Grant and Sumanth contend that trust cues from managers amplify employees' perceived task significance, a key dimension affecting meaningfulness of work, as was argued in Chapter 4. They conducted three studies on samples of students and professional fundraisers. The results confirmed their model of the relationship between prosocial motivation and performance, which was moderated by trust cues and mediated by task significance. Their results held for three distinct performance measures across the three studies.

8.2.2.2 Embrace Servant Leadership to Empower and Inspire Followers

Charismatic leadership is one leadership style for inspiring followers, but another is servant leadership. Robert Greenleaf, an AT&T executive, first used the term servant leadership in a 1970 article (Greenleaf 1970) to describe a leadership style that put followers first. The fact that a nonscholar first introduced and popularized the term led to subsequent confusion about the concept because it did not evolve from typical empirical validation associated with many other leadership constructs (van Dierendonck 2011). The path of servant leadership's evolution does not diminish, however, the appropriateness of the construct for public settings and its compatibility for enhancing public service motivation. The central aspect of the appropriateness of servant leadership to public institutions is that it puts the ideal of service at the center of the leader–follower relationship. This fundamentally alters the way we think about the power of leaders, but in a way appropriate to the constitutional makeup of public institutions, where legitimate power in democratic systems ultimately rests with the governed. Another aspect of servant leadership is its emphasis on the personal growth of followers. Greenleaf's servant-first philosophy puts the needs of others first and emphasizes the leader's role in helping people perform as highly as possible. Dirk Van Dierendonck (2011) emphasizes another way of thinking about the servant-first philosophy: "Greenleaf placed 'going beyond one's self-interest' as a core characteristic of servant leadership" (p. 1230). Servant leadership's philosophy and servant orientation, therefore, also make the style highly compatible with transformational leadership's tactics of individualized consideration and intellectual stimulation.

Although the conceptual underpinnings of servant leadership are not as well established as many other leadership models, six dispositions and behaviors, which offer some guidance for individuals seeking to adopt the style, are generally associated with the construct (Van Dierendonck 2011). These dispositions and behaviors are as follows:

1. *Empowering and developing people* – enabling people to be proactive, giving them a sense of personal power and valuing their personal development.

2. *Humility* – the ability to recognize benefits from the contributions of others and the willingness either to share credit or step back after something has been accomplished.
3. *Authenticity* – behaving with integrity, in ways consistent with one's identity as a person regardless of professional role.
4. *Interpersonal acceptance* – the ability to understand and empathize with others and simultaneously create an atmosphere of trust that others are accepted.
5. *Providing direction* – letting people know what is expected of them and for what they are accountable.
6. *Stewardship* – willingness to take responsibility and act as a caretaker for the institution, epitomizing service and thereby being a role model.

8.2.2.3   Summary

Charismatic and servant leadership styles are particularly well suited for inspiring followers in public organizations because they both serve to reinforce positive self-concepts of followers. To some extent, each leadership style models behaviors that put public service at the center of the leader–follower relationship. Charismatic leaders engender personal commitment to the leader and mission, self-sacrifice from followers, and meaningfulness of the work through expressions of moral conviction and passion. Servant leaders inspire followers by putting the ideal of service at the center of the leader–follower relationship and emphasizing the development of followers. Charismatic and servant leaders are prosocial role models, too. They make a difference through their sustained commitment to the values important to those around them and to the success of the organization and its people (Avolio and Gardner 2005).

8.2.3   *Communicate to Inspire and Build Means-Ends Awareness*

Communication is an integral part of all the theories, strategies, and tactics discussed earlier. Its ubiquity and importance are the reasons why I return to it as the third and final strategy discussed in this chapter. One reason for returning to communication is to highlight and reiterate the need for leaders to pay attention to communication and to use it to elevate employee motivation in their organizations

(Jensen, Moynihan, and Salomonsen 2018). Another reason is to shine light on specific communication tactics not discussed previously in this chapter.

8.2.3.1 Acknowledging Followers' Worth and Collective Efficacy

Employee recognition can come in many forms. In situations involving the production of public or collective goods, the best forms of recognition may be nonpecuniary (see Chapter 6 for more commentary about incentives). In their research on charismatic leadership, Shamir, House, and Arthur (1993) identify several leader behaviors that involved acknowledging follower worth and efficacy: referring to followers' worth and efficacy, referring to collective efficacy, and expressing confidence in followers.

Regardless of the leadership style a leader projects, messages to followers about their worth and efficacy, especially in face-to-face exchanges (Jensen, Moynihan, and Salomonsen 2018), can pay dividends for employee motivation. Communicating to followers about their efficacy can produce the "warm glow" (Andreoni 1990) or satisfaction that comes from helping others. Seeking to tap this sense of satisfaction from helping others recognizes that even people with high public service motivation may bring to their work mixed motives, both altruistic and egoistic.

Although research about warm-glow altruism is modest, and it has been studied in contexts such as donative behavior and charitable giving rather than organizations, some evidence sheds light on motivation in organizations. Mirco Tonin and Michael Vlassopoulos (2010) conducted a field experiment to disentangle the relative contributions of warm-glow and pure altruism. Using student subjects, they found that prosocial motivation was driven wholly by warm-glow altruism and not at all by pure altruism. The other interesting result of their experiment is that warm-glow altruism influenced women, but not men, who were unaffected by any of the treatments. They point to other experimental research that has produced similar gender differences for social preferences to indicate that their results are not anomalous. The gender differences merit additional research.

Experimental research by Adam Grant and Francesca Gino (2010) offers some insights about the mechanisms by which expressions of gratitude influence members' willingness to engage in prosocial behaviors. In four experiments with samples varying from undergraduate and graduate students (experiments 1 and 2), to fundraisers, to undergraduates in different regions of the United States, Grant and Gino tested the mediating effects of agentic and communal interventions on the relationship between expressions of gratitude and prosocial behavior. Agentic mechanisms seek to increase a person's self-efficacy, "the feeling of being capable and competent to act effectively to orchestrate an outcome" (p. 947). Communal mechanisms rely on feelings of social worth being stimulated by expressions of gratitude. "When individuals experience social worth, they feel needed, cared about, and valued by others, which signifies an interpersonal bond or positive relationship" (p. 947). Results from all four experiments led Grant and Gino to conclude that the communal rather than agentic mechanism increased prosocial behavior from expressions of gratitude by beneficiaries. They write, "These findings suggest that when helpers are thanked for their efforts, the resulting sense of being socially valued, more than the feelings of competence they experience, are critical in encouraging them to provide more help in the future" (p. 953).

8.2.3.2 Storytelling

Stories are narratives used to share information and make sense of a situation. Earlier in the book you encountered two stories that conveyed the importance of storytelling as a communications and social process. John DiIulio's (1994) research on the U.S. Bureau of Prisons (BOP, Chapter 3) refers to stories that were influential in that organization for shaping its lore that significantly influenced thousands of staff over many years to work hard and cohesively on behalf of BOP's mission. In that same chapter, you first encountered a story about a meeting between a janitor at NASA and President John F. Kennedy, which stimulated Andrew Carton's research, cited earlier. The story is not only being studied more than fifty years after the reported encounter, but it is being shared in organizations across the federal government.

Stories can be interesting, but the process of storytelling is the dynamic that makes them an important tool for leaders. The influence of stories like those recounted by DiIulio (1994) and Carton (2018) reflects why they are a communication tool for leaders. Stories help us understand that leadership is not about the leader, but rather is a collective process. Although organizations and their leaders must take opportunities to communicate public service values through formal mission statements, informal means such as organizational stories and myths are valuable means for transmitting public values. Laurie Paarlberg, James Perry, and Annie Hondeghem (2008) offer examples from the literature about how stories are used:

> In describing how leaders infuse day-to-day behavior with meaning and purpose, Philip Selznick (1957) described the "elaboration of socially integrating myths" that use the language of "uplift and idealism" to explain what is distinctive about an organization's "aims and methods" (p. 151). Maynard-Moody and Musheno (2003) described how case reviews in staff meetings provided the context for social work staff and supervisors to use storytelling to discuss dilemmas and experiences in ways that heightened the possibility for "responsible action."

Public administration scholars and practitioners are developing a deeper appreciation for narratives because of the recognized power of stories and storytelling. Sonia Ospina and her colleagues at New York University have long championed narrative inquiry as a way to understand better what public administrators do. Mark Bevir (2011) contends that stories help to construct "meaning holism," which places information about behavior, beliefs, and values into its context and history. The powerful influence of this type of explanation leads Bevir to conclude, "Public administration is less about finding formal connections, than about telling stories about beliefs, actions, practices, and their contexts" (2011, 190).

Sonia Ospina and Erica Foldy (2010, 2015) and Kevin Orr and Mike Bennett (2017) help to reveal how storytelling as a communication device facilitates collective leadership in public organizations. Ospina and Foldy developed their generalizations from extended interviews in thirty-eight social change organizations over a five-year period beginning in 2001. Some of the organizations are national, but most are regional or local, including CASA of Maryland, Sacramento Valley Organizing Community, Ohio Valley Environmental Coalition, and Triangle Research Options for Substance Abusers. The issues on which the organizations focus vary, ranging from housing, to the environment, to workers' and human rights, to community development. Orr and Bennett's sample involved interviews between 2008 and 2015 of local council chief executives in different UK councils spanning locations in all four countries of the United Kingdom.

The narratives and stories the interviewees shared with Ospina and Foldy and Orr and Bennett yield several inferences about leader influence. These inferences are summarized here in terms used by Orr and Bennett.

- Stories have a capacity to cut across professional or departmental boundaries and engage people with a shared sense of context and purpose (Orr and Bennett, 2017, 515). The ability of stories to break down boundaries speaks to the capacity of stories to prompt cognitive shifts and influence naming and shaping identity (Ospina and Foldy 2010, 2015).
- Stories invite an emotional connection and commitment to public service helpful for motivating and influencing staff (Orr and Bennett 2017, 520).
- Stories can help challenge and reframe practices and assumptions (Orr and Bennett 2017, 522). Reframing practices and assumptions begins with the power of stories to prompt cognitive shifts, engaging dialog about difference and weaving multiple worlds together through interpersonal relationships (Ospina and Foldy 2010, 2015).
- Stories lend themselves to talking about the public mission of organizations (Orr and Bennett 2017, 515). Engaging dialog about difference sets the stage for conversations about uniqueness, about the publicness of the mission (Ospina and Foldy 2010, 2015).

8.3 Conclusion

Scholars have debated how much leadership matters when it comes to improving organizational performance (Fernandez, Cho, and Perry 2010). In the public sector, we can envision that the effects of leadership may be large, but there is also evidence that, like other arenas, factors such as dissensus about values and other considerations may create a ceiling for the influence of leadership. Even if the effects of leadership on performance range from negligible to 20 percent, the incremental differences leadership can make are worth the effort.

Regardless of the magnitude of leadership's influence on performance, we have good evidence about the levers by which leaders can make a difference. Transformational and sensegiving leadership strategies must attend to three imperatives: mission, inspiration, and communication. A public organization's mission may be a leader's most powerful lever because it is often mission that attracted followers in the first place and mission where prosocial impacts inherently reside. Leaders can be influential agents for magnifying the motivational power of mission. They can seek to strengthen employee mission valence, that is, their perceptions of the attractiveness of the organization's social contribution. Leaders can also develop lines of sight to ultimate aspirations.

Leaders can also play a role in inspiring followers by selecting an authentic leadership style and developing the personal capacities to execute it. Although the means for inspiring followers are myriad, leaders should consider developing their capacities for charismatic and servant leadership styles, which are well suited based on research and the nature of public institutions. A charismatic leadership style is effective for motivating followers through role modeling and inspiration that are key dimensions of transformational leadership. Servant leadership, which puts followers first, is similarly suited to empowering and inspiring followers.

When leaders pursue motivating their followers using mission and inspiration as levers of influence, they are deeply attentive to their role as communicators. But effective communication can itself be a lever for transformational leadership. Communications that acknowledge the worth and collective efficacy of followers can further motivate followers who come to their work for social good. Telling and nurturing stories about the differences an organization and its employees make can also be an effective communications device for motivating membership, role, and performance behaviors that contribute to organizational effectiveness.

Note

1 O'Neill's three questions represent a common rhetorical device, which Antonakis, Fenley, and Liechti (2012) found in their research is a verbal tactic that is positively related to charismatic leadership.

9 | Designing Civil Service to Unleash Public Passion

This book began with a straightforward observation: A significant body of recent social and behavioral science research about public service has laid the foundations for advancing civil service reform. This research has been conducted on different concepts – public service motivation, altruism, and prosocial motivation and behavior. The amount and quality of the research has created a critical mass of intellectual capital. This intellectual capital permits us to rethink civil service system designs, policies, and management practices to change civil service systems around the globe.

Recent reviews of research on public service and prosocial motivation indicate that these topics have garnered more than a thousand studies in recent decades. The book represents two firsts related to this research. It is the first to look systematically across the different streams of research on public service motivation, altruism, and prosocial behavior. It is also the first to synthesize the research across the spectrum of applied questions that public organizations and their leaders and managers confront, including:

- recruiting and selecting staff who will ethically, competently, and persistently pursue public service;
- designing public work to leverage its meaningfulness;
- creating work environments that support intrinsically motivated prosocial behavior;
- compensating and rewarding employees to energize and sustain public service;
- socializing employees for public service missions and values; and
- leading employees for causes greater than themselves.

The new intellectual capital positions public organizations and their leaders and managers as pursuing designs and policies consistent with our aspirations for public service and better fitted to the nature of public institutions. This developing knowledge base potentially supplants motivational practices and assumptions grounded largely in the assumptions of market enterprises. The prospect of a future that simultaneously applies recently developed intellectual capital and pursues positive aspirations for motivation for public service is consistent with the long-term evolution of motivational practices in public institutions. As noted in Chapter 1, an examination of the evolution of public motivational practices from the late nineteenth century to the present tells a revealing story. Although New Public Management (NPM) was perceived by many as ascendant, we discovered that the logic of consequence (March and Olsen 1995) that defined the motivational models associated with NPM is giving way to emergent motivational models. The motivational models ascendant from the late 1970s to the end of the twentieth century, when NPM dominated conversations among scholars and practitioners, turned to practices such as contracting, high-powered incentives, and agentification (Boruvka and Perry 2020). How should the emerging motivational philosophy and practices be characterized? Would a simple label of post-NPM define the new era? Because vestiges of the long-lived bureaucratic era were visible in emerging motivational practices, would it be appropriate to call the emerging era neo-Weberian? The behavioral science evidence this book provides about public service as an instrument to motivate prospective and current staff, together with the normative perspective associated with a public service ethos, led us to characterize this era as "new public service" (Boruvka and Perry 2020; Denhardt and Denhardt 2015).

9.1   A Portfolio for Changing Civil Service Systems

Although I argued earlier that social and behavioral science research has given us a wealth of evidence in recent years that provides a foundation for civil service systems of the future, the proposals presented throughout the book vary from novel to traditional. They are summarized in Table 9.1. The left column in the table provides information on the main policy areas discussed in the book (i.e., recruitment and selection, work design, work environments, compensation and rewards, socializing employees, and leadership). The second and third columns identify specific policies and management practices and describe them briefly. The right column in Table 9.1 specifies which groups or roles are primarily responsible for the policy's implementation.

Table 9.1 *Summary of proposals for reforming civil service, management, and leadership practices*

Chapter theme	Civil service policy/management practice	Description/explanation	Who implements
Selecting for high public service motivation is a priority	Project organizational images to attract high public service motivation prospects	Organizations that project clear images about their missions and how they advance outcomes valued by society generate stronger identification with the organization	Managers
	Shape job advertising to emphasize mission and public values	Job advertisements should include specifically public characteristics like mission and values as a means for projecting organizational images to job candidates	Human resources support Managers
	Screen in candidates with high public service motivation	Use selection procedures, including biographical data, behavioral interviews, and implicit social cognition tests, that predict public service and prosocial motivation	Human resources support Managers Employees/job candidates
	Screen out candidates with motivations likely to crowd out intrinsic or prosocial orientations	• Screen for honesty and corruption • Use realistic job previews • Use probationary periods and alternative selection processes to validate hiring decisions	Human resources support Managers Employees/job candidates

Leveraging the meaningfulness of public work		
Design work to allow for direct contact between employees and service beneficiaries	Connect employees with direct service beneficiaries so they understand the social significance of the work	Human resources support Managers
Use self-persuasion or other self-administered interventions to connect employees to beneficiaries	Self-persuasion relies on employees convincing themselves about the prosocial value of their work. It may be used in jobs for which direct ties to beneficiaries are difficult or impossible	Managers Employees
Incorporate job crafting to increase meaningfulness	Job crafting relies on the initiative of employees to craft their work to add meaning. Job crafting gives the employee discretion in how they frame their work, physically, socially, and cognitively	Employees Managers
Employee career counseling	Career counseling is externally mediated rather than accessed directly from inherent features of the work. Incorporating career counseling interventions can help strengthen employees' pursuit of their callings	Human resources support Managers Employees

Table 9.1 (*cont.*)

Chapter theme	Civil service policy/management practice	Description/explanation	Who implements
Creating a supportive work environment	Establish civil service rule systems that create common pool resources and promote basic psychological needs	Institutional arrangements that select office holders based on merit, rules for conduct with dedication and integrity, acting in accordance with the political and normative order, and serving as stewards for constitutional principles, the rule of law, and professional standards	Civil service laws/rules
	Establish robust learning and growth opportunities	Design opportunities for learning and development throughout the career, leader development up and down the hierarchy, and promoting subjective career success	Human resources support Managers Employees

Developing norms that balance job security and performance	Design and manage job security systems to balance performance and property rights protections for jobs, manage performance management systems for development and performance improvement, build public service into performance management and appraisal systems, and make performance an important criterion for reductions in force	Civil service laws/rules Human resources support Managers Employees
Nurture public service motivation to reinforce ties between organization and employee	Attend to creating an environment for quality communications and performance feedback and satisfying employees' basic psychological needs for competence, autonomy, and relatedness	Executives/leaders Managers Employees
Aligning compensation systems to reinforce public service	Using total compensation as the benchmark for comparisons Using total compensation as the standard for outlays to employees controls the ratio of extrinsic to intrinsic rewards. The goal is to avoid making extrinsic rewards so large that they become behavioral drivers that crowd out public service motivation, thereby sustaining public service as a defining value of government institutions	Civil service laws/rules

Table 9.1 (*cont.*)

Chapter theme	Civil service policy/management practice	Description/explanation	Who implements
	Compensation strategy should incorporate an assessment of alternative, efficiency, and public-service-motivation-adjusted wages into setting base pay	Using alternative methods to benchmark base pay helps to tie base pay to the value of the work	Civil service laws/rules Human resources support
	Pay comparability assessments should use salary surveys and complement them with a variety of additional indicators	Complementing salary surveys with other indicators will permit governments to triangulate what is an externally competitive wage. Indicators such as job application queues and turn-down rates also provide insights into adjustments that could be made in pay rates for public service motivation	Civil service laws/rules Human resources support

| As a compensation strategy, the contest model is best suited for public organizations; the sponsored and tournament mobility models may merit selective use | *Contest mobility* is distinguished by its emphasis on opportunity, where no policies cut off anyone's prospects for elite status or, conversely, for elites to move downward. The contest mobility model has advantages over other models in that it creates rules and an environment to retain talent. The contest model is more efficient and therefore more sustainable under budget constraints. It also creates an environment for sustaining and nurturing public service motivation | Civil service laws/rules
Human resources support |
| As a compensation strategy, public organizations should pursue more pronounced wage dispersion among high-skill occupations and executives | A pay-dispersion problem in public settings is salary compression. The consequence of the relative wage compression is that the public sector has had increasing difficulty attracting and retaining high-skill workers. Relative wage compression is pronounced at the top of the public sector pay range. The essence of this argument is that public pay can be sacrificial, but at extremes, it impedes attracting and retaining high-quality staff | Civil service laws/rules
Human resources support
Managers |

Table 9.1 (*cont.*)

Chapter theme	Civil service policy/management practice	Description/explanation	Who implements
	Ability, skills, and performance collectively are strategic criteria for assessing eligibility for entry and advancement	One way to recognize performance is to build it more robustly into promotional and career advancement processes. Assessments surrounding promotions are more episodic, thorough, and holistic and therefore may be more valid than annual performance reviews that serve both developmental and administrative functions	Civil service laws/rules Human resources support Managers
	When designing incentives, government organizations should emphasize low-powered incentives rather than high-powered incentives	Low-powered incentives are superior to high-powered incentives. Intrinsic motivation can be sustained in the presence of low-powered incentives. Low-powered incentives are more easily sustained in budget-constrained environments, which is the case throughout most of the public sector globally	Civil service laws/rules Human resources support Managers

Providing opportunities to learn public service values	Government organizations should avoid incentives that crowd out public service motivation. Conversely, they should seek opportunities to crowd in prosocial, intrinsic, autonomous motivations	This strategy is a corollary of the low- versus high-powered incentives strategy, but addresses the types of incentives offered to employees. This strategy normatively favors organizational incentives on the autonomous end of the motivation spectrum in contrast to incentives on the controlled end	Civil service laws/rules Human resources support Managers
	Designing onboarding to align organizational and employee public service values	Onboarding is the process of integrating new employees into the organization. Onboarding is strategic, longer term, focused on integrating employees into their new social systems and enhancing their capacity to perform at high levels	Human resources support Executives/leaders Managers Employees
	Create mentoring partnerships to share and reinforce public service values	Mentoring connects new members with established members to promote new member integration and learning about the organization	Human resources support Executives/leaders Managers Employees

Table 9.1 (cont.)

Chapter theme	Civil service policy/management practice	Description/explanation	Who implements
Developing leaders who communicate and model public service values	Clearly articulate mission and vision	individuals' attachments and work effort are elevated when they perceive their values match the organization's mission and vision. Aligning individuals' values and organizational mission relies on organizational signals and transformational leadership that communicates and models values. Leaders are consequential for articulating and activating visions and missions	Executives/leaders Managers
	Strengthen employee mission valence	Mission valence, the salience of an organization's purpose or social contribution for employees, is a critical lever for motivating employee performance, reliable role behavior, and retention. Leaders who establish a clear vision for followers are likely to increase goal clarity and importance and, in turn, mission valence. Leaders who foster a sense of organizational pride also promote increased mission valence	Executives/leaders Managers Employees

Develop lines of sight to ultimate aspirations	Employee understanding of how to contribute to organizational objectives is consequential for work effort. Mechanisms for increasing employees' ability to identify the line of sight include regular communication about organizational mission and goals, employee involvement, and labor–management partnerships	Executives/leaders Managers Employees
Develop leadership styles that inspire followers	Leaders must select an authentic leadership style and develop the personal capacities to execute it	Executives/leaders Managers
Develop and apply charisma to inspire followers	Charismatic leaders are distinguished for their communication and rhetorical skills. They also are set apart by the influence of their personality on followers, their personal attachments to followers, personal vision, and personal dedication to their moral convictions	Executives/leaders Managers

Table 9.1 (*cont.*)

Chapter theme	Civil service policy/management practice	Description/explanation	Who implements
	Embrace servant leadership to empower and inspire followers	Servant leadership puts the ideal of service at the center of the leader–follower relationship. This alters the way we think about the power of leaders in a way appropriate to the constitutional makeup of public institutions. Servant leadership also emphasizes the personal growth of followers	Executives/leaders Managers Employees
	Communicate to inspire and build means-ends awareness	Leaders must pay attention to communication and use it to elevate employee motivation in their organizations	Executives/leaders Managers

Acknowledge followers' worth and collective efficacy	Leader messages to followers about their worth and efficacy can pay dividends for employee motivation. Communicating to followers about their efficacy can produce the "warm glow" or satisfaction that comes from helping others	Executives/leaders Managers Employees
Engage in storytelling	Stories are narratives used to share information and make sense of a situation. Stories help us understand that leadership is not about the leader, but rather is a collective process	Executives/leaders Managers Employees

Potential implementers range from those who establish civil service laws and rules, to decentralized human resources units, to agency and program executives and leaders, and to managers and ultimately employees. In general, each type of implementer is relatively equally represented, and the mix of implementers varies by policy or practice.

The more novel proposals advanced in this book involve explicitly selecting for public service motivation, using self-persuasion to increase the meaningfulness of work, applying total compensation as the benchmark for rewards, and relying on low-powered rather than high-powered incentives. The policy of selecting for public service motivation reflects an underlying shift in perspective shared by other proposals in this book, for example hiring for the organization, not the job (Bowen, Ledford, and Nathan 1991). The logic of hiring for the job is one that fits well with a government of clerks, but is poorly suited for the makeup of the workforce in most governments today, which are usually educated and highly professional (Partnership for Public Service, and the Volcker Alliance 2018). Seeking a high person-organization fit is consistent with theories reviewed in Chapter 2, specifically predisposition-opportunity, attraction–selection–attrition, and person-fit theory. The person-organization fit perspective is a significant break with past practice in most governments globally. This change in perspective has the dual benefit of moving away from dysfunctions associated with job-focused civil service systems (Savas and Ginsburg 1973) and building cultures that rely on public-service-motivated, committed people.

Although some of the proposals in this book may be perceived as novel, others are strikingly familiar and traditional. Traditional law and rule-based civil service systems, job design, onboarding, mentoring, and charismatic and servant leadership are prominent in the literature. These familiar and traditional proposals create their own challenges for generating support among constituencies that need to embrace them as part of a motivational model for the future. Traditional laws and rules for merit systems were under significant pressure for most of the last quarter of the twentieth century. Criticisms of traditional systems have given way to their reexamination (Olsen 2006). Recent research on merit systems (Dahlström, Lapuente, and Teorell 2012; Dahlström and Lapuente 2017), for instance, indicates they are institutional arrangements that permit bureaucrats to speak truth to power to their political masters. The criticisms of features of merit systems, such as excessive job security and generous defined benefit pensions, have simultaneously created waves of adaptations that have diminished some of the excesses of civil service institutional arrangements.

Some of the other traditional proposals offered in this book carry another liability: they are not widely used by governments. Onboarding as a strategic, longer-term process, for example, has not been widely used in government, but may have received momentum from a Partnership for Public Service report (Booz Allen Hamilton 2008), published more than a decade ago. Similar gaps likely exist for the application of other proposals, such as job design and redesign, mentoring, and charismatic and servant leadership development, to which I referred earlier. Although we have little contemporary information about diffusion of these traditional practices, we know from previous, highly visible reforms that diffusion of valued practices is likely (Lah and Perry 2008). Thus, visible applications of processes like onboarding can be expected to diffuse widely.

The third and final category of proposals presented in this book, like many of the ideas mentioned in the previous paragraph, are not widely used in governments, originating from fields outside public administration. I include among these proposals relational job design, job crafting, and career counseling. These proposals are distinguished by their affinity with both the novel and traditional proposals derived from public administration. Relational job design is deeply connected to prosocial motivation, a concept allied with public service motivation (Grant 2007). Career counseling comes into play because of its ability to unlock the motivational power of calling, another concept with a strong connection to public service motivation (Thompson and Christensen 2018).

In Chapter 1, I discussed three types of coherence shared by the ideas presented in this book. One of them, institutional coherence, represents alignment among institutional values like service, giving back and duty, and the models of individual motivation. The second type is theoretical coherence, which means the theories and empirical research are logical, consistent, and sum to a unified whole. Theories advanced across several disciplines and the empirical research they spawned have created a coherent body of compelling evidence. The third form of coherence, synergy, represents consistency across practices that contributes to self-reinforcing effects when they are implemented collectively.

9.2   Change Processes for Advancing the Reform Agenda

Based on the growing body of evidence presented here, the ideas for civil service systems and management practices provide compelling intellectual capital for redesigning and reimagining civil service systems globally (Perry 2020). Evidence-based ideas for change are one part of solving the civil service reform puzzle, as the 1990s comparative civil service research project concluded (Bekke, Perry, and Toonen 1996). The difficulties of changing civil service systems suggest that a need for workable ideas is not the only challenge facing reformers. Change agents must also be mindful of another conclusion from the same comparative research project – civil service systems are artifacts of a variety of external influences and are perpetuated by the systems in which they are nested. This means that reformers must also attend to managing change in public organizations.

Reviews of organizational change research provide useful summaries of what we know about facilitating change processes (Fernandez and Rainey 2006; Kuipers et al. 2014). In this chapter, I discuss two general strategies for civil service reform.

9.2.1   *Leveraging Small Wins to Advance Change Incrementally*

Some governments with long-established civil service systems find themselves today confronting new challenges in an era of hyper-partisanship (Ornstein 2020) and estrangement (Ventriss et al. 2019). These circumstances describe the current state of affairs in the United States. At the federal level, Congressional control is divided between Republicans and Democrats, trust and confidence in the executive is at a low ebb, and stakeholders across the political spectrum are hypervigilant and hyperactive. Prospects for major, comprehensive reforms are near zero.

The circumstances surrounding reform prospects have led two promoters of change, the Partnership for Public Service and the Volcker Alliance (2018), to pursue an incremental change strategy, one predicated on small wins that may build momentum for more significant changes. The Partnership and Alliance have put together a series of recommendations of specific policy, regulatory, and statutory changes to improve federal human resource management. Their joint report, *Renewing America's Civil Service* (Partnership for Public Service, and the Volcker Alliance 2018), provides a road map for incremental change:

> To truly transform the federal workforce, Congress must make some changes to law, particularly in the areas of hiring and compensation. However, much can be done even without legislation to make personnel processes more nimble. The Office of Personnel Management (OPM) and the Office of Management and Budget (OMB) have ample room in their authorities to allow agencies flexibility to innovate, including existing authority for demonstration projects. We also recommend that OPM conduct an expansive review of existing regulations and policies to eliminate rules that are no longer needed and to ensure that all reforms keep the quality of government's service to citizens at the forefront. And Congress, through its oversight function, can provide momentum for modernization by shining a spotlight on both shortcomings and promising solutions.

The report is explicit about the tactics that make change possible: seek rewriting laws only where absolutely necessary (e.g., compensation), decentralize responsibility for introducing change under existing authorities, and showcase major performance gaps and successes.

The change strategy articulated earlier in the text is one that has worked in the past, particularly in the US institutional context. The strategy also receives strong theoretical support in the literatures of public administration and management (Lindblom 1959, 1979; Quinn 1978).

9.2.2 Reform as Comprehensive Change

Comprehensive change sits at the opposite end of the change spectrum from incremental change. Comprehensive change may be more likely in new states or states in transition than in developed states merely because of the needs developing countries may confront to replace traditional governance institutions with institutions that can navigate modern economic, social, political, and technological challenges.

Despite challenges confronting states in the twenty-first century, James March (1981) provided a reality check about expectations for planned organizational change that are worth revisiting here. The relevant takeaways from March's insights are as follows:

- Organizations change continuously and routinely, but change usually cannot be arbitrarily controlled and rarely unfolds as directed.

- "Changes in organizations depend on a few stable processes" (p. 563), among them rule following, problem solving, learning, conflict, and regeneration.
- "Most changes in organizations reflect simple responses to demographic, economic, social, and political forces" (p. 563).
- Everyday, ordinary processes may have unexpected outcomes because of the confusing contexts in which they transpire.

March's insights are helpful for establishing realistic expectations about the speed of change and whether it can be subordinated to rational planning processes and potential opportunities to intervene to shape change.

What we know about countries that have made progress toward comprehensive change, countries such as the former Soviet Republic of Georgia and South Africa, is that they have succeeded in taking incremental steps toward reshaping administrative and governance systems. Research suggests that countries that succeed in transforming themselves in the long run are able to introduce reforms that influence the stable processes to which March refers. Two attributes seem to be prominent and shared by countries that undergo successful transformation: autonomy and professionalism.

9.2.2.1 Autonomy

I have referred on several occasions to autonomy, particularly as it relates to bureaucratic actors, as a positive influence on a variety of individual and organizational outcomes in public bureaucracies. The concept is implicit in Carl Dahlström and Victor Lapuente's (2017) argument that separate incentive structures for civil servants and political actors permit bureaucrats to speak truth to power in their interactions with politicians. Merilee Grindle's (1997) research, which I first highlighted in Chapter 4, provided early evidence about the role of autonomy in explaining high performance in developing countries. Autonomy, particularly with respect to personnel systems, gives civil service leaders opportunities to develop standards and norms to elevate bureaucratic performance.

Grindle's conclusions, based on a study of high and low performing organizational units across six countries, mirrored findings from a fascinating earlier study in a single country, Brazil. Judith Tendler and Sara Freedheim (1994) provide evidence about dynamics that may underlie the autonomy–high performance relationship identified by Grindle. Tendler and Freedheim's case is the turnaround of performance from poor to good in one Brazilian state, Ceará, a highly populated state located in the poor northeast region of the country. The overarching research question they addressed was: "How could a state in a region with such a long and consistent history of mediocre performance 'suddenly' do so well?" (p. 1772). To answer the question, they focused on one high performing program, a rural preventive health program. They discovered three factors at the center of the high performance of the rural preventive health program. The first was that the state government controlled meritocratic hiring of the municipally based workforce of 7,300 health agents and 235 nurse supervisors. The second factor was the creation of a work environment where workers and their supervisors perceived their mission as prestigious and high status. The state government of Ceará created "a sense of 'calling' around these particular jobs through a rigorous process of meritocratic selection and training, unending publicity, and repeated public prizes for good performance" (p. 1773). The third factor was that the commitments of workers led them to take on "self-enlarged" jobs, which became instruments for public benefit because the workers were monitored by the communities in which they were located and they were situated in trusting relationships with their clients. Although workers in the rural preventive health program enjoyed significant autonomy, they were also accountable by virtue of the social relationships that surrounded their work.

Erin McDonnell (2017) also fixes on the importance of autonomy and formalizes its role in the context of her model of interstitial bureaucracy. McDonnell writes about autonomy: "Contrary to the erroneous presumption that organizations everywhere are already thoroughly bureaucratized, in many non-Western contexts *the bureaucratic ethos is the deviant institution,* requiring autonomy to insulate it from the contrary practices of a patronage-based administrative milieu" (p. 497, emphasis in the original).

An intriguing prospect, one that merits additional research, is that the phenomenon made possible by autonomy, that is, interstitial bureaucracy, may pave the way for more significant institutional reforms in the future.

> Bureaucratic interstices foster socially innovative or deviant values, practices, and cultural tools by *clustering a critical mass of proto-bureaucratic human, cognitive, and material resources.* Bureaucratic

interstices are, effectively, a bureaucratic subculture – a loosely bounded numerical minority within a dominant majority, characterized by "a set of modal beliefs, values, norms, and customs associated with a relatively distinct social subsystem (a set of interpersonal networks and institutions) existing within a larger social system and culture" (Fischer 1975: 1323) (McDonnell 2017, p. 494, emphasis in the original).

An unknown is whether bureaucratic interstices are able to move from deviant to dominant, from minority to majority, from social subsystem to social system. This is a theme McDonnell (2020) addresses in a book that builds upon and extends her 2017 *American Sociological Review* article. One way she extends her earlier research is by expanding the scope of countries beyond contemporary Ghana to contemporary Nigeria, mid-twentieth-century Kenya and Brazil, and early twentieth-century China. McDonnell (2020) poses several future research questions that convey a need to explore further the prospects for expanding interstitial niches more widely. Among the research questions she poses with which readers of this book will have an affinity are: "Precisely how big must an initial cluster of distinctiveness be in order to kick off clustering distinctiveness? … Can niches scale up and if so, how? How can these practices spread to other locations within the same state? … Do these mechanics explain the emergence of the bureaucratic ethos within early European state-building?" (Chapter: Conclusion, typescript p. 323).

It is not a leap to envision autonomy, operating independently or through mediating organizations such as bureaucratic interstices, influencing stable processes driving organizational change. Staff who are given autonomy, whether as part of a bureaucratic subculture or culture, are in a better position to embrace rational, performance-oriented rules rather than follow neopatrimonial rules to which they would otherwise be subject. In the context of autonomy, managers are also likely to have more power to enforce rules across their workforce. To the extent that staff or bureaucratic subcultures have the autonomy to apply their cognitive resources, they are more likely to engage in solving problems rather than serving their sponsors. Autonomy is also likely to enhance opportunities for learning and constructive conflict.

9.2.2.2 Professionalism
The concept of profession has typically meant, at a minimum, an occupation subject to specialized training in a body of esoteric knowledge and, perhaps, formal education and certification (Perry 2018).

My use of professionalism here is more expansive. Professionalism is the extent to which competence and integrity are routine expectations for civil servants, and the concept has been widely embraced, for instance, in reforms across Central and Eastern Europe (Neshkova and Kostadinova 2012).

A cluster of distinct practices are often associated with professionalism, among them job competence, political neutrality, merit promotion, and an explicit code of conduct, but they may not all be part of the institutional arrangements in a country and may come into being gradually over time. The politically neutral competence identified with the U.S. federal civil service system, for example, evolved over a period of many years. When the Pendleton Act was passed in 1883, only a very small portion of civil service positions were covered (Van Riper 1958).

Although no comprehensive studies have been conducted of the evolution of professionalism, particularly the cluster of distinct practices referred to earlier, some evidence suggests that the diffusion of professional practices is subject to a variety of institutional processes. Pamela Tolbert and Lynne Zucker (1983) conducted an early study of the institutionalization of change by looking at the diffusion of civil service reforms from 1880 to 1935. Their study looked at US city governments. They found that civil service procedures diffused rapidly and directly when required by the state. This finding is not surprising given that cities are administrative units of states and for many matters subordinate to state law and direction. But even when civil service procedures were not legitimated by the state, they diffused gradually. When reforms were not centrally legitimated by state law, early adopters were motivated by their need to upgrade their administrative capacity and late adopters got on board when the structural form was perceived as legitimate by virtue of widespread adoption by other cities. Tolbert and Zucker's article, which was published the same year as Paul DiMaggio and Walter Powell's (1983) article that addressed the question of what made organizations so similar, identified the three isomorphic processes – coercive, mimetic, and normative – subsequently popularized by DiMaggio and Powell (1983).

A quarter-century after the two influential 1983 studies, T. J. Lah and I investigated the diffusion of the Civil Service Reform Act of 1978 (CSRA) among thirty Organisation for Economic Co-operation and Development (OECD) countries. The Act is legislation originating in the United States during Jimmy Carter's Administration. The Act was multifaceted, introducing comprehensive reforms to the U.S. federal government for the first time in ninety-five years. Among the reforms were merit pay, creation of a rank-in-person executive management system for senior civil servants (Senior Executive Service), and codification of labor–management relations from presidential executive orders into public law. Lah and Perry (2008) observed that the CSRA provisions they studied diffused widely internationally, contrary to expectations grounded in their effectiveness in the United States. The diffusion was explained by mimetic and normative isomorphism that drove countries to adopt CSRA's provisions, either to emulate other countries or conform to judgments about appropriate professional practices.

The two studies discussed earlier offer insights about the routine and continuous change processes in organizations and nation states that might be inferred from March's footnotes on organizational change. Another reason for highlighting them is that they make more transparent the types of gradual change processes behind the stable processes driving change. The isomorphic processes describe multiple channels for introducing new practices that may potentially regenerate the internal machinations of state administrative enterprises. New practices are also a form of learning, albeit imparting learning with varying power, with coercive isomorphism potentially least powerful and possibly destructive, mimetic of modest consequence, and normative most powerful because it is likely to coincide with internalized changes.

Milena Neshkova and Tatiana Kostadinova's (2012) analysis of the effects of civil service reform in Central and Eastern Europe arrived at conclusions consistent with Dahlström and Lapuente's (2017) general thesis about the benefits of distinct career systems and incentives for bureaucrats and politicians. They found that civil service reforms were associated with lower public sector corruption across countries in Central and Eastern Europe, attributing the change to constraints on irresponsible behavior and strengthening of the meritocratic principle. Neshkova and Kostadinova's findings are not definitive evidence for professionalism as a driver for comprehensive change, but they are consistent with a pattern suggesting the value of reforms surrounding civil servant competence and integrity.

9.2.2.3 Summary

Although autonomy and professionalism may be significant drivers for the stable processes that March (1981) identifies as underlying change, they are probably not alone as structural determinants influencing change processes. They are highlighted here, however, because of their prominence in research offering insights about reform and change. Autonomy and professionalism have also been prominent elsewhere in this book with respect to understanding conditions under which public service motivation can develop and flourish. Autonomy and competence are key concepts in self-determination theory, providing both foundations for autonomous motivations like member identification and integration and satisfaction of members' basic psychological needs. McDonnell's (2017) description of attributes of interstitial bureaucracy in Ghana offers strong hints about member attraction, work design, and incentives appearing elsewhere in this book. She writes: "These adaptations of bureaucratic characteristics enabled the niche to carve out a social space of difference, attract and motivate qualified individuals despite low pay, and make its work more predictable by defending against disruptions from entanglement with the larger environment [p. 487] ... Therefore, to attract scarce, high-skilled human resources, niches must offer enticements beyond salary. Nearly all interstitial insiders reported working there despite the salary" (p. 488).

9.2.3 Navigating Comprehensive Change: Georgia and South Africa

Two countries that have made progress toward meaningful and effective comprehensive reform are the former Soviet Republic of Georgia and South Africa. Their relatively rapid progress is highlighted here to illustrate possibilities for reform, the fact reform is difficult and often not linear, and to emphasize the need for additional research that is theory-based and simultaneously attentive to cross-national variations.

9.2.3.1 Georgia

A recent essay in *The Economist* (2017) puts Georgia's progress since the Soviet Union's dissolution in 1990 and the Rose Revolution of 2003 into context. Although Georgia enjoyed double-digit economic growth in the early 2000s, economic growth now stands at about 3 percent. Corruption has declined significantly, setting it apart from other post-Soviet countries. The decline in corruption is eye catching. "Georgia rates better than Italy and close to Spain on Transparency International's corruption perceptions index." *The Economist* also observes that Georgian civil society is strong. Another source (de Waal 2011) touts the efficiency of Georgia's state services, observing admiringly, "You can buy an apartment or obtain a driver's license quickly and without paying a bribe – no mean achievement given the country's traditions and those of its region" (p. 39).

Georgia's ongoing transformation has many roots. My interest here is to focus on those most directly relevant to and underpinning civil service and administrative reforms (Baimenov and Liverakos 2019; Baimenov and Janenova 2019). My inferences depend fully on secondary sources from a modest research literature that is growing slowly. Three factors appear to have influenced the pace and results of civil service and administrative reforms: (1) ministry autonomy that explains variance in results across ministries and magnifies leadership influence; (2) formalization of institutions; and (3) strategic signaling associated with police reform.

David Rinnert (2015) studied Georgia's civil service and administrative reforms using both a research synthesis and semistructured qualitative interviews with ten high-level public officials, most of them former ministers or key ministry staff, and academics. He found that the decentralized nature of reforms and their implementation was a double-edged sword. The autonomy the Georgia central administration granted ministries resulted in large variation in results across ministries, with some ministries realizing high administrative quality over time and others low administrative quality. In the decentralized reform environment, Rinnert found that leadership influence mediated results. Ministries with adept, knowledgeable leaders achieved high administrative quality, and units with poor leaders failed to achieve administrative quality. Rinnert does not identify an alternative course of action, so readers cannot assess whether, for instance, more centralized controls would have produced higher or more uniform administrative quality government-wide. What is known is that autonomy together with quality leadership placed enough discretion in the right hands to support administrative quality.

Another factor that made a difference in Georgia's administrative reforms is a gradual shift away from informality and toward greater institutional formality. Huseyn Aliyev (2014) defines informality as the extent to which informal networks and informal practices constrain the structure of political, economic, and social interaction, a definition that relies heavily on Douglass North's (1991) definition of institutions and informality. The process of formalizing institutions in Georgia was the result of Mikheil Saakashivili's intentional effort to create the type of state resources that McDonnell (2017) identified in the pockets of interstitial bureaucracy she discovered in Ghana. Aliyev (2014) implies that the strong reliance on informal culture in Georgia not only weakened formal state institutions but also fed corruption, which was grounded in informal networks and connections and exchanges of favors. Relying on information from surveys and interviews, Aliyev concludes that the Georgian institution-building reforms were indeed successful in strengthening formal institutions. Although the culture of informality has declined, Aliyev argues that informality has not disappeared but continues to serve an auxiliary role.

In his analysis of civil service and administrative reform, Rinnert argues that the Georgian governance reforms ultimately focused on a small set of ministries, which concentrated resources in the ministries targeted for attention. The downside of this strategy is that it limited widespread implementation of reform. Rinnert observes that the strategy had an upside, and the upside may have been the more influential of the competing influences. The concentrated strategy served as a presidential signal about priorities. An example of the power of the signaling strategy is the reform of policing across Georgia (Light 2014). Police reform appears to have strategically signaled several key messages to the larger society, among them reduction in reliance on informality to constrain relationships and corruption as unacceptable normatively (Light 2014).

9.2.3.2 South Africa

The roots of reform in South Africa are inextricably tied to the country's history of apartheid (Miller 2005). As John Bardill (2000) observes, an essential component of the transition from apartheid to a democratic regime was to change the public sector "from an instrument of discrimination, control and domination to an enabling agency which serves and empowers all the people of the country in a fully accountable and transparent way" (103). Like former Soviet Republic Georgia, institutional reform in South Africa started as a top-down process, triggered and informed by a 1995 *White Paper on the Transformation of the Public Service*, which recommended a Presidential Review Commission. The Commission, created by

President Nelson Mandela in March 1996, issued its report in March 1998.

Karen Miller articulates the twofold agenda for public sector reform that grew from the Presidential Review Commission report in 1998. The reform challenge was magnified not only by apartheid but also by the fragmented and decentralized pre-1998 governance structure. Miller writes: "The problem of poor governance, personnel conflicts, corruption, incompatibility of systems and a low capacity to deliver quality services were problems which the government had to face during the amalgamations of these administrations. The second objective was the restructuring of the senior management echelon" (p. 72).

One path to reform that South Africa's leaders embraced is NPM, the reform movement that I first referred to in Chapter 1. As Robert Cameron's (2009) analysis of the decade following the 1998 Presidential Review Commission report contends, South Africa promulgated tenets of NPM, like agentification and contracting (Boruvka and Perry 2020), but failed to pursue them consistently or to institutionalize them as envisioned by NPM adherents.[1] Cameron argues, for instance, that a framework for decentralization was adopted, but the core central government, particularly the Treasury, was strengthened.[2] The state of affairs Cameron describes appears more closely aligned with the central-local arrangements for the Brazilian state of Ceará, which I described earlier, than a decentralized structure. Cameron also reports that following a period of staff reductions in the 1990s, which accelerated skilled staff attrition, South Africa embarked on strategic growth of its workforce both to create a cadre of middle managers to compete for senior positions and to strengthen professional occupations in its public service. He observes that the strategic workforce growth is "a move away from a minimalist NPM view of the state" (p. 922).

Although South Africa's developmental trajectory since 1994 has not consistently moved toward a more professional public service, promotion of a professional service ethos, one of the eight tenets of the *White Paper on the Transformation of the Public Service* (Department of Public Service and Administration 1995) is an area of progress, particularly since 2000 (Levin 2009). Fernandez (2019) characterizes the administrative reform process since 1994 as "impressive in scale and ambition" (p. 121). At the same time, he observes, "Yet, while notable gains have been achieved, the ANC government continues to struggle to establish a capable and effective public service" (p. 121). His discussion of many challenges to change from the era of apartheid is a sobering reminder that realistic expectations about change likely involve decades and generations. A good example is that a large share of the human capital that came to the new South African public service in 1994 merged from apartheid-era regimes (Fernandez 2019, 131–132). As Fernandez notes, the residual capacity included informal structures from the past. "While changes in formal structure occurred after 1994 in the form of new organizational entities, policies, and procedures, much of the informal structure of the bureaucracy, including norms, values, and practices endured" (p. 132).

It is difficult to definitively characterize South Africa's progress since 1994 on indicators like public service quality and corruption. Fernandez's (2019) analysis, however, offers benchmarks. South Africa's corruption perceptions ranking has declined, for example, but its score has been relatively stable for the last decade and "ranks below all the other BRICS countries and even below G20 member states like Argentina, Indonesia, and Mexico" (Fernandez 2019, 131). South Africa has also been successful in transforming a highly unrepresentative bureaucracy into one that today is highly representative of its society.

The forces underlying any progress on salient indicators are also difficult to identify, but Fernandez's (2019) analysis is the best synthesis of dynamics associated with change to date. Richard Crook (2010) points to nurturing what he calls "islands of effectiveness," localized pockets of effective organizational culture, a concept very similar to McDonnell's (2017) bureaucratic interstices, as a source for potential progress. Crook's focus, however, is the entirety of Africa, and although he refers to South Africa approvingly, he does not identify it as one of the sources for his "islands of effectiveness" construct. Crook also refers to attributes of a public service ethos that converge with the discussion earlier about autonomy and professionalism:

- A sense of commitment to a mission on the part of employees, associated with the belief that they were doing a valued and useful job – hence pride in their job.
- The sense of being part of a team, an enjoyment of the solidarity among work mates.
- Managers who demanded, recognized, and rewarded good work performance, with an open style.
- A sense among employees that they were special and had been selected for their competence.
- Relative organizational autonomy in operational matters (p. 496).

Where South Africa's public service stands with respect to these indicators of public service ethos is uncertain, but the likelihood is that progress, perhaps significant progress, has been made since 1994.

9.2.3.3 Summary

Georgia and South Africa are two countries that have navigated comprehensive change in their public services during the last quarter century. Their progress represents what is possible, even if their examples do not produce models transferable to other countries. The experience in these two countries testifies to the fact that progress is neither linear nor quick. More importantly, Georgia and South Africa also testify that change is possible and a public service ethos can be developed in generations rather than centuries.

9.3　Research to Advance Integrating Public Service Motivation and Civil Service Reform

The processes of change discussed earlier and how to guide institutions and civil service systems toward designs and results that support public service motivation are high priorities for future research. This basic research goal can be facilitated by several discrete research programs. Three high-priority research agendas that provide building blocks for broad reform are discussed here: systematic programs of field experiments, macro-research about variations in national performance, and the dark side of public service motivation.

9.3.1　Systematic Programs of Field Experiments

In Chapter 1, I called attention to the changing reality of the intellectual capital driving civil service reform. The exponential growth in research on public service motivation and related concepts has crossed a critical threshold. As I hope I have shown throughout this book, scholars and practitioners have now built the evidentiary foundations for redesigning civil service systems for the challenges of the twenty-first century. This does not mean that evidence is so abundant we no longer need to pursue basic and applied research to improve motivational outcomes from institutional arrangements of civil service systems, but it does mean we have evidence-based guidance to redesign institutional arrangements with good prospects for successful interventions.

What can we do to fill gaps in the evidence? What courses of action can be taken to produce useable evidence quickly and efficiently? My answer to these questions is that intensive field experiments initiated both across different levels of government (e.g., national, state/provincial, county/municipal) and cross-nationally can go a long way toward producing useable evidence. The type of focused, intensive programs of experiments I have in mind could be led by governmental units with the capacity for and interest in developing evidence for their operations. Partnerships among governments, professional associations, and universities or university consortia is another avenue by which the resources to fill evidence gaps can come together to advance intensive programs of field experiments. The sharing of results from such experiments is critical for incrementally but quickly putting the experiments to broad use.

The report of the Commission on Evidence-Based Policymaking (2017) provides general guidance about ways in which evidence capacity can be expanded, but the focus is largely restricted to the U.S. federal government. We have growing experience with potential models for intensive, experimental initiatives. In Chapter 1, I referred to two evidence-based initiatives that are perceived to have paid dividends: the United Kingdom's Behavioural Insights Team, founded in 2010, and the U.S. Social and Behavioral Sciences Team, created by executive order in 2015. Since its inception, the Behavioural Insights Team has been privatized and now offers its services to government departments for a fee. The Social and Behavioral Insights Team was disbanded on January 21, 2017, upon the transition from President Obama to President Trump. Although responsibilities of the Social and Behavioral Insights Team were not formally handed off, many of their responsibilities were transferred to the Office of Evaluation Sciences in the U.S. General Services Administration (GSA), whose staff and partners represent diverse scientific fields, including economics, psychology, and statistics. The Office of Evaluation Sciences supports GSA's Office of Government-wide Policy's mission to "use policies, evidence, and analysis to help agencies drive efficiency, savings, and improved mission performance" (GSA 2019).

Much of the work of the units referenced earlier focuses on modifications to improve policies (e.g., using social norms to increase tax payments, increasing fine payment rates through text messages, using personalized text messages to low-income students to increase their college enrollment). At least one initiative from the Social and

Behavioral Sciences Team focused on promoting participation of unenrolled service members in the Thrift Savings Plan, a workplace savings plan for federal employees.[3] Although the initiatives were policy-dominated, the spirit behind the experiments pioneered by the Behavioural Insights Team and the Social and Behavioral Sciences Team is transferable to issues confronting civil service systems in both developed and developing countries.

Although my argument here is to expand field experiments, it is important to bear in mind that scholars have already laid the groundwork through experimental research on several fronts. In Chapter 4, for instance, many of the ideas about leveraging the meaningfulness of public work are supported from evidence based on field experiments. The proposals related to leadership similarly were grounded in a relatively large volume of experimental research. Thus, strong experimental evidence is available in many of the areas addressed in this book.

What additional experiments should be undertaken at the outset of a program of intensive field experiments?[4] Several areas rise to the top of a list of priorities. One of these is experimental research related to proposals about employee selection made in Chapter 3. Several selection tests (the dice game, implicit association tests) that appear in research on public service motivation are promising for more extensive use in employee selection. These tests would benefit from more extensive research surrounding their criterion-related validity.

Another proposal from Chapter 3 that merits field experiments is using probationary periods to enhance the selection process. Several facets of this proposal could be illuminated by field experiments. One is what messages to supervisors and managers would encourage them to be more attentive to newcomers during the probationary period. Another facet of the probationary period is the nature of interventions by supervisors that produce better outcomes from this phase of the selection process. The meaning of "better outcomes" is obviously critical. An outcome that immediately comes to mind – departures of staff who are marginally competent and low in public service motivation – would be an important test of the efficacy of monitoring the active interventions during the probationary period.

Another area that could produce payoffs is better understanding of low-powered rewards. The literature refers to low- and high-powered rewards, but it would be helpful to know from field experiments how different types of low-powered rewards are received by employees and what effects they have on behavior. One of these low-powered rewards involves "warm-glow" messages from supervisors and managers. Experiments could be designed to test the influence of different organizational and leader messages about the efficacy of these messages to employees about their efforts to help others.

A third area for which field experiments could produce significant payoffs is performance management. High payoff experiments could be conducted around structures, processes, and messages involving the strengthening of developmental reviews. Improvements of developmental reviews could generate benefits for both performance management generally and performance appraisals specifically. One experimental treatment might be to assign employees randomly to development-only reviews at different junctures during performance periods mandated by law. Such an experiment could help to answer a variety of important questions: What are the attitudinal and behavior outcomes of development-only reviews? Are outcomes sensitive to the frequency of development-only reviews? How are outcomes from development-only reviews affected by reviews that allocate ratings for administrative purposes? Although prior research is voluminous (Harris and Schaubroeck 1988; Jawahar and Williams 1997; Cawley, Keeping, and Levy 1998; Boswell and Boudreau 2002; Pichler 2012), it does not provide clear answers for key questions involving developmental reviews. An intensive program of experiments in a public setting could shed significant light on these important questions.

9.3.2   *Macro-Research about Variations in National Performance*

Systematic programs of field experiments could serve to rapidly advance new civil service policies and management practices. Simultaneous attention to macro-structures and institutional analysis could help to advance our understanding of institutional arrangements that result in outcomes valued by societies – government effectiveness, efficiency, integrity, freedom from corruption, and rule of law. In Chapter 1, I referred to the United Nations Development Program's (UNDP) "New Public Passion" (United Nations Development Program 2015b) initiative, which was predicated on restoring a public service ethos in countries globally. The rationale for the new public passion program was concerns surrounding implementation of the UN's 2030 sustainable development goals. Helen Clark and other UNDP leaders and stakeholders viewed effective public services as crucial for the success of the sustainable development goals, but saw public service, specifically morale and motivation, in crisis across many countries in the developed and developing worlds. Many of the levers envisioned for improving motivation – developing pride and recognition in public service, establishing a merit-based, professional civil service, exercising care in using performance-related pay, promoting a values-based public service, and employee engagement – are integral to proposals in this book. Analysis of macro-institutional arrangements could uncover whether widespread adoption of levers like those listed earlier promote real improvements in outcomes and whether improvements grow exponentially when a multiplicity of the levers are configured together.

A model for this macro-research is the empirical research emanating from the Quality of Government Institute at the University of Gothenburg. Dahlström and Lapuente's (2017) research is a case in point. Their extensive cross-national research about the separation of political and bureaucratic careers and its relationship to government efficiency, effectiveness, and corruption represents one direction for macro-research about the new public service motivational model (Boruvka and Perry 2020). Dahlström and Lapuente's research has opened a window to our understanding of the influence of institutional arrangements offering distinct incentive systems for politicians and bureaucrats. Intensive examination of variations associated with motivational models might pay similar dividends.

Another exemplar for macro-research is the study of high-performance work practices dating to the 1980s. James Combs et al. (2006) conducted a meta-analysis of the high-performance work practice research. Among the questions they asked in the meta-analysis was whether effect sizes were larger when high-performance work practices represented a system versus individual practices. Systems of such practices generated stronger relationships than individual practices. The same may be the case for public motivational practices – pursuing the new public service model systematically may produce larger results.

9.3.3   The "Dark Side" of Public Service Motivation

A review of research on public service motivation (Ritz, Brewer, and Neumann 2016) concluded that most research has focused on positive outcomes associated with the construct, but few scholars have investigated negative outcomes, public service motivation's "dark side." By dark side, they meant negative outcomes (Davis 2018) that may flow to individuals with high public service motivation. James Perry and Lois Wise (1990) raised the issue in their essay, and Laurie Paarlberg, James Perry, and Annie Hondeghem (2008) again called attention to public service motivation's dark side almost two decades later. They pointed to several prospective manifestations of negative outcomes, among them:

- The prospect that seeking out and reenforcing public service values may reduce diversity within the organization and "create an environment in which individuals get lost in the collective" (p. 285).[5]
- Efforts to tap into employees' core values may lead them to feel they are manipulated.
- Pressure to act according to one's public service motivation "may lead to overload, increased job stress, and tensions between work and home life" (p. 285).

Potential negative outcomes have also surfaced in research about concepts allied with public service motivation, such as altruism (Oakley et al. 2012; Furnham et al. 2016), prosocial behavior (Bolino and Grant 2016), and calling (Yaden, McCall, and Ellens 2015).

Carina Schott and Adrian Ritz (2018) observed that despite the attention given to potential negative outcomes early in the evolution of research about public service motivation, few empirical studies have focused on negative outcomes. Most of the research about negative outcomes focuses on employee health and well-being, including stress. The research ironically points to public service motivation as a double-edged sword, simultaneously accounting for positive and negative outcomes. Bangcheng Liu, Kaifeng Yang, and Wei Yu (2015) studied police officers in a large city in eastern China. They found that police officers with higher public service motivation experienced higher mental well-being but lower physical well-being than low public service motivation officers, suggesting a possible trade-off between benefits of public service motivation for coping mentally and costs for physical well-being. In a study of Dutch public employees, Nina Mari van Loon, Wouter Vandenabeele, and Peter Leisink (2015) concluded that the relationship between public service motivation and employee well-being was contingent on the societal impact potential of an employee's work. Public service motivation was associated with higher burnout and lower job satisfaction in people-changing organizations where employees sacrificed themselves for their work. They found the opposite result in people-processing organizations, where low societal impact potential relates to higher burnout and lower job satisfaction because employees experienced frustration when they could not contribute to their desired level.

A subsequent study addressed the public service motivation–well-being relationship, but used a three-wave panel, improving upon the research design of the two 2015 studies. Ulrich Jensen, Lotte Bøgh Andersen, and Ann-Louise Holten (2019) discovered potential ties connecting public service motivation, going to work when ill (presentism), and absenteeism. They found that the strong relationship between public service motivation and presentism could increase subsequent absenteeism, offsetting any performance benefits from going to work when ill.

In addition to the modest volume of research about potential negative outcomes related to employee well-being, two studies of "resigned satisfaction" (Giauque et al. 2012; Quratulain and Khan 2015) raise prospects of negative outcomes. David Giauque et al. (2012) define resigned satisfaction as "the situation surrounding individuals who sense a discrepancy between their work situation and their personal aspiration, and try to counterbalance these negative circumstances by decreasing their level of aspiration" (p. 177). It is "a result of a breach in the contract because the terms and conditions of a reciprocal exchange agreement between employee and employer are not fulfilled" (p. 189). The two studies, one using a sample of Swiss officials and the other a sample from Pakistan, investigated relationships among red tape, public service motivation, and resigned satisfaction and other negative work outcomes. The general thesis of the two studies, that public service motivation either mediates (Giauque et al. 2012) or moderates (Quratulain and Khan 2015) the relationship between red tape and resigned satisfaction, was born out. Although both articles discussed the dark side or negative outcomes, the research designs of the two studies prevented any strong conclusions about public service motivation's association with negative outcomes.

Although scholars have pointed to some "dark sides" associated with public service motivation, in many cases negative outcomes can be satisfactorily managed, especially when managers and employees are aware of them. In Chapter 4, for instance, I referred to Arnold Bakker's research about the job demands-resources model and his suggestions for mitigating burnout and long-term threats to employee well-being from daily exhaustion, which he notes is a real problem for high public service motivation employees (Bakker 2015). His answer for such threats is for managers to be attentive to daily levels of job demands and resources. Bakker offers a number of avenues for employees and attentive managers, some grounded in the logic of job crafting, to mitigate possible exhaustion flowing from excessive job demands or constrained resources for coping (Bakker 2015). The "bright side" of other-oriented motivations may leave leaders, managers, and employees with little choice but to accept the dark with the bright. If this proves to be a reasonable course of action, then research directed toward better understanding negative outcomes and how to mitigate and manage them can be very helpful in guiding stakeholders in addressing the dark side.

In their research synthesis about the dark side of public service motivation, Schott and Ritz (2018) specify propositions to identify and guide research about negative outcomes. I would like to call attention to two general sets of outcomes prominent across their propositions that should receive priority in future research. One outcome is captured by the general label employee well-being, which has already received attention in public service motivation scholarship (Liu, Yang, and Yu 2015; Van Loon, Vandenabeele, and Leisink 2015; Jensen, Andersen, and Holten 2019). Among negatives associated with employee well-being are burnout, stress, and overengagement. The etiology of these psychological and behavioral outcomes may be complex, as existing research suggests, but their investigation can pay dividends for organizations and employees. It seems likely, based on research about both public service motivation and prosocial motivation (Bolino and Grant 2016), that causal processes may be multifaceted. Compassion fatigue, for example, may appear to be a function of caring too much when it may instead be a mismatch between job demands and resources (Klimecki and Singer 2012). Mitigating negative effects of work situations may ultimately require understanding nuances of their etiology.

In light of the nature and role of public institutions, another negative outcome that should be a high priority for future scholarship is potential ties to unethical behavior. Schott and Ritz (2018) identify several classes of such unethical behavior:

- a public servant's commitments may conflict with her/his neutrality or principles of equity and lawfulness;
- strong attachments to values may encourage public servants to use illegal means for organizationally approved ends; and
- public servants may act on moral grounds that justify their blind loyalty to a regime or administrative evil (Adams and Balfour 2014).

C. Daniel Batson et al. (1995) identify another type of unethical behavior and the mechanisms that may trigger it. They conducted two experiments to assess the influence of two decision principles on choices about the welfare of others. One was the principle of justice, tied to simple fairness, derived from John Rawls (1971) writing on political and ethical philosophy. The second principle is empathy-induced altruism. In their experiments, Batson et al. (1995) found that individuals induced to feel empathy were more likely to ignore the principle of justice and allocate resources preferentially to people for whom they felt empathy. The investigators concluded that the two decision principles were independent prosocial motives that sometimes were aligned but at other times conflicted. Their conclusion from the experiments is relevant for public service motivation and public services: "Empathy-induced altruism can, it seems, produce myopia in much the same way as egoistic self-interest. The ultimate goal of egoistic self-interest is to increase one's own welfare; the ultimate goal of altruism is to increase another's welfare. Each of these motives is focused on the welfare of specific persons, so each is potentially at odds with appeals to universal moral principles such as justice" (p. 1053).

Regardless of how desirable it may be for organizations to be populated by members with high public service motivations, the integrity and preservation of public institutions transcends an individual's conformity to their public service identities. Research that helps us to understand the ethical dilemmas that confront actors and potential situations of unethical behavior therefore can contribute to sustaining the integrity of public institutions.

9.4 Conclusion

Research about public service motivation, altruism, and prosocial behavior during the last thirty years has created a stock of intellectual capital that permits us to rethink civil service system designs, policies, and management practices to change civil service systems around the globe. This book has systematically synthesized research across a spectrum of questions that public leaders and managers confront daily. The synthesis provides guidance for policies and management practices to recruit and select staff, design meaningful work, create supportive work environments, compensate and reward employees, and socialize and lead employees for causes greater than themselves.

The policies and practices advanced in this book were selected primarily because I viewed them as consistent with a goal of advancing governance cultures supporting a public service ethos that is increasingly the objective of civil service reforms globally (Crook 2010; United Nations Development Program 2015b). The ultimate arbiter of my judgment about the policies and practices advanced here is their efficacy for advancing constructive outcomes in public service. Empirical judgments could be the result of research from both practicing professional and scholarly communities. We have arrived at the juncture when both real-world experimentation and further scholarly scrutiny are appropriate and important.

Notes

1 Sergio Fernandez (2019) articulates the chief underlying reason for why NPM has not taken off as many presumed it would. He notes that since 1994 two countervailing forces have contended to shape administrative reform. One of these forces, creating a developmental state, requires a strong administrative apparatus. The other force, NPM, favors a minimalist state.

2 Although Robert Cameron (2009) does not explore the organizational dynamics for the failure to decentralize to a greater degree, Paseka Ncholo, former Director-General of the Department of Public Service and Administration, provides context (Ncholo 2000). Ncholo chaired a departmental investigation of provincial government operations. He reports the investigation uncovered extensive evidence of administrative malpractice and poor delegation and coordination, results that are not surprising for a newly revamped administrative system whose capacity is untested. See Paseka Ncholo (2000) for further details. Fernandez (2019) also provides very useful context for understanding the dynamics underlying the progression of reform in South Africa over time. See Fernandez (2019), especially Chapters 2 and 4.

3 The federal agencies represented on the Social and Behavioral Science Team include at least ten cabinet departments and five offices from the

Executive Office of the President (including the Office of Management and Budget). Absent from the list is the federal government's chief personnel agency, the Office of Personnel Management. The Team's membership and reference in the annual report that the unit works "to coordinate the application of social and behavioral science research to advance policy and program goals and better serve the Nation" (Social and Behavioral Sciences Team 2015, VIII) reveal that the Team's priorities were largely directed away from management issues within the federal government.

4 In addition to the types of experimental research I outline here, others have identified excellent opportunities for experiments that extend significantly what I propose. See, for example, McDonnell's (2020) suggestions for experiments in a development context in the concluding chapter of her book. Frederico Finan, Benjamin Olken, and Rohini Pande (2017) offer additional suggestions that also further the agenda discussed here.

5 This negative outcome parallels a similar concern about dynamics associated with the attraction–selection–attrition (ASA) (Schneider 1987), which projects convergence around values espoused by a private organization's founder. See the discussion about ASA theory in Chapter 2.

References

Abner, Gordon B., Sun Young Kim, and James L. Perry. 2017. "Building Evidence for Public Human Resource Management: Using Middle Range Theory to Link Theory and Data." *Review of Public Personnel Administration* 37(2): 139–159.

Abner, Gordon, Jenny Knowles Morrison, James L. Perry, and Bill Valdez. 2019. *Preparing the Next Generation of Federal Leaders: Agency-Based Leadership Development Programs.* Washington, D.C.: IBM Center for the Business of Government.

Adams, Guy B., and Danny L. Balfour. 2014. *Unmasking Administrative Evil.* 3rd ed. Armonk, NY: M.E. Sharpe.

Aguinis, Herman, and Kurt Kraiger. 2009. "Benefits of Training and Development for Individuals and Teams, Organizations, and Society." *Annual Review of Psychology* 60: 451–474.

Alderfer, Clayton P. 1972. *Existence, Relatedness, and Growth: Human Needs in Organizational Settings.* New York, NY: Free Press.

Aliyev, Huseyn. 2014. "The Effects of the Saakashvili Era Reforms on Informal Practices in the Republic of Georgia." *Studies of Transition States and Societies* 6(1): 19–33.

Allen, Tammy D., Lillian T. Eby, Mark L. Poteet, Elizabeth Lentz, and Lizzette Lima. 2004. "Career Benefits Associated with Mentoring for Protégés: A Meta-analysis." *Journal of Applied Psychology* 89(1): 127–136.

Anderfuhren-Biget, Simon, Frédéric Varone, and David Giauque. 2014. "Policy Environment and Public Service Motivation." *Public Administration* 92(4): 807–825.

Andersen, Lotte Bøgh, Bente Bjørnholt, Louise Ladegaard Bro, and Christina Holm-Petersen. 2018. "Leadership and Motivation: A Qualitative Study of Transformational Leadership and Public Service Motivation." *International Review of Administrative Sciences* 84(4): 675–691.

Andersen, Lotte Bøgh, Tor Eriksson, Nicolai Kristensen, and Lene Holm Pedersen. 2012. "Attracting Public Service Motivated Employees: How to Design Compensation Packages." *International Review of Administrative Sciences* 78(4): 615–641.

Andersen, Lotte Bøgh, Eskil Heinesen, and Lene Holm Pedersen. 2014. "How Does Public Service Motivation among Teachers Affect Student Performance in Schools?" *Journal of Public Administration Research and Theory* 24(3): 651–671.

Andersen, Lotte Bøgh, Thomas Pallesen, and Heidi Houlberg Salomonsen. 2013. "Doing Good for Others and/or for Society? The Relationships between Public Service Motivation, User Orientation and University Grading." *Scandinavian Journal of Public Administration* 17(3): 23–44.

Anderson, Jon Lee. 2018. "The Diplomat Who Quit the Trump Administration." *The New Yorker*, May 28. www.newyorker.com/magazine/2018/05/28/the-diplomat-who-quit-the-trump-administration

Andreoni, James. 1990. "Impure Altruism and Donations to Public Goods: A Theory of Warm-Glow Giving." *Economic Journal* 100(401): 464–477.

Andrews, Rhys. 2010. "Organizational Social Capital, Structure and Performance." *Human Relations* 63: 583–608.

Antonakis, John, Marika Fenley, and Sue Liechti. 2012. "Learning Charisma: Transform Yourself into the Person Others Want to Follow." *Harvard Business Review* 90(6): 127–130, 147.

Arieli, Sharon, Adam M. Grant, and Lilach Sagiv. 2014. "Convincing Yourself to Care about Others: An Intervention for Enhancing Benevolence Values." *Journal of Personality* 82(1): 15–24.

Arnold, Edwin W., and Clyde J. Scott. 2002. "Does Broad Banding Improve Pay System Effectiveness?" *Southern Business Review* 27(2): 1–8.

Aronson, Elliot. 1999. "The Power of Self-persuasion." *American Psychologist* 54(11): 875–884.

Arrington, Karen Quinnelly. 2008. "What Social Workers Make." *Alabama State Board of Social Work Examiners Semi-Annual Newsletter*, January.

Ashforth, Blake E., and Kreiner, Glen E. 1999. "'How Can You Do It?': Dirty Work and the Challenge of Constructing a Positive Identity." *Academy of Management Review* 24(3): 413–434.

Ashraf, Nava, Oriana Bandiera, and Kelsey B. Jack. 2014. "No Margin, No Mission? A Field Experiment on Incentives for Public Service Delivery." *Journal of Public Economics* 120(C): 1–17.

Ashraf, Nava, Oriana Bandiera, and Scott S. Lee. 2014. "Awards Unbundled: Evidence from a Natural Field Experiment." *Journal of Economic Behavior & Organization* 100(C): 44–63.

Asseburg, Julia. 2018. "Work-Family Conflict in the Public Sector: The Impact of Public Service Motivation and Job Crafting." Kiel, Hamburg: ZBW – Leibniz Information Centre for Economics. http://hdl.handle.net/10419/183185

Asseburg, Julia, Judith Hattke, David Hensel, Fabian Homberg, and Rick Vogel. 2020. "The Tacit Dimension of Public Sector Attraction in

Multi-Incentive Settings." *Journal of Public Administration Research and Theory* 30(1): 41–59.

Asseburg, Julia, Fabian Homberg, and Rick Vogel. 2018. "Recruitment Messaging, Environmental Fit and Public Service Motivation: Experimental Evidence on Intentions to Apply for Public Sector Jobs." *International Journal of Public Sector Management* 31(6): 689–709.

Avolio, Bruce J., and William L. Gardner. 2005. "Authentic Leadership Development: Getting to the Root of Positive Forms of Leadership." *The Leadership Quarterly* 16(3): 315–338.

Baimenov, Alikhan, and Saltanat Janenova. 2019. "The Emergence of a New Model? Trajectories of Civil Service Development in the Former Soviet Union Countries." In *Public Service Excellence in the 21st Century*, edited by Alikhan Baimenov and Panos Liverakos, 105–143. Singapore: Palgrave Macmillan.

Baimenov, Alikhan, and Panos Liverakos, eds. 2019. *Public Service Excellence in the 21st Century*. Singapore: Palgrave Macmillan.

Bakker, Arnold B. 2015. "A Job Demands–Resources Approach to Public Service Motivation." *Public Administration Review* 75(5): 723–732.

Bandura, Albert. 1977. *Social Learning Theory*. Englewood Cliffs, NJ: Prentice-Hall.

1986. *Social Foundations of Thought and Action: A Social Cognitive Theory*. Englewood Cliffs, NJ: Prentice-Hall.

Banerjee, Abhijit V., Raghabendra Chattopadhyay, Esther Duflo, Daniel Keniston, and Nina Singh. 2014. "Can Institutions Be Reformed from Within? Evidence from a Randomized Experiment with the Rajasthan Police." NBER Working Paper 17912. Cambridge, MA: National Bureau of Economic Research.

Banerjee, Ritwik, Tushi Baul, and Tanya Rosenblat. 2015. "On Self-selection of the Corrupt into the Public Sector." *Economics Letters* 127: 43–46.

Banuri, Sheheryar, and Philip Keefer. 2015. "Was Weber Right? The Effects of Pay for Ability and Pay for Performance on Pro-Social Motivation, Ability and Effort in the Public Sector." Policy Research Working Paper 7261. Washington, D.C.: The World Bank. https://openknowledge.worldbank.org/handle/10986/21993

2016. "Pro-social Motivation, Effort and the Call to Public Service." *European Economic Review* 83: 139–164.

Bardill, John E. 2000. "Towards a Culture of Good Governance: The Presidential Review Commission and Public Service Reform in South Africa." *Public Administration and Development* 20: 103–117.

Barfort, Sebastian, Nikolaj A. Harmon, Frederik G. Hjorth, and Asmus Leth Olsen. 2019. "Sustaining Honesty in Public Service: The Role of Selection." *American Economic Journal: Economic Policy* 11(4): 96–123.

Barley, Stephen R., and Gideon Kunda. 1992. "Design and Devotion: Surges of Rational and Normative Ideologies of Control in Managerial Discourse." *Administrative Science Quarterly* 37(3): 363–399.

Barnard, Chester I. 1938. *The Functions of the Executive.* Cambridge, MA: Harvard University Press.

Bartol, Kathryn M., Wei Liu, Xiangquan Zeng, and Kelu Wu. 2009. "Social Exchange and Knowledge Sharing among Knowledge Workers: The Moderating Role of Perceived Job Security." *Management and Organization Review* 5(2): 223–240.

Bass, Bernard M. 1990. "From Transactional to Transformational Leadership: Learning to Share the Vision." *Organizational Dynamics* 18(3): 19–31.

Bateman, Thomas S., and Bruce Barry. 2012. "Masters of the Long Haul: Pursuing Long-Term Work Goals." *Journal of Organizational Behavior* 33: 984–1006.

Batson, C. Daniel. 1994. "Why Act for the Public Good? Four Answers." *Personality and Social Psychology Bulletin* 20(5): 603–610.

Batson, C. Daniel, Tricia Klein, Lori Highberger, and Laura Shaw. 1995. "Immorality from Empathy-induced Altruism: When Compassion and Justice Conflict." *Journal of Personality and Social Psychology* 68(6): 1042–1054.

Batson, C. Daniel, and Laura L. Shaw. 1991. "Evidence for Altruism: Toward a Pluralism of Prosocial Motives." *Psychological Inquiry* 2(2): 107–122.

Bauer, Talya N. 2010. *Onboarding New Employees: Maximizing Success.* Washington, D.C.: Society for Human Resource Management Foundation. www.shrm.org/hr-today/trends-and-forecasting/special-reports-and-expert-views/Documents/Onboarding-New-Employees.pdf

Bekke, Hans A. G. M., James L. Perry, and Theo A. J. Toonen. 1996. "Conclusion: Assessment of Progress and a Research Agenda." In *Civil Service Systems in Comparative Perspective*, edited by Hans A. G. M. Bekke, James L. Perry, and Theo A. J. Toonen, 318–332. Bloomington, IN: Indiana University Press.

Bellé, Nicola. 2013. "Experimental Evidence on the Relationship between Public Service Motivation and Job Performance." *Public Administration Review* 73(1): 143–153.

2014. "Leading to Make a Difference: A Field Experiment on the Performance Effects of Transformational Leadership, Perceived Social Impact, and Public Service Motivation." *Journal of Public Administration Research and Theory* 24(1): 109–136.

Bellé, Nicola, and Paola Cantarelli. 2015. "Monetary Incentives, Motivation, and Job Effort in the Public Sector: An Experimental Study with Italian

Government Executives." *Review of Public Personnel Administration* 35(2): 99–123.

Berg, Justin M., Jane E. Dutton, and Amy Wrzesniewski. 2008. "What Is Job Crafting and Why Does It Matter?" In Theory-to-Practice Briefing. Ann Arbor, MI: Ross School of Business, University of Michigan. http://positiveorgs.bus.umich.edu/wp-content/uploads/What-is-Job-Crafting-and-Why-Does-it-Matter1.pdf

2013. "Job Crafting and Meaningful Work." In *Purpose and Meaning in the Workplace*, edited by Bryan J. Dik, Zinta S. Byrne, and Michael F. Steger, 81–104. Washington, D.C.: American Psychological Association.

Berinato, Scott. 2010. "You Have to Lead from Everywhere." *Harvard Business Review* 11: 76–79.

Bertelli, Anthony M. 2006. "Motivation Crowding and the Federal Civil Servant: Evidence from the U.S. Internal Revenue Service." *International Public Management Journal* 9(1): 3–23.

Bevir, Mark. 2011. "Public Administration as Storytelling." *Public Administration* 89(1): 183–195.

Bierhoff, Hans Werner. 2002. *Prosocial Behaviour.* London: Psychology Press.

Biggs, Andrew G., and Jason Richwine. 2012. "Finding Answers to the Public Compensation Question." *Public Administration Review* 72(5): 780–781. 2014. *Overpaid or Underpaid? A State-by-State Ranking of Public-Employee Compensation.* AEI Economic Policy Working Paper 2014-04. Washington, D.C.: American Enterprise Institute.

Block, Stephen R., and Steven Rosenberg. 2002. "Toward an Understanding of Founder's Syndrome: An Assessment of Power and Privilege among Founders of Nonprofit Organizations." *Nonprofit Management and Leadership* 12: 353–368.

Bolino, Mark C., and Adam M. Grant. 2016. "The Bright Side of Being Prosocial at Work, and the Dark Side, Too: A Review and Agenda for Research on Other-Oriented Motives, Behavior, and Impact in Organizations." *The Academy of Management Annals* 10: 599–670.

Bolino, Mark C., William H. Turnley, and Todd Averett. 2003. "Going the Extra Mile: Cultivating and Managing Employee Citizenship Behavior." *Academy of Management Executive* 17(3): 60–71.

Booz Allen Hamilton. 2008. *Getting On Board: A Model for Integrating and Engaging New Employees.* Washington, D.C.: Partnership for Public Service. https://ourpublicservice.org/wp-content/uploads/2008/05/c04bbbb3d5c41dfdb39f779dbc8003da-1403634756.pdf

Borjas, George J. 2003. "Wage Structures and the Sorting of Workers into the Public Sector." In *For the People, Can We Fix Public Service?*, edited by John D. Donahue and Joseph S. Nye, Jr., 29–54. Washington, D.C.: The Brookings Institution.

Boruvka, Elise, and James L. Perry. 2020. "Understanding Evolving Public Motivational Practices: An Institutional Analysis." *Governance* 33(3): 565–584.

Boswell, Wendy R., and John W. Boudreau. 2001. "How Leading Companies Create, Measure and Achieve Strategic Results through 'Line of Sight'." *Management Decision* 39(10): 851–860.

2002. "Separating the Developmental and Evaluative Performance Appraisal Uses." *Journal of Business and Psychology* 16(3): 391–412.

Bottomley, Paul, Ahmed Mohammed Sayed Mostafa, Julian Seymour Gould-Williams, and Filadelfo León-Cázares. 2016. "The Impact of Transformational Leadership on Organizational Citizenship Behaviours: The Contingent Role of Public Service Motivation." *British Journal of Management* 27(2): 390–405.

Bowen, David E., Gerald E. Ledford, and Barry R. Nathan. 1991. "Hiring for the Organization, Not the Job." *Academy of Management Executive* 5(4): 35–51.

Boyte, Harry C., and Nancy N. Kari. 1996. *Building America: The Democratic Promise of Public Work*. Philadelphia, PA: Temple University Press.

Bozeman, Barry, and Mary K. Feeney. 2009a. "Public Management Mentoring: A Three-Tier Model." *Review of Public Personnel Administration* 29(2): 134–157.

2009b. "Public Management Mentoring: What Affects Outcomes?" *Journal of Public Administration Research and Theory* 19(2): 427–452.

Bozeman, Barry, and Xuhong Su. 2015. "Public Service Motivation Concepts and Theory: A Critique." *Public Administration Review* 75(5): 700–710.

Brans, Marleen, and Annie Hondeghem. 2005. "Competency Frameworks in the Belgian Governments: Causes, Construction and Contents." *Public Administration* 83(4): 823–837.

Breaugh, James A. 2009. "The Use of Biodata for Employee Selection: Past Research and Future Directions." *Human Resources Management Review* 19(3): 219–231.

Breaugh, Jessica, Kerstin Alfes, and Adrian Ritz. 2019. "Strength in Numbers? Understanding the Effect of Collective PSM in Team Level Performance." Working paper. Berlin: Hertie School of Government.

Breaugh, Jessica, Adrian Ritz, and Kerstin Alfes. 2018. "Work Motivation and Public Service Motivation: Disentangling Varieties of Motivation and Job Satisfaction." *Public Management Review*, 20(10): 1423–1443.

Brehm, John O., and Scott Gates. 1997. *Working, Shirking, and Sabotage: Bureaucratic Response to a Democratic Public*. Ann Arbor, MI: University of Michigan Press.

Brewer, Gene A. 2003. "Building Social Capital: Civic Attitudes and Behavior of Public Servants." *Journal of Public Administration Research and Theory* 13(1): 5–25.

Brewer, Gene A., and Gene A. Brewer, Jr. 2011. "Parsing Public/Private Differences in Work Motivation and Performance: An Experimental Study." *Journal of Public Administration Research and Theory* 21(suppl 3): i347–i362.

Brewer, Gene A., and J. Edward Kellough. 2016. "Administrative Values and Public Personnel Management: Reflections on Civil Service Reform." *Public Personnel Management* 45(2): 171–189.

Brewer, Gene A., and Sally Coleman Selden. 1998. "Whistle Blowers in the Federal Civil Service: New Evidence of the Public Service Ethic." *Journal of Public Administration Research and Theory* 8(3): 413–439.

Brief, Arthur P., and Stephan J. Motowidlo. 1986. "Prosocial Organizational Behaviors." *Academy of Management Review* 11(4): 710–725.

Bright, Leonard. 2007. "Does Person-Organization Fit Mediate the Relationship between Public Service Motivation and the Job Performance of Public Employees?" *Review of Public Personnel Administration* 27(4): 361–379.

2008. "Does Public Service Motivation Really Make a Difference on the Job Satisfaction and Turnover Intentions of Public Employees?" *American Review of Public Administration* 38(2): 149–166.

2016. "Public Service Motivation and Socialization in Graduate Education." *Teaching Public Administration* 34(3): 284–306.

Bromberg, Daniel E. and Étienne Charbonneau. 2020. "Public Service Motivation, Personality, and the Hiring Decisions of Public Managers: An Experimental Study." *Public Personnel Management* 49(2): 193–217.

Bronkhorst, Babette, Bram Steijn, and Brenda Vermeeren. 2015. "Transformational Leadership, Goal Setting, and Work Motivation: The Case of a Dutch Municipality." *Review of Public Personnel Administration* 35(2): 124–145.

Bryce, Andrew. 2018. "Finding Meaning through Work: Eudaimonic Well-Being and Job Type in the US and UK." Working Papers 2018004. Department of Economics, The University of Sheffield.

Buchanan, Bruce, II. 1974. "Building Organizational Commitment: The Socialization of Managers in Work Organizations." *Administrative Science Quarterly* 19(4): 533–546.

Buchanan, Bruce. 1975. "Red-Tape and the Service Ethic: Some Unexpected Differences Between Public and Private Managers." *Administration & Society* 6(4): 423–444.

Bunderson, J. Stuart, and Jeffery A. Thompson. 2009. "The Call of the Wild: Zookeepers, Callings, and the Double-Edged Sword of Deeply Meaningful Work." *Administrative Science Quarterly* 54(1): 32–57.

Burbano, Vanessa C. 2016. "Social Responsibility Messages and Worker Wage Requirements: Field Experimental Evidence from Online Labor Marketplaces." *Organization Science* 27(4): 1010–1028.

Burgess, Simon, and Marisa Ratto. 2003. "The Role of Incentives in the Public Sector: Issues and Evidence." *Oxford Review of Economic Policy* 19(2): 285–300.

Burns, James MacGregor. 1978. *Leadership*. New York, NY: Harper Collins.

Cable, Daniel M., and Timothy A. Judge. 1996. "Person–Organization Fit, Job Choice Decisions, and Organizational Entry." *Organizational Behavior and Human Decision Processes* 67(3): 294–311.

Caillier, James Gerard. 2015. "Towards a Better Understanding of Public Service Motivation and Mission Valence in Public Agencies." *Public Management Review* 17(9): 1217–1236.

2017. "The Impact of High-Quality Workplace Relationships in Public Organizations." *Public Administration* 95: 638–653.

Caldwell, David F., Jennifer A. Chatman, and Charles O'Reilly. 1990. "Building Organizational Commitment: A Multifirm Study." *Journal of Occupational Psychology* 63: 245–261.

Callen, Michael, Saad Gulzar, Ali Hasannain, Yasir Khan, and Arman Rezaee. 2015. "Personalities and Public Sector Performance: Evidence from a Health Experiment in Pakistan." National Bureau of Economic Research Working Paper 21180. Cambridge, MA: National Bureau of Economic Research.

Cameron, Kim S. 2008. "Positively Deviant Organizational Performance and the Role of Leadership Values." *The Journal of Values-Based Leadership* 1(1): 1–17. http://scholar.valpo.edu/jvbl/vol1/iss1/8

Cameron, Kim S., and Marc Lavine. 2006. *Making the Impossible Possible*. San Francisco, CA: Berrett Koehler.

Cameron, Robert. 2009. "New Public Management Reforms in the South African Public Service: 1999–2009." *Journal of Public Administration* 1(Special Issue): 910–942.

Carpenter, Daniel P. 2010. *Reputation and Power: Organizational Image and Pharmaceutical Regulation in the FDA*. Princeton, NJ: Princeton University Press.

Carpenter, Jacqueline, Dennis Doverspike, and Rosanna F. Miguel. 2012. "Public Service Motivation as a Predictor of Attraction to the Public Sector." *Journal of Vocational Behavior* 80(2): 509–523.

Carr, Carlin. 2013. "Mentoring: The Key to Unlocking India's Demographic Dividend?" *The Guardian*. Friday, December 27, 2013. www.theguardian.com/global-development-professionals-network/2013/dec/27/india-youth-unemployment-mentoring

Carton, Andrew M. 2018. "'I'm Not Mopping the Floors, I'm Putting a Man on the Moon': How NASA Leaders Enhanced the Meaningfulness of Work by Changing the Meaning of Work." *Administrative Science Quarterly* 63(2): 323–369.

Cassar, Lea, and Stephan Meier. 2018. "Nonmonetary Incentives and the Implications of Work as a Source of Meaning." *Journal of Economic Perspectives* 32(3): 215–238.

Cawley, Brian D., Lisa M. Keeping, and Paul E. Levy. (1998). "Participation in the Performance Appraisal Process and Employee Reactions: A Meta-Analytic Review of Field Investigations." *Journal of Applied Psychology* 83(4): 615–633.

Celani, Anthony, and Parbydyal Singh. 2011. "Signaling Theory and Applicant Attraction Outcomes." *Personnel Review* 40(2): 222–238.

Cerasoli, Christopher P., Jessica M. Nicklin, and Michael T. Ford. 2014. "Intrinsic Motivation and Extrinsic Incentives Jointly Predict Performance: A 40-Year Meta-Analysis." *Psychological Bulletin* 140(4): 980–1008.

Chatman, Jennifer A. 1991. "Matching People and Organizations, Selection and Socialization in Public Accounting Firms." *Administrative Science Quarterly* 36(3): 459–484.

Chen, Chung-An and Barry Bozeman. 2013. "Understanding Public and Nonprofit Managers' Motivation Through the Lens of Self-Determination Theory." *Public Management Review* 15(4): 584–607.

Chen, Chung-An, Don-Yun Chen, Zhou-Peng Liao, and Ming-Feng Kuo. 2019. "Winnowing Out High-psm Candidates: The Adverse Selection Effect of Competitive Public Service Exams." *International Public Management Journal*. https://doi.org/10.1080/10967494.2019.1658663

Choi, Do Lim. 2004. "Public Service Motivation and Ethical Conduct." *International Review of Public Administration* 8(2): 99–106.

Choi, Yujin, and Il Hwan Chung. 2017. "Attraction-Selection and Socialization of Work Values: Evidence from Longitudinal Survey." *Public Personnel Management* 46(1): 66–88.

Christensen, Robert K., Laurie Paarlberg, and James L. Perry. 2017. "Public Service Motivation Research: Lessons for Practice." *Public Administration Review* 77(4): 529–542.

Christensen, Robert K., Steven W. Whiting, Tobin Im, Eunju Rho, Justin M. Stritch, and Jungho Park. 2013. "Public Service Motivation, Task, and Non-Task Behavior: A Performance Appraisal Experiment with Korean MPA and MBA Students." *International Public Management Journal* 16(1): 28–52.

Christensen, Robert K., and Bradley Wright. 2011. "The Effects of Public Service Motivation on Job Choice Decisions: Disentangling the Contributions of Person–Organizational Fit and Person–Job Fit." *Journal of Public Administration Research and Theory* 21(4): 723–743.

Chronus. 2019. "Top 10 Mentoring Program Best Practices." https://chronus.com/blog/top-10-mentoring-program-best-practices

Clements, Benedict, Sanjeev Gupta, Shamsuddin Tareq, and Izabela Karpowicz. 2010. "Evaluating Government Employment and Compensation." IMF Technical Notes and Manuals 10/15. Washington, D.C.: International Monetary Fund.

Clerkin, Richard M., and Jerrell D. Coggburn. 2012. "The Dimensions of Public Service Motivation and Sector Work Preferences." *Review of Public Personnel Administration* 32(3): 209–235.

Cohen, David K., and Richard J. Murnane. 1985. *The Merits of Merit Pay.* Washington, D.C.: National Institute of Education.

Colby, Ann, and William Damon. 1992. *Some Do Care: Contemporary Lives of Moral Commitment.* New York, NY: Free Press.

Combs, James, Younmei Liu, Angela Hall, and David Ketchen. 2006. "How Much Do High-Performance Work Practices Matter? A Meta-Analysis of Their Effects on Organizational Performance." *Personnel Psychology* 59: 501–528.

Commission on Evidence-Based Policymaking. 2017. *The Promise of Evidence-based Policymaking.* Washington, D.C.: Commission on Evidence-Based Policymaking. https://www.cep.gov/report/cep-final-report.pdf

Condrey, Steve E., Rex L. Facer, and Jared J. Llorens. 2012. "Getting It Right: How and Why We Should Compare Federal and Private Sector Compensation." *Public Administration Review* 72(5): 784–785.

Connelly, Brian L., S. Trevis Certo, R. Duane Ireland, and Christopher R. Reutzel. 2011. "Signaling Theory: A Review and Assessment." *Journal of Management* 37(1): 39–67.

Cooper-Thomas, Helena D., and Neil Anderson. 2002. "Newcomer Adjustment: The Relationship Between Organizational Socialization Tactics, Information Acquisition and Attitudes." *Journal of Occupational and Organizational Psychology* 75, 423–437.

Cooper-Thomas, Helena D., Annalies Van Vianen, and Neil Anderson. 2004. "Changes in Person-Organization Fit: The Impact of Socialization Tactics on Perceived and Actual P-O Fit." *European Journal of Work and Organizational Psychology* 13(1): 52–78.

Crook, Richard C. 2010. "Rethinking Civil Service Reform in Africa: 'Islands of Effectiveness' and Organisational Commitment." *Commonwealth & Comparative Politics* 48(4): 479–504.

Dahlström, Carl, and Victor Lapuente. 2017. *Organizing Leviathan: Politicians, Bureaucrats, and the Making of Good Government.* Cambridge, UK: Cambridge University Press.

Dahlström, Carl, Victor Lapuente, and Jan Teorell. 2012. "The Merit of Meritocratization: Politics, Bureaucracy, and the Institutional Deterrents of Corruption." *Political Research Quarterly* 65(3): 656–668.

Dal Bó, Ernesto, Frederico Finan, and Martín A. Rossi. 2013. "Strengthening State Capabilities: The Role of Financial Incentives in the Call to Public Service." *The Quarterly Journal of Economics* 128(3): 1169–1218.

Danzer, Alexander M., and Peter J. Dolton. 2011. "Total Reward in the UK in the Public and Private Sectors." Discussion Paper No 5656. Bonn: Forschungsinstitut zur Zukunft der Arbeit (Institute for the Study of Labour).

Davis, Randall S. 2018. "The 'Dark Side' of the Public Workplace: Counterproductive Workplace Behavior and Environmental Negativity in Public Administration Research." In *Handbook of American Public Administration*, edited by Edmund C. Stazyk and H. George Frederickson, 205–220. Cheltenham, UK: Edward Elgar.

Davis, Trenton J., and Gerald T. Gabris. 2008. "Strategic Compensation Utilizing Efficiency Wages in the Public Sector to Achieve Desirable Organizational Outcomes." *Review of Public Personnel Administration* 28: 327–348.

Deci, Edward L. 1971. "Effects of Externally Mediated Rewards on Intrinsic Motivation." *Journal of Personality and Social Psychology* 18(1): 105–115.

Deci, Edward L., Richard Koestner, and Richard M. Ryan. 1999. "A Meta-Analytic Review of Experiments Examining the Effects of Extrinsic Rewards on Intrinsic Motivation." *Psychological Bulletin* 125(6): 627–668.

Deci, Edward L., and Richard M. Ryan. 1985. *Intrinsic Motivation and Self-determination in Human Behavior*. New York, NY: Plenum.

2000. "Intrinsic and Extrinsic Motivations: Classic Definitions and New Directions." *Contemporary Educational Psychology* 25: 54–67.

Deckop, John R., Robert Mangel, and Carol C. Cirka. 1999. "Getting More Than What You Pay For: Organizational Citizenship Behavior and Pay-for-Performance Plans." *Academy of Management Journal* 42(4): 420–428.

De Dreu, Carsten K. W. 2006. "Rational Self-interest and Other Orientation in Organizational Behavior: A Critical Appraisal and Extension of Meglino and Korsgaard (2004)." *Journal of Applied Psychology* 91(6): 1245–1252.

Denhardt, Janet V., and Robert B. Denhardt. 2015. "The New Public Service Revisited." *Public Administration Review* 75(5): 664–672.

Denhardt, Robert B. 1993. *The Pursuit of Significance: Strategies for Managerial Success in Public Organizations*. Belmont, CA: Wadsworth.

Department of Public Service and Administration. 1995. "White Paper on the Transformation of the Public Service, Notice 1227 of 1995." South African Government Gazette No. 16838, Pretoria. www.dpsa.gov.za/dpsa2g/documents/acts&regulations/frameworks/white-papers/wpstoc.pdf

Deserranno, Erika. 2019. "Financial Incentives as Signals: Experimental Evidence from the Recruitment of Village Promoters in Uganda." *American Economic Journal: Applied Economics* 11(1): 277–317.

Desimone, Laura M., Andrew C. Porter, Michael S. Garet, Kwang Suk Yoon, and Beatrice F. Birman. 2002. "Effects of Professional Development on

Teacher's Instruction: Results from a Three-Year Longitudinal Study." *Education Evaluation and Policy Analysis* 24: 81–112.

De Waal, Thomas. 2011. *Georgia's Choices for Charting a Future in Uncertain Times*. Washington, D.C.: Carnegie Endowment for International Peace.

Dickson, Matt, Fabien Postel-Vinay, and Hélène Turon. 2014. "The Lifetime Earnings Premium in the Public Sector: The View from Europe." *Labour Economics* 31: 141–161.

DiIulio, John D., Jr. 1994. "Principled Agents: The Cultural Bases of Behavior in a Federal Government Bureaucracy." *Journal of Public Administration Research and Theory* 4(3): 277–318.

Dik, Bryan J., and Ryan D. Duffy. 2009. "Calling and Vocation at Work: Definitions and Prospects for Research and Practice." *The Counseling Psychologist* 37(3): 424–450.

Dik, Bryan J., Ryan D. Duffy, and Brandy M. Eldridge. 2009. "Calling and Vocation in Career Counseling: Recommendations for Promoting Meaningful Work." *Professional Psychology: Research and Practice* 40(6): 625–632.

DiMaggio, Paul J., and Walter W. Powell. 1983. "The Iron Cage Revisited: Institutional Isomorphism and Collective Rationality in Organizational Fields." *American Sociological Review* 48(2): 147–160.

Dur, Robert A. J., and Max van Lent. 2019. "Socially Useless Jobs." *Industrial Relations* 58: 3–16.

Dutton, Jane E., Janet M. Dukerich, and Celia V. Harquail. 1994. "Organizational Images and Member Identification." *Administrative Science Quarterly* 39(2): 239–263.

Earnest, David R., David G. Allen, and Ronald S. Landis. 2011. "Mechanisms Linking Realistic Job Previews with Turnover: A Meta-Analytic Path Analysis." *Personnel Psychology* 64(4): 865–897.

Eby, Lillian T., Tammy D. Allen, Sarah C. Evans, Thomas Ng, and David L. DuBois. 2008. "Does Mentoring Matter? A Multidisciplinary Meta-Analysis Comparing Mentored and Non-mentored Individuals." *Journal of Vocational Behavior* 72(2): 254–267.

Ehrich, Lisa C., and Brian C. Hansford. 2008. "Mentoring in the Public Sector." *Practical Experiences in Professional Education* 11(1): 1–16.

Elliott, Robert H., and Allen L. Peaton. 1994. "The Probationary Period in the Selection Process: A Survey of Its Use at the State Level." *Public Personnel Management* 23(1): 47–59.

Esteve, Marc, and Christian Schuster. 2019. *Motivating Public Employees*. Cambridge, UK: Cambridge University Press.

Esteve, Marc, Diemo Urbig, Arjen van Witteloostuijn, and George Boyne. 2016. "Prosocial Behavior and Public Service Motivation." *Public Administration Review* 76(1): 177–187.

Esteve, Marc, Arjen Van Witteloostuijn, and George Boyne. 2015. "The Effects of Public Service Motivation on Collaborative Behavior: Evidence from Three Experimental Games." *International Public Management Journal* 8(2): 171–189.

Etzioni, Amitai. 1988. *The Moral Dimension: Toward a New Economics.* New York, NY: Free Press.

Feeley, John D. 2018. "Why I Can No Longer Serve This President." *The Washington Post*, March 9. www.washingtonpost.com/opinions/why-i-could-no-longer-serve-this-president/2018/03/08/f444f086-225c-11e8-86f6-54bfff693d2b_story.html

Fehrler, Sebastian, and Michael Kosfeld. 2014. "Pro-social Missions and Worker Motivation: An Experimental Study." *Journal of Economic Behavior and Organization* 100(April): 99–110.

Feintzeig, Rachel. 2014. "U.S. Struggles to Draw Young, Savvy Staff." *Wall Street Journal*, June 10.

Fernandez, Sergio. 2019. *Representative Bureaucracy and Performance: Public Service Transformation in South Africa.* Cham, Switzerland: Palgrave Macmillan.

Fernandez, Sergio, Yoon Jik Cho, and James L. Perry. 2010. "Exploring the Link between Integrated Leadership and Public Sector Performance." *The Leadership Quarterly* 21(2): 308–323.

Fernandez, Sergio, and Hal G. Rainey. 2006. "Managing Successful Organizational Change in the Public Sector." *Public Administration Review* 66(2): 168–176.

Ferraro, Fabrizio, Jeffrey Pfeffer, and Robert I. Sutton. 2005. "Economics Language and Assumptions: How Theories Can Become Self-fulfilling." *Academy of Management Review* 30(1): 8–24.

Finan, Frederico, Benjamin A. Olken, and Rohini Pande. 2017. "The Personnel Economics of the Developing State." *Handbook of Economic Field Experiments* 2: 467–514.

Fine, Saul. 2010. "Cross-cultural Integrity Testing as a Marker of Regional Corruption Rates." *International Journal of Selection and Assessment* 18(3): 251–259.

Finer, Herman. 1941. "Administrative Responsibility in Democratic Government." *Public Administration Review* 1(4): 335–350.

Fischer, Claude S. 1975. "Toward a Subcultural Theory of Urbanism." *American Journal of Sociology* 80(6): 1319–1341.

Fisher, Cynthia D. 1986. "Organizational Socialization: An Integrative Review." *Research in Personnel and Human Resource Management* 4: 101–145.

Forde, Chris. 2001. "Temporary Arrangements: The Activities of Employment Agencies in the UK." *Work, Employment and Society* 15(3): 631–644.

Francois, Patrick. 2000. "'Public Service Motivation' as an Argument for Government Provision." *Journal of Public Economics* 78(3): 275–299.

Frank, Robert H. 1996. "What Price the Moral High Ground?" *Southern Economic Journal* 63(1): 1–17.

Frey, Bruno S. 1997. *Not Just for the Money: An Economic Theory of Personal Motivation*. Cheltenham, UK: Edward Elgar.

Frey, Bruno S., and Reto Jegen. 2001. "Motivation Crowding Theory." *Journal of Economic Surveys* 15(5): 589–611.

Frey, Bruno S., and Margit Osterloh. 2005. "Yes, Managers Should Be Paid Like Bureaucrats." *Journal of Management Inquiry* 14(1): 96–111.

Friedrich, Carl J. 1935. Responsible Government Service under the American Constitution. In *Problems of the American Public Service*, by Carl J. Friedrich et al., Monograph no. 7. New York: McGraw-Hill.

Friel, Brian. 2008. "Intelligent Design: How Your Workplace Is Designed Can Have a Big Impact on How Things Get Done." *Government Executive*, May 7. www.govexec.com/management/2008/05/intelligent-designk/26843/

Furnham, Adrian, Luke Treglown, Gillian Hyde, and Geoff Trickey. 2016. "The Bright and Dark Side of Altruism: Demographic, Personality Traits, and Disorders Associated with Altruism." *Journal of Business Ethics* 134(3): 359–368.

Gailmard, Sean, and John W. Patty. 2007. "Slackers and Zealots: Civil Service, Policy Discretion, and Bureaucratic Expertise." *American Journal of Political Science* 51(4): 873–889.

Gans-Morse, Jordan, Alexander Kalgin, Andrei Klimenko, Dmitriy Vorobyev, and Andrei Yakovlev. 2019. "A Tough Test of Generalizability: Does Public Service Motivation Predict Sectoral Career Preferences in Russia?" Paper presented at the Elevating Public Service Motivation Conference, Aspen Grove, UT, September 26–28.

2020. "Public Service Motivation as a Predictor of Corruption, Dishonesty, and Altruism." Unpublished paper supported by the Equality Development and Globalization Studies (EDGS) program at Northwestern University and the Russian Academic Excellence Project "5-100." Evanston, IL: Northwestern University.

Georgellis, Yannis, Elisabetta Iossa, and Vurain Tabvuma. 2011. "Crowding Out Intrinsic Motivation in the Public Sector." *Journal of Public Administration Research and Theory* 21(3): 473–493.

Gerhart, Barry, and Sara L. Rynes. 2003. *Compensation: Theory, Evidence and Strategic Implications*. Thousand Oaks, CA: Sage.

Ghosal, Sumantra. 2005. "Bad Management Theories Are Destroying Good Management Practices." *Academy of Management Learning and Education* 4(1): 75–91.

Ghosh, Rajashi, and Thomas G. Reio, Jr. 2013. "Career Benefits Associated with Mentoring for Mentors: A Meta-Analysis." *Journal of Vocational Behavior* 83(1): 106–116.

Giauque, David, Simon Anderfuhren-Biget, and Frédéric Varone. 2013. "HRM Practices, Intrinsic Motivators, and Organizational Performance in the Public Sector." *Public Personnel Management* 42(2): 123–150.

Giauque, David, Adrian Ritz, Frédéric Varone, and Simon Anderfuhren-Biget. 2012. "Resigned but Satisfied: The Negative Impact of Public Service Motivation and Red Tape on Work Satisfaction." *Public Administration* 90(1): 175–193.

Goodsell, Charles T. 2004. *The Case for Bureaucracy*. 4th ed.. Washington, D.C.: CQ Press.

2011. *Mission Mystique: Belief Systems in Public Agencies*. Washington, D.C.: CQ Press.

Gould-Williams, Julian S., Ahmed Mohammed Sayed Mostafa, and Paul Bottomley. 2015. "Public Service Motivation and Employee Outcomes in the Egyptian Public Sector: Testing the Mediating Effect of Person–Organization Fit." *Journal of Public Administration Research and Theory* 25(2): 597–622.

Govloop. 2017. *Your Guide to Effective Onboarding in Government*. www.govloop.com/resources/guide-effective-onboarding-government/

Graeber, David. 2013. "On the Phenomenon of Bullshit Jobs: A Work Rant." *Strike! Magazine* 3: 1–6.

Grant, Adam M. 2007. "Relational Job Design and the Motivation to Make a Prosocial Difference." *Academy of Management Review* 32(2): 393–417.

2008a. "Does Intrinsic Motivation Fuel the Prosocial Fire? Motivational Synergy in Predicting Persistence, Performance, and Productivity." *Journal of Applied Psychology* 93(1): 48–58.

2008b. "Employees without a Cause: The Motivational Effects of Prosocial Impact in Public Service." *International Public Management Journal* 11(1): 48–66.

2012. "Leading with Meaning: Beneficiary Contact, Prosocial Impact, and the Performance Effects of Transformational Leadership." *Academy of Management Journal* 55(2): 458–476.

Grant, Adam M., and Justin M. Berg. 2011. "Prosocial Motivation at Work: When, Why, and How Making a Difference Makes a Difference." In *The Oxford Handbook of Positive Organizational Scholarship*, edited by Gretchen M. Spreitzer and Kim S. Cameron, 28–44. New York, NY: Oxford University Press.

Grant, Adam M., Elizabeth M. Campbell, Grace Chen, Keenan Cottone, David Lapedis, and Karen Lee. 2007. "Impact and the Art of Motivation Maintenance: The Effects of Contact with Beneficiaries on Persistence

Behavior." *Organizational Behavior and Human Decision Processes* 103(1): 53–67.

Grant, Adam M., and Francesca Gino. 2010. "A Little Thanks Goes a Long Way: Explaining Why Gratitude Expressions Motivate Prosocial Behavior." *Journal of Personality and Social Psychology* 98(6): 946–955.

Grant, Adam M., and David A. Hofmann. 2011. "Outsourcing Inspiration: The Performance Effects of Ideological Messages from Leaders and Beneficiaries." *Organizational Behavior and Human Decision Processes* 116(2): 173–187.

Grant, Adam M. and Sharon K. Parker. 2009. "Redesigning Work Design Theories: The Rise of Relational and Proactive Perspectives." *Academy of Management Annals* 3(1): 317–375.

Grant, Adam M., and John J. Sumanth. 2009. "Mission Possible? The Performance of Prosocially Motivated Employees Depends on Manager Trustworthiness." *Journal of Applied Psychology* 94(4): 927–944.

Greenleaf, Robert K. [1970] 2003. "The Servant as Leader." In *The Servant-Leader Within: A Transformative Path*, edited by Hamilton Beazley, Julie Beggs, and Larry C. Spears, 31–74. Mahwah, NJ: Paulist Press.

Greenwald, Anthony G., and Calvin K. Lai. 2020. "Implicit Social Cognition." *Annual Review of Psychology* 71: 419–445.

Gregg, Paul, Paul A. Grout, Anita Ratcliffe, Sarah Smith, and Frank Windmeijer. 2011. "How Important Is Pro-social Behaviour in the Delivery of Public Services?" *Journal of Public Economics* 95(7–8): 758–766.

Grindle, Merilee S. 1997. "Divergent Cultures? When Public Organizations Perform Well in Developing Countries." *World Development* 25(4): 481–495.

Gross, Hellen P., Julia Thaler, and Vera Winter. 2019. "Integrating Public Service Motivation in the Job-Demands-Resources Model: An Empirical Analysis to Explain Employees' Performance, Absenteeism, and Presenteeism." *International Public Management Journal* 22(1): 176–206.

Hackman, J. Richard, and Greg R. Oldham. 1976. "Motivation through the Design of Work: Test of a Theory." *Organizational Behavior and Human Performance* 16(2): 250–279.

1980. *Work Redesign*. Reading, MA: Addison-Wesley.

Hackman, J. Richard, Greg Oldham, Robert Janson, and Kenneth Purdy. "A New Strategy for Job Enrichment." *California Management Review* 17(4): 57–71.

Hall, Douglas T., and Dawn E. Chandler. 2005. "Psychological Success: When the Career Is a Calling." *Journal of Organizational Behavior: The International Journal of Industrial, Occupational and Organizational Psychology and Behavior* 26(2): 155–176.

Hamidullah, Madinah F., Gregg G. Van Ryzin, and Huafang Li. 2016. "The Agreeable Bureaucrat: Personality and PSM." *International Journal of Public Sector Management* 29(6): 582–595.

Hanna, Rema, and Shing-Yi Wang. 2017. "Dishonesty and Selection into Public Service: Evidence from India." *American Economic Journal: Economic Policy* 9(3): 262–290.

Harris, Michael M., and John Schaubroeck. 1988. "A Meta-Analysis of Self-supervisor, Self-peer, and Peer-supervisor Ratings." *Personnel Psychology* 41(1): 43–62.

Hasnain, Zahid, Nick Manning, and Jan Henryk Pierskalla. 2014. "The Promise of Performance Pay? Reasons for Caution in Policy Prescriptions in the Core Civil Service." *The World Bank Research Observer* 29(2): 235–264.

Hatmaker, Deneen M. 2015. "Bringing Networks In: A Model of Organizational Socialization in the Public Sector." *Public Management Review* 17(8): 1146–1164.

Hatmaker, Deneen M., and Hyun Hee Park. 2014. "Who Are All These People? Longitudinal Changes in New Employee Social Networks within a State Agency." *The American Review of Public Administration* 44(6): 718–739.

Hawley, Willis D. 1985. "Designing and Implementing Performance-based Career Ladder Plans." *Educational Leadership* 43(3): 57–61.

Herzberg, Frederick. 1968. "One More Time: How Do You Motivate Employees?" *Harvard Business Review* 46(1): 53–62.

Heslin, Peter A., Gary P. Latham, and Don Van de Walle. 2005. "The Effect of Implicit Person Theory on Performance Appraisals." *Journal of Applied Psychology* 90(5): 842–856.

Higgins, Monica C., and Kathy E. Kram. 2001. "Reconceptualizing Mentoring at Work: A Developmental Network Perspective." *Academy of Management Review* 26: 264–288.

Hirschman, Albert O. 1970. *Exit, Voice, and Loyalty: Responses to Decline in Firms, Organizations, and States.* Cambridge, MA: Harvard University Press.

Holmstrom, Bengt, and Paul Milgrom. 1987. "Aggregation and Linearity in the Provision of Intertemporal Incentives." *Econometrica* 55(2): 303–328.

Holt, Stephen B. 2018. "For Those Who Care: The Effect of Public Service Motivation on Sector Selection." *Public Administration Review* 78(3): 457–471.

Horton, Sylvia. 2008. "History and Persistence of an Idea and an Ideal." In *Motivation in Public Management: The Call of Public Service*, edited by James L. Perry and Annie Hongeghem, 17–32. Oxford, UK: Oxford University Press.

Houston, David J. 2006. "'Walking the Walk' of Public Service Motivation: Public Employees and Charitable Gifts of Time, Blood, and Money." *Journal of Public Administration Research and Theory* 16(1): 67–86.

Hu, Jing, and Jacob B. Hirsh. 2017. "Accepting Lower Salaries for Meaningful Work." *Frontiers in Psychology* 8: Article 1649, 1–10.

Hur, Hyunkang. 2019. "Job Security Matters: A Systematic Review and Meta-Analysis of the Relationship between Job Security and Work Attitudes." *Journal of Management & Organization* 1–31.

Hur, Hyunkang, and James L. Perry. 2016. "Evidence-based Change in Public Job Security Policy: A Research Synthesis and Its Practical Implications." *Public Personnel Management* 5(3): 264–283.

2020. "Job Security Rule Changes and Employee Organizational Commitment." *Review of Public Personnel Administration* 40(4): 641–668.

Im, Tobin, Jesse W. Campbell, and Jisu Jeong. 2016. "Commitment Intensity in Public Organizations: Performance, Innovation, Leadership and PSM." *Review of Public Personnel Administration* 36(3): 219–239.

Ingraham, Patricia Wallace. 2006. "Building Bridges over Troubled Waters: Merit as a Guide." *Public Administration Review* 66: 486–495.

Irvine, Renwick, Robert Chambers, and Rosalind Eyben. 2004. "Learning from Poor People's Experience: Immersions." Lessons for Change in Policy & Organisations No. 13. Brighton: Institute of Development Studies. www.researchgate.net/profile/Rosalind_Eyben/publication/265679047_Learning_from_poor_people%27s_experience_immersions/links/54fa16f80cf23e66f03115a3/Learning-from-poor-peoples-experience-immersions.pdf

Jacobsen, Christian B., Johan Hvitved, and Lotte B. Andersen. 2014. "Command and Motivation: How the Perception of External Interventions Relates to Intrinsic Motivation and Public Service Motivation." *Public Administration* 92: 790–806.

Jang, Chyi-Lu. 2012. "The Effect of Personality Traits on Public Service Motivation: Evidence from Taiwan." *Social Behavior and Personality*, 40(5): 725–734.

Jans, Nicholas, and Judy Frazer-Jans. 2004. "Career Development, Job Rotation, and Professional Performance." *Armed Forces & Society* 30(2): 255–277.

Jawahar, I. M., and Charles R. Williams. 1997. "Where All the Children Are Above Average: The Performance Appraisal Purpose Effect." *Personnel Psychology* 50(4): 905–925.

Jensen, Ulrich T. 2018. "Does Perceived Societal Impact Moderate the Effect of Transformational Leadership on Value Congruence? Evidence from a Field Experiment." *Public Administration Review* 78(1): 48–57.

Jensen, Ulrich T., and Lotte Bøgh Andersen. 2015. "Public Service Motivation, User Orientation, and Prescription Behaviour: Doing Good for Society or for the Individual User?" *Public Administration* 93(3): 753–768.

Jensen, Ulrich Thy, Lotte Bøgh Andersen and Ann-Louise Holten. 2019. "Explaining a Dark Side: Public Service Motivation, Presenteeism, and Absenteeism." *Review of Public Personnel Administration* 39(4): 487–510.

Jensen, Ulrich T., Lotte Bøgh Andersen, and Christian Bøtcher Jacobsen. 2019. "Only When We Agree! How Value Congruence Moderates the Impact of Goal-Oriented Leadership on Public Service Motivation." *Public Administration Review* 79(1): 12–24.

Jensen, Ulrich T., Donald P. Moynihan, and Heidi H. Salomonsen. 2018. "Communicating the Vision: How Face-to-Face Dialogue Facilitates Transformational Leadership." *Public Administration Review* 78(3): 350–361.

Jin, Myung, Bruce McDonald, and Jaehee Park. 2016. "Followership and Job Satisfaction in the Public Sector: The Moderating Role of Perceived Supervisor Support and Performance-oriented Culture." *International Journal of Public Sector Management* 29(3): 218–237.

Jin, Myung H., Bruce McDonald, Jaehee Park, and Kang Yang Trevor Yu. 2019. "Making Public Service Motivation Count for Increasing Organizational Fit: The Role of Followership Behavior and Leader Support as a Causal Mechanism." *International Review of Administrative Sciences* 85(1): 98–115.

Jordan, Todd, and R. Paul Battaglio, Jr. 2014. "Are We There Yet? The State of Public Human Resource Management Research." *Public Personnel Management* 43(1): 25–57.

Jorgensen, Torben Beck, and Mark R. Rutgers. 2014. "Tracing Public Values Change: A Historical Study of Civil Service Job Advertisements." *Contemporary Readings in Law and Social Justice* 6(2): 59–80.

Jose, Jinoy. 2019. "Resignations in the IAS. What Is Troubling India's Elite Officers?" *The Hindu Business Line*, September 27. www.thehindubusinessline.com/blink/know/resignations-in-the-ias-what-is-troubling-indias-elite-officers/article29528239.ece

Kaiser, Lutz. 2014. "Job Satisfaction and Public Service Motivation." IZA Discussion Paper No. 7935. http://ftp.iza.org/dp7935.pdf

Karl, Katherine A., and Barbara Peat. 2004. "A Match Made in Heaven or a Square Peg in a Round Hole? How Public Service Educators Can Help Students Assess Person-Environment Fit." *Journal of Public Affairs Education* 10(4): 265–277.

Katz, Daniel. 1964. "The Motivational Basis of Organizational Behavior." *Behavioral Science* 9(2): 131–146.

Katz, Eric. 2018a. "Leaked Memo: Trump Admin to Boost Use of Private Prisons While Slashing Federal Staff." *Government Executive*, January 25.

www.govexec.com/management/2018/01/trump-administration-looks-boost-use-private-prisons-while-slashing-federal-staff/145496/

2018b. "OPM Calls on Agencies to Implement Coaching Programs for Employees." *Government Executive*, October 3. www.govexec.com/management/2018/10/opm-calls-agencies-implement-coaching-programs-employees/151767/

Katz, Lawrence F., and Alan B. Krueger. 1991. "Changes in the Structure of Wages in the Public and Private Sectors." No. w3667. Cambridge, MA: National Bureau of Economic Research.

Kaufman, Herbert. 1969. "Administrative Decentralization and Political Power." *Public Administration Review* 29(1): 3–15.

Kelley, Caroline. 1999. "The Motivational Effect of School-Based Performance Awards." *Journal of Personnel Evaluation in Education* 12(4): 309–326.

Kelman, Steve. 2015. "How Do We Get Public Servants to Want to Serve the Public?" *FCW*. http://fcw.com/blogs/lectern/2015/04/kelman-psm.aspx?m=1

Kelman, Steven. 1988. "Why Public Ideas Matter." In *The Power of Public Ideas*, edited by Robert Reich, 31–53. Cambridge, MA: Harvard University Press.

Kerckhoff, Alan C. 1995. "Institutional Arrangements and Stratification Processes in Industrial Societies." *Annual Review of Sociology* 21(1): 323–347.

Kettl, Donald F. 2016. *Managing Risk, Improving Results: Lessons for Improving Government Management from GAO's High-Risk List*. Washington, D.C.: IBM Center for the Business of Government. www.businessofgovernment.org/report/managing-risk-improving-results-lessons-improving-government-management-gao%E2%80%99s-high-risk-list

Kim, Sangmook. 2012. "Does Person–Organization Fit Matter in the Public Sector? Testing the Mediating Effect of Person–Organization Fit in the Relationship between Public Service Motivation and Work Attitudes." *Public Administration Review* 72(6): 830–840.

Kim, Sangmook, Wouter Vandenabeele, Bradley E. Wright, Lotte Bøgh Andersen, Francesco Pablo Cerase, Robert K. Christensen, Celine Desmarais et al., 2013. "Investigating the Structure and Meaning of Public Service Motivation across Populations: Developing an International Instrument and Addressing Issues of Measurement Invariance." *Journal of Public Administration Research and Theory* 23(1): 79–102.

Kiser, Larry, and Elinor Ostrom. 1982. "The Three Worlds of Political Action." In *Strategies of Political Inquiry*, edited by Elinor Ostrom, 179–222. Beverley Hills, CA: Sage Publications.

Kjeldsen, Anne Mette. 2014. "Dynamics of Public Service Motivation: Attraction–Selection and Socialization in the Production and Regulation of Social Services." *Public Administration Review* 74(1): 101–112.

Kjeldsen, Anne Mette, and Christian Bøtcher Jacobsen. 2013. "Public Service Motivation and Employment Sector: Attraction or Socialization." *Journal of Public Administration Research and Theory* 23(4): 899–926.

Klein, Howard J., and Natasha A. Weaver. 2000. "The Effectiveness of an Organizational-Level Orientation Training Program in the Socialization of New Hires." *Personnel Psychology* 53(1): 47–66.

Klimecki, Olga, and Tania Singer. 2012. "Empathic Distress Fatigue Rather Than Compassion Fatigue? Integrating Findings from Empathy Research in Psychology and Neuroscience." In *Pathological Altruism*, edited by Barbara Oakley, Ariel Knafo, Guruprasad Madhavan, and David Sloan Wilson, 368–384. New York, NY: Springer.

Klitgaard, Robert. 1988. *Controlling Corruption*. Berkeley, CA: University of California Press.

Knoke, David, and Christine Wright-Isak. 1982. "Individual Motives and Organizational Incentive Systems." *Research in the Sociology of Organizations* 1(2): 209–254.

Kosfeld, Michael, and Susanne Neckermann. 2011. "Getting More Work for Nothing? Symbolic Awards and Worker Performance." *American Economic Journal: Microeconomics* 3(3): 86–99.

Kraimer, Maria L., Sandy J. Wayne, Robert C. Liden, and Raymond T. Sparrowe. 2005. "The Role of Job Security in Understanding the Relationship between Employees' Perceptions of Temporary Workers and Employees' Performance." *Journal of Applied Psychology* 90(2): 389–398.

Kristof-Brown, Amy L., Ryan D. Zimmerman, and Erin C. Johnson. 2005. "Consequences of Individuals' Fit at Work: A Meta-Analysis of Person-Job, Person-Organization, Person-Group, and Person-Supervisor Fit." *Personnel Psychology* 58: 281–342.

Krogsgaard, Julie Alsøe, Pernille Thomsen, and Lotte Bøgh Andersen. 2014. "Only If We Agree? How Value Conflicts Moderate the Relationship between Transformational Leadership and Public Service Motivation." *International Journal of Public Administration* 37(12): 895–907.

Kroll, Alexander, Leisha DeHart-Davis, and Dominick Vogel. 2019. "Mechanisms of Social Capital in Organizations: How Team Cognition Influences Employee Commitment and Engagement." *The American Review of Public Administration* 49(7): 777–791.

Krueger, Alan B. 1988a. "Are Public Sector Workers Paid More Than Their Alternative Wage? Evidence from Longitudinal Data and Job Queues." In *When Public Sector Workers Unionize*, edited by Richard Freeman and B. Casey Ichniowski, 217–240. Chicago, IL: University of Chicago Press. 1988b. "The Determinants of Queues for Federal Jobs." *Industrial and Labor Relations Review* 41(4): 567–581.

Krueger, Alan B., and Lawrence H. Summers. 1988. "Efficiency Wages and the Inter-Industry Wage Structure." *Econometrica* 56: 259–293.

Kuipers, Ben S., Malcolm Higgs, Walter Kickert, Lars Tummers, Jolien Grandia, and Joris Van der Voet. 2014. "The Management of Change in Public Organizations: A Literature Review." *Public Administration* 92(1): 1–20.

Lachance, Janice R. 2017. "Commentary: Public Service Motivation: Lessons from NASA's Janitor." *Public Administration Review* 77(4): 542–543.

Lah, T. J., and James L. Perry. 2008. "The Diffusion of the Civil Service Reform Act of 1978 in OECD Countries: A Tale of Two Paths to Reform." *Review of Public Personnel Administration* 28(3): 282–299.

Lambright, W. Henry. 2016. "Reflections on Leadership: Jean-Jacques Dordain of the European Space Agency." *Public Administration Review* 76(3): 507–511.

Latham, Gary P., and Edwin A. Locke. 1991. "Self-regulation through Goal Setting." *Organizational Behavior and Human Decision Processes* 50(2): 212–247.

Lavigna, Bob. 2009. "Getting Onboard: Integrating and Engaging New Employees." *Government Finance Review* 25(3): 65–70.

Lawler, Edward E. 1994. "From Job-based to Competency-based Organizations." *Journal of Organizational Behavior* 5: 3–15.

Lazear, Edward P. 1999. "Personnel Economics: Past Lessons and Future Directions." *Journal of Labor Economics* 17(2): 199–236.

Lazear, Edward P., and Sherwin Rosen. 1981. "Rank-Order Tournaments as Optimum Labor Contracts." *Journal of Political Economy* 89(5): 841–864.

Lazear, Edward P., and Kathryn L. Shaw. 2007. "Personnel Economics: The Economist's View of Human Resources." *The Journal of Economic Perspectives* 21(4): 91–114.

Leana, Carrie, Eileen Appelbaum, and Iryna Shevchuk. 2009. "Work Process and Quality of Care in Early Childhood Education: The Role of Job Crafting." *Academy of Management Journal* 52(6): 1169–1192.

Lee, Geon, and Do Lim Choi. 2016. "Does Public Service Motivation Influence the Intention to Work in the Public Sector? Evidence from Korea." *Review of Public Personnel Administration* 36(2): 145–163.

LeGrand, Julian. 2003. *Motivation, Agency and Public Policy: Of Knights and Knaves, Pawns and Queens.* Oxford, UK: Oxford University Press.

2010. "Knights and Knaves Return: Public Service Motivation and the Delivery of Public Services." *International Public Management Journal* 13(1): 56–71.

Leisink, Peter. 2004. "Do Public Personnel Policies Nourish Public Service Motivation?" Paper presented at the EGPA Annual Conference: Study Group 3: Public Personnel Policies, Llubljana, Slovenia, September 1–4.

Leisink, Peter, and Bram Steijn. 2008. "Recruitment, Attraction, and Selection." In *Motivation in Public Management: The Call of Public*

Service, edited by James L. Perry and Annie Hondeghem, 118–135. Oxford, UK: Oxford University Press.

Levin, Richard. 2009. "Transforming the Public Service to Support the Developmental State." *Journal of Public Administration* 1(Special Issue): 943–968.

Light, Matthew. 2014. "Police Reforms in the Republic of Georgia: The Convergence of Domestic and Foreign Policy in an Anti-corruption Drive." *Policing and Society* 24(3): 318–345.

Light, Paul C. 2008. *A Government Ill Executed: The Decline of the Federal Service and How to Reverse It.* Cambridge, MA: Harvard University Press.

Light, Paul C. 2020. "Catch-22 Government: Federal Performance in Peril." In *Public Service and Good Governance for the 21st Century*, edited by James L. Perry, 14–42. Philadelphia, PA: University of Pennsylvania Press.

Lindblom, Charles E. 1959. "The Science of Muddling Through." *Public Administration Review* 19(2): 79–88.

1979. "Still Muddling, Not Yet Through." *Public Administration Review* 39: 517–526.

Linos, Elizabeth. 2018. "More Than Public Service: A Field Experiment on Job Advertisements and Diversity in the Police." *Journal of Public Administration Research and Theory* 28(1): 67–85.

Lipsky, Michael. 2010. *Street-Level Bureaucracy: Dilemmas of the Individual in Public Service.* 30th Anniversary Expanded Edition. New York, NY: Russell Sage Foundation.

Liu, Bangcheng, Thomas Li-Ping Tang and Kaifeng Yang. 2015. "When Does Public Service Motivation Fuel the Job Satisfaction Fire? The Joint Moderation of Person–Organization Fit and Needs–Supplies Fit." *Public Management Review* 17(6): 876–900.

Locke, Edwin A. 1991. "The Motivation Sequence, the Motivation Hub, and the Motivation Core." *Organizational Behaviors and Human Decision Processes* 50: 288–299.

Locke, Edwin A., and Gary P. Latham. 1990. "Work Motivation and Satisfaction: Light at the End of the Tunnel." *Psychological Science* 1(4): 240–246.

Lu, Chang-qin, Dan-yang Du, Xiao-min Xu, and Rui-fang Zhang. 2017. "Revisiting the Relationship between Job Demands and Job Performance: The Effects of Job Security and Traditionality." *Journal of Occupational and Organizational Psychology* 90: 28–50.

Lunney, Kellie. 2016. "Longer Probationary Periods for New Defense Hires." *Government Executive.* www.govexec.com/management/2016/10/longer-probationary-periods-new-defense-hires/132088/

March, James G. 1981. "Footnotes to Organizational Change." *Administrative Science Quarterly* 26(4): 563–577.

March, James G., and Herbert A. Simon. 1958. *Organizations.* New York, NY: John Wiley and Sons.

March, James G., and Johan P. Olsen. 1989. *Rediscovering Institutions*. New York, NY: Free Press.

1995. *Democratic Governance*. New York, NY: Free Press.

Marvel, John D., and William D. Resh. 2019. "An Unconscious Drive to Help Others? Using the Implicit Association Test to Measure Prosocial Motivation." *International Public Management Journal* 22(1): 29–70.

Maslow, A. H. 1943. "A Theory of Human Motivation." *Psychological Review* 50: 370–396.

Maynard-Moody, Steven, and Michael Musheno. 2000. "State Agent or Citizen Agent: Two Narratives of Discretion." *Journal of Public Administration Research and Theory* 10(2): 329–358.

2003. *Cops, Teachers, Counselors: Stories from the Front Lines of Public Service*. Ann Arbor, MI: University of Michigan Press.

2009. *Cops, Teachers, Counselors: Stories from the Front Lines of Public Service*. Ann Arbor, MI: University of Michigan Press.

McDonnell, Erin Metz. 2017. "Patchwork Leviathan: How Pockets of Bureaucratic Governance Flourish within Institutionally Diverse Developing States." *American Sociological Review* 82(3): 476–510.

2020. *Patchwork Leviathan: Pockets of Bureaucratic Effectiveness in Developing States*. Princeton, NJ: Princeton University Press.

McKissen, Dustin. 2019. "Want to Attract Talented Workers? Find a Better Way to Tell Your City's Story." *Governing*, February 19. www.governing.com/gov-institute/voices/col-attracting-talented-workforce-city-marketing.html

Meglino, Bruce M., and Audrey Korsgaard. 2004. "Considering Rational Self-interest as a Disposition: Organizational Implications of Other Orientation." *Journal of Applied Psychology* 89(6): 946–959.

Meyer, Herbert H., Emanuel Kay, and John R. P. French, Jr. 1965. "Split Roles in Performance Appraisal." *Harvard Business Review* 43(1): 123–129.

Meyer, John W., and Brian Rowan. 1977. "Institutional Organizations: Formal Structure as Myth and Ceremony." *American Journal of Sociology* 83: 340–363.

Meyer-Sahling, Jan-Hinrik, Kim Sass Mikkelsen, and Christian Schuster. 2019. "The Causal Effect of Public Service Motivation on Ethical Behavior in the Public Sector: Evidence from a Large-Scale Survey Experiment." *Journal of Public Administration Research and Theory* 29(3): 445–459.

Meyer-Sahling, Jan-Hinrik, Christian Schuster, and Kim Sass Mikkelsen. 2018. *Civil Service Management in Developing Countries: What Works? Evidence from a Survey with 23,000 Civil Servants in Africa, Asia, Eastern Europe and Latin America*. Report for the UK Department for International Development (DFID). London: University of Nottingham and University College London.

Miao, Qing, Nathan Eva, Alexander Newman, and Gary Schwarz. 2019. "Public Service Motivation and Performance: The Role of Organizational Identification." *Public Money & Management* 39(2): 77–85.

Miao, Qing, Alexander Newman, Gary Schwarz, and Brian Cooper. 2018. "How Leadership and Public Service Motivation Enhance Innovative Behavior." *Public Administration Review* 78(1): 71–81.

Milkovich, George M. and John W. Boudreau. 1997. *Human Resource Management*. 8th ed.. Chicago, IL: Irwin.

Milkovich, George T., and Jerry M. Newman. 1999. *Compensation*. 6th ed.. Boston, MA: Irwin/McGraw-Hill.

Miller, Gary J., and Andrew B. Whitford. 2007. "The Principal's Moral Hazard: Constraints on the Use of Incentives in Hierarchy." *Journal of Public Administration and Theory* 17: 213–233.

Miller, Karen. 2005. *Public Sector Reform: Governance in South Africa*. Aldershot, England: Ashgate.

Mintzberg, Henry. 1979. *The Structuring of Organizations*. Englewood Cliffs, NJ: Prentice-Hall.

Mostafa, Ahmed Mohammed Sayed, and Filadelfo Leon-Cazares. 2016. "Public Service Motivation and Organizational Performance in Mexico: Testing the Mediating Effects of Organizational Citizenship Behaviors." *International Journal of Public Administration* 39(1): 40–48.

Moynihan, Donald P. 2008. "The Normative Model in Decline? Public Service Motivation in the Age of Governance." In *Motivation in Public Management: The Call of Public Service*, edited by James L. Perry and Annie Hondeghem, 247–267. Oxford, UK: Oxford University Press.

2013. "Does Public Service Motivation Lead to Budget Maximization? Evidence from an Experiment." *International Public Management Journal* 16(2): 179–196.

Moynihan, Donald P., and Sanjay K. Pandey. 2007. "The Role of Organizations in Fostering Public Service Motivation." *Public Administration Review* 67(1): 40–53.

Mulgan, Richard. 2007. "Truth in Government and the Politicization of Public Service Advice." *Public Administration* 85(3): 569–586.

Munsi, Pallabi. 2019. "Government Staffers Follow Lead of American Diplomats Who Are Stepping Down in Protest, Putting Pressure on India's PM." *The Daily Dose*, October 13. www.ozy.com/the-new-and-the-next/indias-bureaucrats-are-following-americas-diplomats-by-quitting-in-protest/96926/

Muralidharan, Karthik, and Venkatesh Sundararaman. 2011. "Teacher Performance Pay: Experimental Evidence from India." *Journal of Political Economy* 119(1): 39–77.

Murnane, Richard, and David Cohen. 1986. "Merit Pay and the Evaluation Problem: Why Most Merit Pay Plans Fail and a Few Survive." *Harvard Educational Review* 56(1): 1–18.

Naff, Katherine C., and John Crum. 1999. "Working for America: Does Public Service Motivation Make a Difference?" *Review of Public Personnel Administration* 19(4): 5–16.

National Academy of Public Administration. 1991. *Modernizing Federal Classification: An Opportunity for Excellence.* Washington, D.C.: National Academy of Public Administration.

2017. *No Time to Wait: Building a Public Service for the 21st Century.* Washington, D.C.: National Academy of Public Administration. www.napawash.org/uploads/Academy_Studies/No-Time-to-Wait_Building-a-Public-Service-for-the-21st-Century.pdf

2018. *No Time to Wait, Part 2: Building a Public Service for the 21st Century.* Washington, D.C.: National Academy of Public Administration. www.napawash.org/uploads/Academy_Studies/NTTW2_09192018_WebVersion.pdf

National Research Council. 1991. *Pay for Performance: Evaluating Performance Appraisal and Merit Pay.* Washington, D.C.: National Academy Press.

Ncholo, Paseka. 2000. "Reforming the Public Service in South Africa: A Policy Framework." *Public Administration and Development* 20: 87–102.

Neshkova, Milena I., and Tatiana Kostadinova. 2012. "The Effectiveness of Administrative Reform in New Democracies." *Public Administration Review* 72(3): 324–333.

Neumann, Oliver. 2016. "Does Misfit Loom Larger than Fit? Experimental Evidence on Motivational Person-Job Fit, Public Service Motivation, and Prospect Theory." *International Journal of Manpower* 37(5): 822–839.

North, Douglass. 1991. "Institutions." *The Journal of Economic Perspectives* 5(1): 97–112.

Oakley, Barbara, Ariel Knafo, Guruprasad Madhavan, and David Sloan Wilson, eds. 2012. *Pathological Altruism.* New York, NY: Springer.

Oberfield, Zachary. 2014. *Becoming Bureaucrats: Socialization at the Front Lines of Government Service.* Philadelphia, PA: University of Pennsylvania Press.

Ogrysko, Nicole. 2019. "Absent Civil Service Reform, Agencies Scoring Small Wins on Workforce Challenges." *Federal News Network.* https://federalnewsnetwork.com/workforce/2019/10/absent-civil-service-reform-agencies-scoring-small-wins-on-workforce-challenges/

Olsen, Asmus Leth, Frederik Hjorth, Nikolaj Harmon, and Sebastian Barfort. 2019. "Behavioral Dishonesty in the Public Sector." *Journal of Public Administration Research and Theory* 29(4): 572–590.

O'Leary, Rosemary. 2020. *The Ethics of Dissent: Managing Guerilla Government.* 3rd ed.. Thousand Oaks, CA: Congressional Quarterly.

Olsen, Johan P. 2006. "Maybe It Is Time to Rediscover Bureaucracy." *Journal of Public Administration Research and Theory* 16(1): 1–24.

O'Neill, Paul H. 2012. "Truth, Transparency, and Leadership." *Public Administration Review* 72(1): 11–12.

Organ, Dennis W., and Katherine Ryan. 1995. "A Meta-Analytic Review of Attitudinal and Dispositional Predictors of Organizational Citizenship Behavior." *Personnel Psychology* 48(4): 775–802.

Ornstein, Norman. 2020. "Political Disruption: Is America Headed toward Uncontrollable Extremism or Partisan Goodwill." In *Public Service and Good Governance for the 21st Century*, edited by James L. Perry, 87–101. Philadelphia, PA: University of Pennsylvania Press.

Orr, Kevin, and Mike Bennett. 2017. "Relational Leadership, Storytelling, and Narratives: Practices of Local Government Chief Executives." *Public Administration Review* 77(4): 515–527.

Ospina, Sonia M., and Erica Gabrielle Foldy. 2010. "Building Bridges from the Margins: The Work of Leadership in Social Change Organizations." *Leadership Quarterly* 21(2): 292–307.

2015. "Enacting Collective Leadership in a Shared-Power World." In *Handbook of Public Administration.* 3rd ed., edited by James L. Perry and Robert K. Christensen, 489–507. San Francisco, CA: Jossey-Bass.

Ostroff, Cheri, and Steve W. J. Kozlowksi. 1992. "Organizational Socialization as a Learning Process: The Role of Information Acquisition." *Personnel Psychology* 45(4): 849–874.

Paarlberg, Laurie E. 2007. "The Impact of Customer Orientation on Government Employee Performance." *International Public Management Journal* 10(2): 201–231.

Paarlberg, Laurie E., and Bob Lavigna. 2010. "Transformational Leadership and Public Service Motivation: Driving Individual and Organizational Performance." *Public Administration Review* 70(5): 710–718.

Paarlberg, Laurie E., and James L. Perry. 2007. "Values Management, Aligning Individual Values and Organization Goals." *American Review of Public Administration* 37(4): 387–408.

Paarlberg, Laurie E., James L. Perry, and Annie Hondeghem. 2008. "From Theory to Practice: Strategies for Applying Public Service Motivation." In *Motivation in Public Management: The Call of Public Service*, edited by James L. Perry and Annie Hondeghem, 268–293. Oxford, UK: Oxford University Press.

Park, Sung Min, and Hal G. Rainey. 2008. "Leadership and Public Service Motivation in U.S. Federal Agencies." *International Public Management Journal* 11(1): 109–142.

Parkyn, Michael B. 2006. "Making More Mike Stranks – Teaching Values in the United States Marine Corps." In *Leading with Values*, edited by Edward D. Hess and Kim S. Cameron, 213–233. New York, NY: Cambridge University Press.

Partnership for Public Service. 2019. *Public Service Leadership Model*. https:// ourpublicservice.org/our-work/public-service-leadership-model/

Partnership for Public Service and Grant Thornton. 2010. *Closing the Gap: Seven Obstacles to a First-Class Federal Workforce*. https:// ourpublicservice.org/wp-content/uploads/2010/08/9eed0aa3e456c80ff25 08b783def0951-1402951808.pdf

Partnership for Public Service, and The Volcker Alliance. 2018. *Renewing America's Civil Service*. www.volckeralliance.org/ recommendations-renewing-americas-civil-service

PDRI. 2010. *The Weakest Link: How Strengthening Assessment Leads to Better Federal Hiring*. Washington, D.C.: Partnership for Public Service.

Peach, Eric K., and T. D. Stanley. 2009. "Efficiency Wages, Productivity and Simultaneity: A Meta-Regression Analysis." *Journal of Labor Research* 30(3): 262–268.

Pedersen, Mogens Jin. 2013. "Public Service Motivation and Attraction to Public versus Private Sector Employment: Academic Field of Study as Moderator?" *International Public Management Journal* 16(3): 357–385.

2015. "Activating the Forces of Public Service Motivation: Evidence from a Low-intensity Randomized Survey Experiment." *Public Administration Review* 75(5): 734–746.

Penner, Louis A., John F. Dovidio, Jane A. Piliavin, and David A. Schroeder. 2005. "Prosocial Behavior: Multilevel Perspectives." *Annual Review of Psychology* 56(1): 365–392.

Perry, James L. 1986. "Merit Pay in the Public Sector: The Case for a Failure of Theory." *Review of Public Personnel Administration* 7(1): 57–69.

1996. "Measuring Public Service Motivation: An Assessment of Construct Reliability and Validity." *Journal of Public Administration Research and Theory* 6: 5–22.

1997. "Antecedents of Public Service Motivation." *Journal of Public Administration Research and Theory* 7(2): 181–197.

2000. "Bringing Society In: Toward a Theory of Public-Service Motivation." *Journal of Public Administration Research and Theory* 10: 471–448.

2014. "The Motivational Bases of Public Service: Foundations for a Third Wave of Research." *Asia Pacific Journal of Public Administration* 36(1): 34–47.

2017. "Know Your Values and Be Prepared: An Interview with Paul H. O'Neill." *Public Administration Review* 77(1): 131–134.

2018. "The 2017 John Gaus Award Lecture: What If We Took Professionalism Seriously?" *PS: Political Science & Politics* 51(1): 93–102.

2019. "Public Service Motivation: Research Bibliography." https://psm.indiana.edu/

2020. "Introduction." In *Public Service and Governance for the 21st Century*, edited by James L. Perry. Philadelphia, PA: University of Pennsylvania Press.

Perry, James L., and Neal D. Buckwalter. 2010. "The Public Service of the Future." *Public Administration Review* 70(S1): S238–S245.

Perry, James L., Trent Engbers, and So Yun Jun. 2009. "Back to the Future? Performance-Related Pay, Empirical Research, and the Perils of Persistence." *Public Administration Review* 69(1): 39–51.

Perry, James L., Debra Mesch, and Laurie Paarlberg. 2006. "Motivating Employees in a New Governance Era: The Performance Paradigm Revisited." *Public Administration Review* 66(4): 505–514.

Perry, James L., and Lyman W. Porter. 1982. "Factors Affecting the Context for Motivation in Public Organizations." *Academy of Management Review* 7(1): 89–98.

Perry, James L., and Hal G. Rainey. 1988. "The Public-Private Distinction in Organization Theory: A Critique and Research Strategy." *Academy of Management Review* 13(2): 182–201.

Perry, James L., and Wouter Vandenabeele. 2008. "Behavioral Dynamics: Institutions, Identities, and Self-Regulation." In *Motivation in Public Management: The Call of Public Service*, edited by James L. Perry and Annie Hondeghem, 56–79. Oxford, UK: Oxford University Press.

Perry, James L., and Lois R. Wise. 1990. "The Motivational Bases of Public Service." *Public Administration Review* 50(3): 367–373.

Phillips, Jean M. 1998. "Effects of Realistic Job Previews on Multiple Organizational Outcomes: A Meta-Analysis." *Academy of Management Journal* 41(6): 673–690.

Pichler, Shaun. 2012. "The Social Context of Performance Appraisal and Appraisal Reactions: A Meta-Analysis." *Human Resource Management* 51(5): 709–732.

Pierson, Paul. 2000. "Increasing Returns, Path Dependence, and the Study of Politics." *American Political Science Review* 94(2): 251–267.

Piliavin, Jane Allyn, and Hong-Wen Charng. 1990. "Altruism: A Review of Recent Theory and Research." *Annual Review of Sociology* 16(1): 27–65.

Piotrowski, Suzanne J., and David H. Rosenbloom. 2002. "Nonmission-Based Values in Results-Oriented Public Management: The Case of Freedom of Information." *Public Administration Review* 62(6): 643–657.

Podgursky, Michael J., and Matthew G. Springer. 2007. "Teacher Performance Pay: A Review." *Journal of Policy Analysis and Management* 26(4): 909–950.

Podsakoff, Philip M., Scott B. MacKenzie, Julie Beth Paine, and Daniel G. Bachrach. 2000. "Organizational Citizenship Behaviors: A Critical Review of the Theoretical and Empirical Literature and Suggestions for Future Research." *Journal of Management* 26(3): 513–563.

Pounian, Charles A. and Jeffrey J. Fuller. 1996. "Compensating Public Employees." In *Handbook of Public Administration*. 2nd ed., edited by James L. Perry, 405–423. San Francisco, CA: Jossey-Bass.

Pratkanis, Anthony and Elliot Aronson. 2001. *Age of Propaganda: The Everyday Use and Abuse of Persuasion*. New York, NY: Freeman.

Premack, Steven L., and John P. Wanous. 1985. "A Meta-Analysis of Realistic Job Preview Experiments." *Journal of Applied Psychology* 70(4): 706–719.

Quinn, James Brian. 1978. "Strategic Change: 'Logical Incrementalism'." *Sloan Management Review* 20(1): 7–21.

Quratulain, Samina, and Abdul Karim Khan. 2015. "How Does Employees' Public Service Motivation Get Affected? A Conditional Process Analysis of the Effects of Person–Job Fit and Work Pressure." *Public Personnel Management* 44(2): 266–289.

Rainey, Hal G. 1982. "Reward Preferences Among Public and Private Managers: In Search of the Service Ethic." *American Review of Public Administration* 16(4): 288–302.

1983. "Public Agencies and Private Firms: Incentives, Goals and Individual Roles." *Administration and Society* 15(2): 207–242.

Rainey, Hal G., and Paula Steinbauer. 1999. "Galloping Elephants: Developing Elements of a Theory of Effective Government Organizations." *Journal of Public Administration Research and Theory* 9(1): 1–32.

Rasul, Imran, and Daniel Rogger. 2015. "The Impact of Ethnic Diversity in Bureaucracies: Evidence from the Nigerian Civil Service." *American Economic Review* 105(5): 457–461.

Rawls, John. 1971. *A Theory of Justice*. Cambridge, MA: Harvard University Press.

Reilly, Thom. 2012. *Rethinking Public Sector Compensation: What Ever Happened to the Public Interest?* Armonk, NY: M.E. Sharpe.

Resh, William G., John D. Marvel, and Bo Wen. 2018. "The Persistence of Prosocial Work Effort as a Function of Mission Match." *Public Administration Review* 78(1): 116–125.

Rhodes, Jean, Òscar Prieto-Flores, and Justin Preston. 2017. "Youth Mentoring Is Rapidly Expanding across Europe: Here's One Reason." *The Chronicle of Evidence-based Mentoring*, September 21. www.evidencebasedmentoring. org/youth-mentoring-expanding-across-europe-heres/

Rhodes, Rod A. W. 1996. "The New Governance: Governing without Government." *Political Studies*, 44 (4): 652–667.

Richwine, Jason. 2012. "Government Employees Work Less than Private-Sector Employees." Backgrounder 2724. September 11. http://thf_media. s3.amazonaws.com/2012/pdf/b2724.pdf

Riccucci, Norma. 2005. *Management Matters: Street-Level Bureaucrats and Welfare Reform.* Washington, D.C.: Georgetown University Press.

Rinnert, David. 2015. "The Politics of Civil Service and Administrative Reforms in Development – Explaining within-Country Variation of Reform Outcomes in Georgia after the Rose Revolution." *Public Admininstration and Development* 35: 19–33.

Risher, Howard, and Adam J. Reese. 2016. *Primer on Total Compensation in Government.* Alexandria, VA: International Public Management Association for Human Resources. www.ipma-hr.org/stay-informed/bookstore/bookstore-product/primer-on-total-compensation-in-government

Risher, Howard H., and Brigitte W. Schay. 1994. "Grade Banding: The Model for Future Salary Programs?" *Public Personnel Management* 23(2): 187–199.

Ritz, Adrian, Gene Brewer, and Oliver Neumann. 2016. "Public Service Motivation: A Systematic Literature Review and Outlook." *Public Administration Review* 76(3): 414–426.

Ritz, Adrian, and Christian Waldner. 2011. "Competing for Future Leaders: A Study of Attractiveness of Public Sector Organizations to Potential Job Applicants." *Review of Public Personnel Administration* 31(3): 291–316.

Roediger, Ant, Jason LaBresh, Victoria Lee, Rainer Strack, and Jenny Huang. 2019. *Building the Government Workforce of the Future*, May 23. www.bcg.com/publications/2019/building-government-workforce-of-the-future.aspx

Rosenbaum, James E. 1979. "Tournament Mobility: Career Patterns in a Corporation." *Administrative Science Quarterly* 24: 220–241.

1984. *Career Mobility in a Corporate Hierarchy.* New York, NY: Academic Press.

Rousseau, Denise M. 2012. "Envisioning Evidence-based Management." In *The Oxford Handbook of Evidence-Based Management*, edited by Denise M. Rousseau, 3–24. Oxford, UK: Oxford University Press.

Rousseau, Denise M., and Miguel R. Olivas-Luján. 2015. "Evidence-based Management." In *Wiley Encyclopedia of Management*, edited by Cary L. Cooper, 1–3. Hoboken, NJ: Wiley.

Rushton, J. Philippe, Roland D. Chrisjohn, and G. Cynthia Fekken. 1981. "The Altruistic Personality and the Self-Report Altruism Scale." *Personality and Individual Differences* 2(4): 293–302.

Ryan, Richard M., and James P. Connell. 1989. "Perceived Locus of Causality and Internalization: Examining Reasons for Acting in Two Domains." *Journal of Personality and Social Psychology* 57(5): 749–761.

Ryan, Richard. M., and Edward L. Deci. 2000. "Self-determination Theory and the Facilitation of Intrinsic Motivation, Social Development, and Well-Being." *American Psychologist* 55(1): 68–78.

Ryu, Geunpil. 2017. "Rethinking Public Service Motivation from the Perspective of Person–Environment Fit: Complementary or Supplementary Relationship?" *Review of Public Personnel Administration* 37(3): 351–368.

Saks, Alan M., and Blake E. Ashforth. 1997. "Socialization Tactics and Newcomer Information Acquisition." *International Journal of Selection and Assessment* 5(1): 48–61.

Salajegheh, Sanjar, Morteza Mouseli, and Ali Moradpour Jaghdari. 2016. "Assessment of the Relationship between Public Service Motivation and Job Performance of Imam Khomeini Relief Foundation (IKRF) Staff Considering Mediating Role of Person-Organization Fit (a Case Study of Hormozgan, Kerman and Bushehr Provinces)." *International Journal of Humanities and Cultural Studies* 2350–2361. Special Issue, May 2016.

Sanabria-Pulido, Pablo. 2018. "Public Service Motivation and Job Sector Choice: Evidence from a Developing Country." *International Journal of Public Administration* 41(13): 1107–1118.

Savas, Emanuel S., and Sigmund G. Ginsburg. 1973. "The Civil Service: A Meritless System?" *The Public Interest* 32: 70–85.

Schneider, Benjamin. 1987. "The People Make the Place." *Personnel Psychology*, 40(3): 437–453.

2001. "Fits about Fit." *Applied Psychology* 50(1): 141–152.

Schneider, Benjamin, Harold W. Goldstein, and D. Brent Smith. 1995. "The ASA Framework: An Update." *Personnel Psychology* 48: 747–773.

Schott, Carina, and Adrian Ritz. 2018. "The Dark Sides of Public Service Motivation: A Multi-Level Theoretical Framework." *Perspectives on Public Management and Governance* 1(1): 29–42.

Schuster, Jay R., and Patricia K. Zingheim. 1992. *The New Pay: Linking Employee and Organizational Performance.* San Francisco, CA: Jossey-Bass.

Scott, William R. 1987. "The Adolescence of Institutional Theory." *Administrative Science Quarterly* 32(4): 493–511.

Seligman, Martin E. P., Tayyab Rashid, and Acacia C. Parks. 2006. "Positive Psychotherapy." *American Psychologist* 61(8): 774.

Selznick, Philip. 1957. *Leadership in Administration.* Berkeley, CA: University of California Press.

Shamir, Boas. 1991. "Meaning, Self and Motivation in Organizations." *Organization Studies* 12(3): 405–424.

Shamir, Boas, Robert J. House, and Michael B. Arthur. 1993. "The Motivational Effects of Charismatic Leadership: A Self-Concept Based Theory." *Organization Science* 4(4): 577–594.

Shim, Dong Chul, Hyun Hee Park, and Tae Ho Eom. 2015. "Street-Level Bureaucrats' Turnover Intention: Does Public Service Motivation Matter?" *International Review of Administrative Sciences* 83(3): 563–582.

Smith, Jason. 2016. "The Motivational Effects of Mission Matching: A Lab-Experimental Test of a Moderated Mediation Model." *Public Administration Review* 76: 626–637.

Social and Behavioral Sciences Team. 2015. *Annual Report.* Washington, D.C.: Executive Office of the President National Science and Technology Council.

Solow, Robert. 1979. "Another Possible Source of Wage Stickiness." *Journal of Macroeconomics* 1(1): 79–82.

Spence, Michael. 1973. "Job Market Signaling." *The Quarterly Journal of Economics* 87(3): 355–374.

Staats, Elmer B. 1982. "Governmental Performance in Perspective: Achievements and Challenges." In *Improving the Accountability and Performance of Government.* Washington, D.C.: The Brookings Institution.

Stazyk, Edmund C. 2013. "Crowding Out Public Service Motivation? Comparing Theoretical Expectations with Empirical Findings on the Influence of Performance-Related Pay." *Review of Public Personnel Administration* 33(3): 252–274.

Stazyk, Edmund C., and Randall S. Davis. 2015. "Taking the 'High-Road': Does Public Service Motivation Alter Ethical Decision Making Processes?" *Public Administration* 93(3): 627–645.

Steger, Michael F., Bryan J. Dik, and Ryan D. Duffy. 2012. "Measuring Meaningful Work: The Work and Meaning Inventory (WAMI)." *Journal of Career Assessment* 20(3): 322–337.

Steger, Michael. F., Bryan J. Dik, and Y. Shim. 2019. "Assessing Meaning and Satisfaction at Work." In *The Oxford Handbook of Positive Psychology Assessment.* 2nd ed., edited by Shane J. Lopez, 373–388. Oxford, UK. Oxford University Press

Steijn, Bram. 2008. "Person–Environment Fit and Public Service Motivation." *International Public Management Journal* 11(1): 13–27.

Stier, Max. 2011. Written Testimony Prepared for The House Committee on Oversight and Government Reform Subcommittee on Federal Workforce, U.S. Postal Service and Labor Policy Hearing, "Are Federal Workers Underpaid?" Washington, D.C.: Partnership for Public Service, March 9.

Stiglitz, Joseph E. 2002. "Information and the Change in the Paradigm in Economics." *American Economic Review* 92: 460–501.

Sun, Rusi, Shuyang Peng, and Sanjay K. Pandey. 2014. "Testing the Effect of Person-Environment Fit on Employee Perceptions of Organizational Goal Ambiguity." *Public Performance & Management Review* 37(3): 465–495.

Tang, Shu-Hua, and Vernon C. Hall. 1995. "The Overjustification Effect: A Meta-Analysis." *Applied Cognitive Psychology* 9: 365–404.

Taylor, Jeannette. 2014. "Public Service Motivation, Relational Job Design, and Job Satisfaction in Local Government." *Public Administration* 92(4): 902–918.

Taylor, Jeannette, and Ranald Taylor. 2009. "Do Governments Pay Efficiency Wages? Evidence from a Selection of Countries." Paper presented at the 2009 International Public Service Motivation Research Conference, Bloomington, IN, June 7–9.

2010. "Working Hard for More Money or Working Hard To Make a Difference? Efficiency Wages, Public Service Motivation, and Effort." *Review of Public Personnel Administration* 31(1): 67–86.

Tendler, Judith, and Sara Freedheim. 1994. "Trust in a Rent-Seeking World: Health and Government Transformed in Northeast Brazil." *World Development* 22(12): 1771–1791.

Teo, Stephen T. T., David Pick, Matthew Xerri, and Cameron Newton. 2016. "Person–Organization Fit and Public Service Motivation in the Context of Change." *Public Management Review* 18(5): 740–762.

Tepe, Markus. 2016. "In Public Servants We Trust? A Behavioural Experiment on Public Service Motivation and Trust among Students of Public Administration, Business Sciences and Law." *Public Management Review* 18(4): 508–538.

The Economist. 2017. "Georgia, a Model of Reform, Is Struggling to Stay Clean." *The Economist*, June 29. www.economist.com/europe/2017/06/29/georgia-a-model-of-reform-is-struggling-to-stay-clean

Thelen, Kathleen. 1999. "Historical Institutionalism in Comparative Politics." *Annual Review of Political Science* 2: 369–404.

Thompson, James R., and Rob Seidner. 2009. "A New Look at Paybanding and Pay for Performance." In *Innovations in Human Resource Management: Getting the Public's Work Done in the 21st Century*, edited by Hannah S. Sistare, Myra Howze Shiplett, and Terry E. Buss, 147–169. Armonk, NY: M.E. Sharpe.

Thompson, Jeffrey A., and Robert K. Christensen. 2018. "Bridging the Public Service Motivation and Calling Literatures." *Public Administration Review* 78(3): 444–456.

Tims, Maria, Daantje Derks, and Arnold B. Bakker. 2016. "Job Crafting and Its Relationships with Person–Job Fit and Meaningfulness: A Three-Wave Study." *Journal of Vocational Behavior* 92: 44–53.

Tolbert, Pamela S., and Lynne G. Zucker. 1983. "Institutional Sources of Change in the Formal Structure of Organizations: The Diffusion of Civil Service Reform, 1880–1935." *Administrative Science Quarterly* 28: 22–39.

Tonin, Mirco, and Michael Vlassopoulos. 2010. "Disentangling the Sources of Pro-socially Motivated Effort: A Field Experiment." *Journal of Public Economics* 94(11–12): 1086–1092.

Tonon, Joseph M. 2008. "The Costs of Speaking Truth to Power: How Professionalism Facilitates Credible Communication." *Journal of Public Administration Research and Theory* 18(2): 275–295.

Tummers, Lare G., and Eva Knies. 2013. "Leadership and Meaningful Work in the Public Sector." *Public Administration Review* 73(6): 859–868.

Turner, Ralph H. 1960. "Sponsored and Contest Mobility and the School System." *American Sociological Review* 25(6): 855–867.

Underhill, Christina M. 2006. "The Effectiveness of Mentoring Programs in Corporate Settings: A Meta-Analytical Review of the Literature." *Journal of Vocational Behavior* 68: 292–307.

United Nations Development Program. 2015a. *Public Service Motivation and the SDGs: An Unacknowledged Crisis?* Singapore: UNDP Global Centre for Public Service Excellence.

2015b. *The SDGs and New Public Passion: What Really Motivates the Civil Service?* Singapore: UNDP Global Centre for Public Service Excellence.

U.S. Department of Justice. 2014. "Federal Prison System: FY 2014 Congressional Budget Buildings and Facilities." www.justice.gov/sites/default/files/jmd/legacy/2013/12/26/bop-bf-justification.docx

U.S. General Services Administration. 2019. "Office of Evaluation Services." www.gsa.gov/about-us/organization/office-of-governmentwide-policy/office-of-evaluation-sciences

U.S. Government Accountability Office. 2014. *Management of New Prison Activations Can Be Improved.* Washington, D.C.: U.S. Government Accountability Office. GAO-14-709. www.gao.gov/assets/670/665417.pdf

2017. *High-Risk Series: Progress on Many High-Risk Areas, While Substantial Efforts Needed on Others.* Washington, D.C.: U.S. Government Accountability Office. GAO-17-317. www.gao.gov/assets/690/682765.pdf

U.S. Merit Systems Protection Board. 2005. *The Probationary Period: A Critical Assessment Opportunity.* Washington, D.C.: U.S. Merit Systems Protection Board.

2018. *The Roles of Feedback, Autonomy, and Meaningfulness in Employee Performance Behaviors.* Washington, D.C.: U.S. Merit Systems Protection Board, Office of Policy and Evaluation.

U.S. Office of Personnel Management. 2019a. *Assessment & Selection: Realistic Job Previews.* Washington, D.C.: U.S. Office of Personnel Management. www.opm.gov/policy-data-oversight/assessment-and-selection/other-assessment-methods/realistic-job-previews/

2019b. *Training and Development.* www.opm.gov/policy-data-oversight/training-and-development/career-development/#url=Individual-Learning-Accounts

Vandenabeele, Wouter. 2007. "Toward a Public Administration Theory of Public Service Motivation." *Public Management Review* 9(4): 545–556.

2008. "Government Calling: Public Service Motivation as an Element in Selecting Government as an Employer of Choice." *Public Administration* 86(4): 1089–1105.

2011. "Who Wants to Deliver Public Service? Do Institutional Antecedents of Public Service Motivation Provide an Answer?" *Review of Public Personnel Administration* 31(1): 87–107.

2014. "Explaining Public Service Motivation: The Role of Leadership and Basic Needs Satisfaction." *Review of Public Personnel Administration* 34(2): 153–173.

Van de Walle, Steven, Bram Steijn, and Sebastian Jilke. 2015. "Extrinsic Motivation, PSM and Labour Market Characteristics: A Multilevel Model of Public Sector Employment Preference in 26 Countries." *International Review of Administrative Sciences* 81(4): 833–855.

van Dierendonck, Dirk. 2011. "Servant Leadership: A Review and Synthesis." *Journal of Management* 37(4): 1228–1261.

Van Loon, Nina, Anne Mette Kjeldsen, Lotte Bøgh Andersen, Wouter Vandenabeele, and Peter Leisink. 2018. "Only When the Societal Impact Potential Is High? A Panel Study of the Relationship between Public Service Motivation and Perceived Performance." *Review of Public Personnel Administration* 38(2): 139–166.

Van Loon, Nina Mari, Wouter Vandenabeele, and Peter Leisink. 2015. "On the Bright and Dark Side of Public Service Motivation: The Relationship between PSM and Employee Wellbeing." *Public Money & Management* 35(5): 349–356.

Van Maanen, John. 1975. "Police Socialization: A Longitudinal Examination of Job Attitudes in an Urban Police Department." *Administrative Science Quarterly* 20(2): 207–228.

Van Maanen, John, and Edgard H. Schein. 1979. "Toward a Theory of Organizational Socialization." *Research in Organizational Behavior* 1: 209–264.

Van Riper, Paul P. 1958. *History of the United States Civil Service*. Evanston, IL: Row, Peterson and Company.

van Witteloostuijn, Arjen, Marc Esteve, and George Boyne. 2017. "Public Sector Motivation *ad fonts*: Personality Traits as Antecedents of the Motivation to Serve the Public Interest." *Journal of Public Administration Research and Theory* 27(1): 20–35.

Ventriss, Curtis, James L. Perry, Tina Nabatchi, H. Brinton Milward, and Jocelyn M. Johnston. 2019. "Democracy, Public Administration, and Public Values in an Era of Estrangement." *Perspectives on Public Management and Governance* 2(4): 275–282.

Verkuil, Paul R. 2017. *Valuing Bureaucracy: The Case for Professional Government*. Cambridge, UK: Cambridge University Press.

Vinzant, Janet C. 1998. "Where Values Collide: Motivation and Role Conflict in Child and Adult Protective Services." *American Review of Public Administration* 28(4): 347–366.

Viswesvaran, Chockalingam, and Deniz S. Ones. 2000. "Perspectives on Models of Job Performance." *International Journal of Selection and Assessment* 8(4): 216–226.

Vogel, Dominik, and Alexander Kroll. 2016. "The Stability and Change of PSM-Related Values across Time: Testing Theoretical Expectations against Panel Data." *International Public Management Journal* 19(1): 53–77.

Vogel, Dominik, and Jurgen Willems. 2020. "The Effects of Making Public Service Employees Aware of Their Prosocial and Societal Impact: A Microintervention." *Journal of Public Administration Research and Theory* 30(3): 485–503.

Volcker Alliance. 2018. *Preparing Tomorrow's Public Service: What the Next Generation Needs*. New York, NY: Volcker Alliance. www.volckeralliance. org/sites/default/files/attachments/Preparing%20Tomorrow%27s%20 Public%20Service.pdf

Vyse, Graham. 2019. "'Choose Purpose': Cities Launch Ad Campaigns to Attract More Applicants." *Governing*, February 13. www.governing.com/ topics/workforce/gov-state-local-government-cities-recruitment-hiring-employees.html

Wagner, Erich. 2019. "OPM Proposes Legislation to Clarify Probationary Periods, Expand Hiring Eligibility." *Government Executive*. www.govexec. com/management/2019/06/opm-proposes-legislation-clarify-probationary-periods-expand-hiring-eligibility/157788/

Waldner, Christian. 2012. "Do Public and Private Recruiters Look for Different Employees? The Role of Public Service Motivation." *International Journal of Public Administration* 35(1): 70–79.

Wanous, John P. 1989. "Installing a Realistic Job Preview: Ten Tough Choices." *Personnel Psychology* 42(1): 117–134.

1992. *Organizational Entry: Recruitment, Selection, Orientation, and Socialization of Newcomers*. Reading, MA: Prentice Hall/Addison-Wesley.

Warren, Dave C., and Li-Ting Chen. 2013. "The Relationship between Public Service Motivation and Performance." In *Meta-Analysis for Public Management and Policy*, edited by Evan Ringquist, 442–474. San Francisco, CA: Jossey-Bass.

Waterhouse, Jennifer, Erica French, and Naomi Puchala. 2014. "The Impact of Socialization on Graduates' Public Service Motivation – A Mixed Method Study." *Australian Journal of Public Administration* 73(2): 247–259.

Weibel, Antoinette, Katja Rost, and Margit Osterloh. 2010. "Pay for Performance in the Public Sector – Benefits and (Hidden) Costs." *Journal of Public Administration Research and Theory* 20(2): 387–412.

Welbourne, Theresa M., Diane E. Johnson, and Amir Erez. 1998. "The Role-Based Performance Scale: Validity Analysis of a Theory-based Measure." *Academy of Management Journal* 41(5): 540–555.

Weske, Ulrike, Adrian Ritz, Carina Schott, and Oliver Neumann. 2019. "Attracting Future Civil Servants with Public Values? An Experimental Study on Employer Branding." *International Public Management Journal* https://doi.org/10.1080/10967494.2018.1541830

Whalen, Cortney, and Mary E. Guy. 2008. "Broadbanding Trends in the States." *Review of Public Personnel Administration* 28(4): 349–366.

Wilthagen, Ton, and Frank Tros. 2004. "The Concept of 'Flexicurity': A New Approach to Regulating Employment and Labour Markets." *TRANSFER: European Review of Labour and Research* 10(2): 166–186.

World Bank. 2003. *Grass Roots Immersion Program (GRIP) in India: Notes and Photographic Record of the Salt Workers Team (English)*. Washington, D.C.: World Bank. http://documents.worldbank.org/curated/en/329241468041988326/Grass-Roots-Immersion-Program-GRIP-in-India-Notes-and-photographic-record-of-the-salt-workers-team

2016. *How Shanghai Does It: Insights and Lessons from the Highest-Ranking Education System in the World*. Washington, D.C.: World Bank.

Wright, Bradley E. 2001. "Public-Sector Work Motivation: A Review of the Current Literature and a Revised Conceptual Model." *Journal of Public Administration Research and Theory* 11(4): 559–586.

2004. "The Role of Work Context in Work Motivation: A Public Sector Application of Goal and Social Cognitive Theories." *Journal of Public Administration Research and Theory* 14(1): 59–78.

2007. "Public Service and Motivation: Does Mission Matter?" *Public Administration Review* 67(1): 54–64.

2008. "Methodological Challenges Associated with Public Service Motivation Research." In *Motivation in Public Management: The Call of Public Service*, edited by James L. Perry and Annie Hondeghem, 80–98. Oxford: Oxford University Press.

Wright, Bradley E., and Robert K. Christensen. 2010. "Public Service Motivation: A Longitudinal Analysis of the Job Attraction-Selection-Attrition Model." *International Public Management Journal* 13(2): 155–176.

Wright, Bradley E., Robert K. Christensen, and Kimberley Roussin Isett. 2013. "Motivated to Adapt? The Role of Public Service Motivation as Employees Face Organizational Change." *Public Administration Review* 73(5): 738–747.

Wright, Bradley E., Robert K. Christensen, and Sanjay K. Pandey. 2013. "Measuring Public Service Motivation: Exploring the Equivalence of Existing Global Measures." *International Public Management Journal* 16(2): 197–223.

Wright, Bradley E., and Adam M. Grant. 2010. "Unanswered Questions about Public Service Motivation: Designing Research to Address Key Issues of Emergence and Effects." *Public Administration Review* 70(5): 691–700.

Wright, Bradley E., Donald P. Moynihan, and Sanjay K. Pandey. 2012. "Pulling the Levers: Transformation Leadership, Public Service Motivation and Mission Valence." *Public Administration Review* 72(2): 206–215.

Wright, Bradley E., and Sanjay K. Pandey. 2008. "Public Service Motivation and the Assumption of Person–Organization Fit: Testing the Mediating Effect of Value Congruence." *Administration & Society* 40(5): 502–521.

2011. "Public Organizations and Mission Valence: When Does Mission Matter?" *Administration & Society* 43(1): 22–44.

Wrzesniewski, Amy, and Jane E. Dutton. 2001. "Crafting a Job: Revisioning Employees as Active Crafters of Their Work." *Academy of Management Review* 26(2): 179–201.

Xu, Chengwei, and Chung-An Chen. 2017. "Moving from Public Service Motivation (PSM) to Moviation for Public Service (MPS): Through the Lens of Self-Determination Theory." In *Self-Determination Theory (SDT): Perspective, Applications and Impact*, edited by Susan L. Wade, 1–8. Hauppauge, NY: Nova Science.

Yaden, David Bryce, Theo D. McCall, and J. Harold Ellens. 2015. *Being Called: Scientific, Secular, and Sacred Perspectives*. Santa Barbara, CA: Praeger.

Yates, Sally Q. 2016. "Reducing Our Use of Private Prisons." In Memorandum for Acting Director of the Federal Bureau of Prisons. www.justice.gov/archives/opa/file/886311/download

Zarychta, Alan, Tara Grillos, and Krister P. Andersson. 2020. "Public Sector Governance Reform and the Motivation of Street-Level Bureaucrats in Developing Countries." *Public Administration Review* 80(1): 75–91.

Zingheim, Patricia K., and Jay R. Schuster. 2002. "Pay Changes Going Forward." *Compensation & Benefits Review* 34(4): 48–53.

Zweimüller, Josef, and Erling Barth. 1994. "Bargaining Structure, Wage Determination, and Wage Dispersion in 6 OECD Countries." *Kyklos* 47: 81–93.

Index

Printed in the United States
By Bookmasters